To Jokes,

An inspiring book to an inspiring friend.

Happy Birthday!

Love,

Larry

BENJAMIN JOSÉ "BENGIE" MOLINA is a former Major League Baseball catcher who has played for the Anaheim Angels, the Toronto Blue Jays, the San Francisco Giants, and the Texas Rangers. His brothers, Yadier and José, are also Major League catchers. Bengie holds two World Championship rings and two Gold Glove Awards. He lives with his family in Arizona.

JOAN RYAN is an award-winning journalist and author whose work has earned her thirteen Associated Press Sports Editors awards, a National Headliner Award, and the Women's Sports Foundation's Journalism Award. Her book *Little Girls in Pretty Boxes* was named one of the Top 100 Sports Books of All Time by *Sports Illustrated* and one of the Top 50 Sports Books by the *Guardian*. Joan now works as a media consultant to the San Francisco Giants.

MOLINA

THE STORY OF THE FATHER WHO RAISED AN UNLIKELY BASEBALL DYNASTY

BENGIE MOLINA

WITH JOAN RYAN

SIMON & SCHUSTER PAPERBACKS

NEW YORK LONDON TORONTO SYDNEY NEW DELHI

Simon & Schuster Paperbacks
An Imprint of Simon & Schuster, Inc.
1230 Avenue of the Americas
New York, NY 10020

First Simon & Schuster trade paperback edition June 2016

Interior design by Ruth Lee-Mui

Manufactured in the United States of America

1 3 5 7 9 10 8 6 4 2

The Library of Congress has cataloged the hardcover edition as follows:

Molina, Bengie, 1974–
Molina : the story of the father who raised an unlikely baseball dynasty / Bengie Molina with Joan Ryan.
pages cm
1. Molina, Benjamin. 2. Fathers—Puerto Rico. 3. Fathers and sons. 4. Molina, Bengie, 1974– 5. Baseball—Puerto Rico.
I. Ryan, Joan, 1959– II. Title.
GV865.M6M65 2015
796.357092—dc23
[B] 2014043223

ISBN 978-1-4516-4104-2
ISBN 978-1-4516-4105-9 (pbk)
ISBN 978-1-4516-4106-6 (ebook)

All photographs courtesy of the author, except images on p. 13 of the insert, which are courtesy of Angels Baseball.

For Pai and Mai, my lifelong inspirations.

And for my brothers, Cheo and Yadier.

I love you all and may God continue to bless you.

—Bengie

For my father, Bob Ryan

—Joan

"Baseball is about going home, and how hard it
is to get there and how driven is our need."

A. BARTLETT GIAMATTI

PROLOGUE

THE LIFE WE recognize as uniquely ours begins with our first memory. This memory surely isn't random. There has to be a reason why our brains, so many years later, retrieve a particular moment and present it to us as the opening scene of our lives. It is the baseline by which we measure everything else.

This is my earliest memory.

I am four or five years old. My father is a second baseman on a semipro baseball team in the town of Utuado. I call him Pai, short for Papi. He is kind of a small guy compared to the other players, but he is like a giant to me. He wears superhero clothes like in my comic books: tight shirt and pants that show off his muscles. He has special shoes that make marks in the dirt when he walks. His arms and shoulders look like they could yank a palm tree straight out of its roots. His face is as hard as the bricks holding up our clapboard house.

I am in the dugout. I'm sure it is the first time Pai allows me to stay with him and the other men. I like how the men in the dugout smell. It's different from Mai—my mother—who smells like soap and cooking oil. It's different even from the tangy, metal smell of Pai when he comes home from the factory. The men in the dugout smell like grass and Winstons and sweat. I like, too, how they talk to each other, as if everything is a joke, and I like how their faces turn serious when they press a helmet onto their heads and pull a bat from the rack at the end of the bench.

I am gripping the chain-link fence that separates the players' bench from the field and watching everything. The game is dragging on into the tenth inning. The men have stopped joking. Everybody seems worn-out and angry.

Pai picks up a bat. It is his turn.

"I'm going to hit a home run to left field," he says. "We're all going to go home. I'm tired of this game."

I look out to left field. The fence seems a million miles away.

"No, no," one of the men says. "Go to right! It's shorter!"

The right-field fence is the close one. Even I can see that.

"He's pitching me away," my father says. "I've got to go to left."

He walks to the plate and digs in to the batter's box. I hear people clapping and shouting my father's name that is also my name: "Bengie! Let's go, Bengie!" The pitcher winds up and throws. Pai swings.

The ball sails into left field. It keeps rising. The left fielder races back. The ball begins to fall. The left fielder runs faster. He stretches out his arm and it looks as if he's going to catch the ball. Then I see the ball hit the top of the fence and bounce over.

A home run.

I watch Pai round the bases, the biggest grin on his face. The men rush from the dugout toward home plate. They are yelling and jumping. I run with them. I am also yelling and jumping.

"Get him! Somebody get him!" I hear Mai scream from the stands, terrified that I will be trampled.

Pai crosses the plate and, in the midst of the celebration, shouts, "Where is he?" His eyes land on me, and his face lights up. He scoops me up in his arms and swings me onto his broad shoulders. I hear the people chanting, "Bengie! Bengie!" I think the cheers are for me. I can feel Pai's shoulders under my legs. He grips both my ankles in one strong workman's hand. The men are hugging him and me at once—his shoulders and my legs.

We are like one person.

One big baseball man.

I am so happy. I want to stay there forever.

That's the opening scene of my life. A ballpark. A dugout. And my father.

I don't know if a person can decide the course of his life at the age of four or five. But I believe I did. I wanted to wear those clothes. Play on a field like that. Know what those men knew. I wanted to hear Pai talk to me the way he talked to them.

I heard stories that Pai had dreamed of making it to the Major Leagues. He had been a great baseball player in his day. One of the best in Puerto Rico. Famous, even. People told stories about how he played second base like a scorpion, scuttling from side to side in the blink of an eye. They told how he gripped the bat so far up the handle you swore he would poke himself in the belly when he swung, and how even with this crazy grip he still hit home runs. Our house was filled with his trophies.

Everyone thought he'd make it to the Major Leagues like Roberto Clemente, Puerto Rico's national hero. But he never did. He never even got to the minor leagues.

Instead he spent almost forty years working at a factory.

I don't recall exactly when, but I decided I would make it to the Major Leagues. As his oldest son and namesake, I would make Pai's dream come true through me. I would erase his failure with my success.

I was a child, with a child's magical thinking. I didn't know that millions of boys dream of making it to the Major Leagues, and almost nobody does. Think about how many of your childhood friends ended up wearing a Major League uniform. Probably none. The odds are astronomical.

And my odds, as it turned out, were particularly bad. I wasn't a natural athlete like my father. He was pure and fluid and self-assured. I had minimal natural talent; I was a box of parts requiring assembly. I wasn't strong like Pai, either. I was short and skinny and, at least back then, had none of his grit. Every criticism scraped my thin skin.

Still, I kept imagining a day when Pai would rush onto the field in some Major League stadium after I had hit a game-winning home run. In my mind, it looked a lot like the moment at home plate when Pai scooped me onto his shoulders. One big baseball man. I spent my life trying to recapture that moment, that perfect connection with my father. It drove me.

Maybe every son is driven by his need to secure his father's respect. For me, I think, it was more than that. My father was the best man I knew. Sometimes he seemed not like a real man to me. He was something else. Ask anyone in the barrio. They will tell you so many things about him on the baseball field.

They'll tell you, too, that he had three sons. And that he taught these sons everything he knew about baseball.

They will tell you that José, Yadier, and I all became catchers.

And that against all odds, *all three* of these boys made it to the Major Leagues.

And that against greater odds—no three brothers in the history of baseball have ever done this—Benjamín's sons earned two World Series rings each.

They will also tell you that our father was a better ballplayer than any of us.

Everyone in the barrio has a story about Benjamín Molina Santana.

Now I will tell you mine.

I will begin at the end.

My father died at the age of fifty-eight on the field by the tamarind trees across the street from our house. It was his field. He measured the base paths and lined them with handfuls of white chalk from a bag he kept in the carport. He raked the infield dirt. He poured sand into mud puddles after the rains.

My brothers and I grew up on that field. Our lives were framed by its baselines. Even years later I could have walked every inch of it in the dark and known exactly where I was. I'd know how many steps from the edge of the dirt to the light pole in the middle of left field, which, if you weren't careful, could bring a sprint for a fly ball to a sudden and painful stop. I'd know how to slide into home plate to make sure I wouldn't cut my legs on the exposed, spiky ends of the backstop fence.

The story of my father is, in many ways, the story of Puerto Rican baseball. Our best players emerged from rutted fields that once grew sugarcane. They cut bats from tree branches and as children wore paper bags for fielding gloves. They sharpened their eyes by hitting dried seeds. They tuned in to radio broadcasts of Major League games, listening for mentions of Hiram Bithorn and El Divino Loco and Roberto Clemente.

My father's love for baseball grew from these deep roots. Our love for the game grew from his. But baseball was so much more than a game for us, though I didn't understand this until later. Baseball was the means by which my quiet, shy, and macho father could show the depth of his love for us.

If you had stumbled upon my father's funeral in the tiny barrio of Kuilan, you would have thought a governor had died instead of a factory worker. Thousands turned out. Streets were closed. The outpouring of affection and grief and respect that day was the most amazing thing I have ever seen.

After the funeral, as Pai's friends recalled his extraordinary talent, they told me about his Major League aspirations and the shocking decision he eventually made, something neither he nor Mai had ever told my brothers and me. I realized then that I didn't know my father. At least, I didn't know him beyond being my father. At the funeral and for months and years after, I talked with my aunts and uncles, with Pai's old teammates, the boys he coached and his coworkers at the factory where he worked for more than thirty years.

I learned what had happened that kept him from playing in the United States. I learned what he had really been teaching my brothers and me all those hours and years on the baseball field. And I came to understand that the least of my father's legacy is that he put three sons in the Major Leagues.

During one of my visits to Puerto Rico after Pai died, his friend

Vitin told me he had been given the task of collecting the belongings from my father's body at the hospital. He found three things in his pockets.

A Little League rulebook.

A measuring tape.

And a lotto ticket.

I didn't know it at the time, but they would be my guideposts in telling you about the poor factory worker in Puerto Rico who was behind the most unlikely dynasty in baseball.

PART 1

I WAS BORN on a summer Saturday, the year the Oakland A's won their third World Series in a row. The last-place team in the division that year was the lowly California Angels. I smile to think of my father reading the baseball box scores while he waited in the hospital that day, not knowing that his wrinkly newborn would be the starting catcher for the Angels when they won their first World Series championship twenty-eight years later.

California was a long way off, of course, in both distance and imagination. The hospital was in Río Piedras, the only local hospital that would take Mai without insurance. But Mai and Pai lived at that time in Vega Alta, where Mai grew up. The town's nickname is *El Pueblo de los Nangotaos*, The Town of Squatters. It received its name from the workers who squatted by the railroad tracks as they waited for the train to take them to the sugarcane fields. Much was made of the nickname when my brothers and I became catchers.

Vega Alta is a town in the district of Dorado. You might have heard of the beaches of Dorado. They stretch for miles along the northern coastline west of San Juan and once belonged to the Rockefellers. They are still beautiful, kept clean and sparkling for tourists who flock to the beach resorts and golf courses.

But that's not our Dorado.

Our Dorado is inland, where the roads are narrow and rutted, and the concrete-block houses are so close you could stand at your bathroom sink and almost reach into your neighbor's cabinet for a toothbrush. The eaves of the flat-roofed houses are painted in faded shades of aqua, pink, and yellow and make you think of rows of girls in Easter dresses. There are iron bars across the doors and windows to keep out the street criminals who seem to multiply every year. Faded work shirts and underwear hang from clotheslines. Old ladies in loose cotton *batas* sit in plastic chairs by their front doors, their calloused brown feet swollen from the heat. Hard-faced men in short sleeves drink beer and play dominoes in open-air bars.

Our barrio is Espinosa. Our sector in Espinosa is Kuilan, marked with a handmade sign off Calle Marvella. Maybe the neighborhood looks poor and rough to outsiders. I can't say. I can only see it through my eyes. The same hard rains that rut the roads and rust the chain-link fences turn every dropped seed into some beautiful living thing. We have huge trees called *flamboyan* with enormous branches that arch over the streets and bloom with bright orange or red flowers that look like orchids. There are avocado, banana, and tamarind trees. There are trees called *pomerosa* with red fruit that smell like perfume. Even the iron bars on the windows and doors are beautiful, all swirls and geometry, each home's pattern different, a reflection of the spirit of the family inside. A few blocks from our house, near the San Juan Cement Company, is a jungle on a hill that stretches like an outfield wall around our little piece of Dorado.

If you ask me the name of the street I grew up on, where Mai still lives, I can't tell you. It has no address. The street has a name, I think, but nobody uses it. In much of Dorado, you give directions by landmarks: the ball field, the market, the church, the bar. Our mail goes to Mami's house in Vega Alta. Everybody in Mai's family—brothers, sisters, nieces, and nephews—gets their mail there. Titi Norma lives there now.

No one remembers where Pai's people had been before Dorado or how we ended up there. My great-aunt Clara Virgen said she once heard we originally came from Morovis, a town about ten minutes from Dorado. But all anyone knows now is Dorado and Espinosa and Kuilan. Pai's family goes back generations, and almost nobody has left. Three of Pai's sisters live on the same plot of land their parents and grandparents lived on before them. Titi Clara Virgen lives there, too. Two of Pai's brothers live half a mile away. And on and on. The town is so packed with cousins, aunts and uncles, half brothers, and half sisters that you can't walk to La Marketa without running into a blood relative.

My aunt Alejandra tells the story of falling in love with a boy at school. One day he followed her home. Alejandra's mother came running out the door.

"What is he doing here?" she asked.

"This is my friend," Alejandra said.

"That is your brother!"

The boy was the son of Alejandra's father, who had left years earlier and started a new family.

My great-aunt Clara Virgen said her father skipped out on her family, too. He left behind a wife and four children. One of them was a boy named Francisco. This was Pai's father.

Francisco's family was poor, like everyone else in Espinosa in the late 1920s. By then, Puerto Rico had been a province of the United States for two decades, part of the spoils from Spain at the end of the Spanish-American War. Sugar and tobacco companies had come in and bought up farmland. Families that once had grown plenty of food for themselves now worked in the sugarcane fields and sugar mills.

Francisco's mother took whatever work she could find. "What didn't she work in?" Clara Virgen told me. "If she had to pick grapefruit, she picked grapefruit. If she had to lay fertilizer, she laid fertilizer. She would do everything to support us." In her small yard, she grew pigeon peas, sweet potatoes, *panapen* (breadfruit), bananas, and plantains, and raised pigs and chickens. She bought cornmeal, rice, and fish at the market. The house had no electricity or running water. Clara Virgen and her sisters fetched water from a local well, filling huge lard cans that they carried on their heads. There was so much work at home that most girls left school after second grade. "I learned to read and write," Clara Virgen said. "Thank God for that."

Francisco and her other brothers stayed in school longer, maybe until sixth grade, Clara Virgen guessed. Francisco was quiet and kind. He'd walk to town with a rag and a brush and shine shoes to make money for the family. He cut sugarcane. He laid fertilizer alongside his mother. Eventually he landed a job at a grocery store. Francisco put so much of himself into work that he found little time for dating.

Then he met Luz Maria. She was in her early twenties, divorced and the mother of three children. She lived with her mother, a woman so well known and well loved that everyone in Kuilan, including

Francisco, knew her simply as Mama. When Francisco met Luz Maria, he liked her immediately. She was sweet like Mama, despite the tragedy in her life. One day not long after her divorce, Luz Maria's ex-husband showed up at Mama's house, yelling about taking the children away. Mama hid the children in her room. The ex-husband forced his way past Luz Maria, searched the house, and dragged the crying children out from underneath Mama's bed. He forced them into his car and drove away. Luz Maria collapsed into Mama's arms. She had no money to fight her husband in court. She never saw her children again.

Francisco married Luz Maria and moved into Mama's house, and the couple soon began a family that would grow to thirteen children. My father was the second child and first son.

He was born at home in 1950 into the hands of the neighborhood midwife. Mama fell utterly in love with her grandson. He was light-skinned and had slightly slanted eyes. She called him Chino. Three more children were born in Mama's house while Francisco and Luz Maria lived there.

Pai was six when Francisco and Luz Maria, pregnant with their sixth child, announced they had saved enough money to move into a house down the road. Mama cried. She had become so attached to little Chino that she couldn't bear to let him go. She asked Francisco and Luz Maria if she could keep him with her. They would be living so close by. They could see him every day. After some discussion, they agreed.

"It's not as if my parents gave him up," Tío Chiquito told me when I sat with him one day after Pai died. "It's just that Mama kept him."

Mama took in other grandchildren as well, about eight in all over the years for various reasons. The tiny house was noisy, a bustling village with Mama as the busy, benevolent mayor. Mama dispatched the grandkids on assorted chores throughout the day, hustling them out with a happy "Get to work!" Some fetched water from the cistern at the side of the house or, when there had been no rain, from the nearby spring or neighborhood well. Some picked pigeon peas and dug up sweet potatoes. Others fed the cow and chickens and collected eggs. Some shucked corn from the field and set the kernels in the sun to dry.

"Ay, *bendito,* aren't you ever going to finish?" Mama would tease one child or another.

Mama was never without a kerchief on her head and an apron over her *bata.* In the kitchen, she ground the dried corn into flour on a hand mill, which she fried up into *surullitos,* or mixed with milk for a cornmeal mush called *funche.* When the children played *gallitos* in the yard, swinging strings weighted with algaroba seeds at each other, they could hear the clatter of her sewing machine rise and fall like a train passing through town.

Benjamín helped Mama with the chores like a little man, like he was her protector. He shot dark looks at his cousins when they showed the slightest disrespect. "Benjamín was good from the time he was born," Tío Chiquito told me. "He was a being that was born with light. With grace. Mama brought him up almost as if he were a relic. He didn't get out of Mama's hands. Benjamín never left Mama's hands."

Mama didn't hide the fact that Pai was her favorite. She whacked the other grandchildren with a broomstick or a branch from the guava tree. If neither was at hand, she'd deliver a good knuckle-thump on the boys' heads. On the rare occasions she disciplined Pai, she tapped him on the arm with two fingers. On Three Kings Day, a Christmas-like celebration every January 6 in Puerto Rico (and other Latin countries), Mama would give the grandchildren homemade rag dolls and inexpensive toy guns or maracas. She gave Pai a new watch. When she caught one of the other grandchildren wearing the watch one day, she hit him. Mama made sure Benjamín had the best shoes and clothes, though by all accounts he never asked for anything. He was kind and shy like Francisco, barely saying a word even among family.

When there was a celebration, Mama cooked up some chicken, and all her children and grandchildren descended on the house. There might be a bottle of local moonshine making the rounds. One of the men inevitably took out a small guitar with double strings called a *cuatro.* Others had maracas, bongo drums, and a homemade *marimbola*—a kind of box with flat strips of metal cut from a car chassis and plucked like a bass. There might be a *guira* made from a coffee can. They'd play traditional *jibara* music. Everyone would sing and dance.

But not Benjamín. He was reserved and serious. He always seemed older than he was. People would laugh sometimes to see such a dry face on a young child.

The only place he seemed to loosen up was on the baseball field.

MY BROTHER JOSÉ—whom we call Cheo—and I ran home from elementary school every day and waited for Pai. We lived at that time in Vega Alta, in a barrio called Ponderosa, just west of Dorado. Our house balanced on stacks of bricks, with wooden steps to the front door. It had a small sitting room, a kitchen, and two bedrooms—one for Mai and Pai, and one where Cheo and I shared a bed. The bathroom had a copper pipe protruding from the wall and delivered only cold water. The floor in the sitting room had two holes big enough to watch the roosters from next door wander beneath us looking for shade.

Pai's shoulders filled the doorway when he walked through,

arriving home from the factory. He always wore a collared shirt. Mai pressed it every morning. He wouldn't put it on until right before he left because the house was hot and humid. I'd eat cereal in front of the TV as Pai, fresh from the shower, padded around bare-chested. Mai made him eggs and boiled hot dogs and coffee. Sometimes I'd go into the bathroom and watch him shave. I'd watch him tie his shoes and hear him wish for ones with more protection around the toes.

I didn't yet know he was going to work. I didn't think of him as having a life beyond baseball and us. Mai worked, too, but I didn't think about where she went, either. Before we were old enough for school, they dropped us off every morning at our grandmothers' homes—Cheo to Mai's mother, me to Pai's. Sometimes I pretended to be asleep in the car because I knew Pai would carry me inside, place me on Abuelita's couch, and kiss me on the forehead. Soon I understood they worked at factories, Pai at Westinghouse and Mai at General Electric.

When Pai got home, Cheo and I already had our gloves in our laps.

"*Bendición,*" we said.

"*Dios te bendiga,*" Pai answered. *May God bless you.*

There were no hugs and kisses. Just the respectful greeting between children and elders.

Pai set his empty Tupperware container on the kitchen counter; Mai would fill it with the night's leftovers for Pai's lunch the next day. Pai sank into the big chair and unlaced his shoes. Mai barked at him from the kitchen not to leave them in the middle of the floor like he always did.

"You're lucky I come home at all!" Pai barked back.

They went back and forth. But Pai was smiling. And I could see that Mai was smiling, too, just a little, like she was trying not to. This was their routine. They almost never touched each other. I rarely saw them kiss. Pai would never show affection in front of other people.

Mai would make a show sometimes of trying to kiss him in public just to get him going. He'd shoo her away. But at the end of the night, they always walked together into the bedroom.

Mai handed Pai a plate of pork chops or fried beef, and he turned on our black-and-white TV to the Mexican comedy *El Chavo del Ocho.* Cheo and I plopped onto the floor next to him. We'd watch *El Chavo,* but we also watched Pai. We loved seeing his face relaxed. Sometimes he laughed so hard we could see the food in his mouth. He didn't laugh much the rest of the time. He still had the serious face he had as a child. He wasn't a talker. He was the sort of man who told you something once. We never had big discussions. He told us to do our homework and respect Mai and take off our muddy clothes on the back patio by the washer and dryer. When he was angry, he'd look straight into our eyes and not move a muscle. We'd stop whatever we were doing.

Mai was a different story. She was outgoing and opinionated. She was the yeller and the hitter. She'd whack us with whatever she could reach—a spoon, a hanger, the back of her hand. We'd run away and she'd chase us—especially Yadier when he came along. He was the happy hellion. Cheo and I were rules followers, me especially as the oldest. Yadier was all about having fun. He'd tease Mai, grabbing her by the waist and whirling her around to dance when she was sputtering mad. Sometimes she'd end up laughing and dancing; she saw a lot of herself in Yadier. But when she had it in her head to wallop us, there was no distracting her. I remember one time Cheo and I wouldn't stop fighting. Mai came after me with a belt, and I crawled under the bed. "Don't worry. You have to come out sometime," she said. When the sun set and the house was quiet, I slithered out, curled up on the bed, still in my baseball uniform, and fell asleep. All of a sudden I was under siege. Mai was whipping my legs.

"I told you I was going to get you! Don't ever run from me!"

There were times she'd put the belt to my back and I'd have two long marks that made an X. When I went outside without a shirt my friends would laugh. "What'd you do now?" Their mothers were the same, and most of the fathers, too. Even the teachers hit us. In sixth-grade English, Mrs. Cuello would walk around the classroom with her hands behind her back as she delivered the lesson. If you weren't paying attention, she'd sneak up and karate-chop your neck. I was extremely introverted and hated speaking in class, much less standing up in the front of the room. When I refused one day, Mrs. Cuello yanked me up to the board, her big old nails digging into my neck. Another time she hurled an eraser at me; I ducked and it hit my cousin Mandy, leaving a rectangle of white chalk on his forehead.

So Mai wasn't unusual in her physical punishments. She was tough. Nothing intimidated her, not even the roaches and rats that infested the houses in our barrio. You'd open a cabinet and a dozen roaches would scatter. We'd find rats almost every morning in the traps Mai set on the kitchen floor or in the patches of glue she placed under the sink and behind the stove. She had no problem picking up the dead ones—or stepping on a live one if she had to. I once saw Mai twist the neck and snap off the head of a live screaming chicken when nobody else had the stomach to do it. She plunged the body in boiling water, plucked the feathers, and gutted it. Pai, on the other hand, got the heebie-jeebies around a dog or cat. When Mai got a small dog after my brothers and I left home, she asked Pai to give him a bath in the plastic tub outside. He took the dog outside and sprayed him with a hose from five feet away. When Mai saw him, she yanked the hose away and turned it on Pai.

"You like that shower now?" she said.

Pai ran away, dripping wet, yelling at her to stop.

"Don't even think about going in the house like that!"

Mai was hard-core. She had to deal with four boys. All of us and Pai.

After *El Chavo,* Pai retreated to the bedroom, changed into his sneakers, and emerged with a canvas bag of bats and balls. Titi Graciella told me Pai went crazy with happiness when I was born because he'd have a son he could take to the baseball field with him. Cheo was born less than a year later. As he grew up, Cheo became handsome, with kind eyes and a sturdy athlete's body. Like Mai, he seemed always to be smiling. I was serious like Pai. But that's where the resemblance ended. Pai was built like a block of granite, with a flat, squarish face and cropped hair. I was skinny with a long face, a big nose, a gap between my two front teeth, and crazy kinky hair that Luis the barber would yank so hard my neck would snap back. I'd cry until Pai gave me one of his looks. For as long as I can remember, I cringed when I looked at myself in the mirror.

We piled into the old Toyota and drove to the baseball field, which was a few blocks from that house in Ponderosa. Every town in our part of Puerto Rico had and still has two landmarks: a church and a baseball field. My two brothers and I were baptized in the big church on the Vega Alta town square. My baptism and communion were pretty much the extent of my church experience. My parents weren't even married in a church. Church weddings cost too much.

As a child, on the few occasions I found myself in the Vega Alta church, I didn't feel that God would live in such a place. The door was thick and heavy, and when it closed behind me, I imagined being sealed inside an enormous crypt, cut off from everything alive.

The ball field was a different story.

There was grass and sun and, from that earliest memory of Pai hitting the home run, I believed baseball fields were places where magical things happened. Pai's lessons about the game only deepened that belief. He told us that the foul lines don't really stop at the outfield fence but go on forever, into infinity. And it was possible, Pai said, for a baseball game to last forever if a team managed to keep getting on base or no team scored. So baseball could defy space and time. That sounded more like God than anything I heard in church.

The baseball field always seemed like an extension of our house, even before we moved back to Espinosa and lived right across the street from the park by the tamarind trees. Pai cared for the baseball fields the way Mai cared for our houses. He brought a rake to clear the rocks and smooth the infield divots. He brought enormous, ten-inch-thick sponges and a wheelbarrow of sand to sop up rainwater. Sometimes he brought gasoline and set the puddles on fire.

He'd push a nail into the dirt by home plate and attach a string. He'd tie the other end to the base of the outfield foul pole. He sprinkled chalk one handful at a time along the string to make straight baselines. Then he'd measure the batter's box and chalk that, too.

Pai had a system for teaching us baseball. He introduced one skill at a time, making sure we mastered it before moving on to the next. First, he taught us how to catch a ball. For days and weeks, we did nothing but play catch. *Two hands. Get in front of the ball.* He didn't yell. He talked. He was loose and comfortable. He talked more in one afternoon on the baseball field than in a week at home. He seemed somehow softer on the field. He even moved differently, with more lightness and grace. He was uncomfortable with affection, but on the field he'd sling his arm around us or pat our faces when we did something well or he wanted to lift our spirits.

After Cheo and I could catch the ball almost every time, he taught us how to stand in the batter's box. *Get balanced. Feet apart, knees bent nice and light. Lift your hands. Be ready to hit. See the ball, hit the ball. See it, hit it! See it, hit it! C'mon!*

We were ready to swing for the fences, the way we'd seen Pai and the other men do. *No,* he said. *You learn first how to bunt.*

He showed us how to hold the bat so the pitch wouldn't hit our fingers. *Here's how you drop the bat to the meet the ball.*

Finally we got to swing.

Eyes on the ball. Let the ball come to you. Wait for it. See it. Then hit it hard somewhere. As hard as you can. Keep your hands on the bat. Keep your body straight, straight, straight. Okay, you're turning away from the ball. A lot of players make that mistake.

Sometimes he pitched beans, corn kernels, or bottle caps. He could make them dip and cut, and you had to watch closely to hit them.

He taught us to run the bases—when to round first base, when to run right through it, how to slide. I was light and fast, one of the fastest in my school. I loved running the bases. An irony, I know, given my reputation later as the slowest man in the Major Leagues.

Then he taught us pitching. *Rest your glove on your chest. Pick a spot on your catcher. Leg high. Push off. Throw it hard. Down the middle of the plate. Right into the glove. Throw strikes. Keep it simple.*

He taught us fielding last. Despite his groundskeeping, the field was still rutted and rocky enough that he was afraid we'd get hurt by a bad bounce. *Watch it all the way into the glove. Play the ball—don't let the ball play you. Bend! Put your glove on the dirt. Stay low. Set your feet.*

He told us not to feel defeated when we missed the ball or made a bad throw. *Be humble. This is a hard game. The players who succeed are the ones who learn from their failures and then toss them aside. Don't dwell. Move on. Focus on the next play.*

He said whatever good plays we made or good hits we got didn't matter unless they helped the team win. *Every time you put on a uniform it's to learn and to win.* Our own performance was meaningless, because baseball wasn't an individual sport. *Your teammates are your brothers. How can you help them win? How can you help them be better?* Pai had no use for players who called attention to themselves or worried about their own stats and accolades.

Be prepared and ready to play, he told us again and again. *If you're not prepared, you're cheating the game and hurting your teammates. If you lose doing all the right things, you can hold your head high.*

When Pai was at work, Cheo and I played on our own. In our street games, the strike zone was a cardboard square taped to a signpost or a chalked square on the side of the house. We wrapped electrical tape around crumpled paper for balls and used broomsticks for bats. We played entire games either by ourselves or with the neighborhood boys—two-on-two, three-on-three. Every boy we knew played baseball. We didn't get many games on television then. Mostly the playoffs and the World Series. My favorite player was Pete Rose, because he played the way Pai taught us: all out. I never risked my Pete Rose in the baseball card games we played in the schoolyard. There was a number on the back of the cards on the top right-hand corner. We challenged each other, one card against another; the highest-numbered card won. Pete Rose stayed safely in my metal lunch box.

In the street with our broomsticks, I *was* Pete Rose. I crouched at the plate like he did. But more times than not, I missed the ball or dribbled it back to whoever was pitching. I couldn't wait to play on a real team with real pitchers and real uniforms. That's when I'd show what I could do.

When I was six and old enough for Little League, I couldn't find a team that had room for me. Some of Pai's coworkers said their sons hadn't found teams, either.

Pai found out there was room in the league in Kuilan. So he started his own team there, in the park where he had played as a boy. Pai signed up all of his coworkers' kids and all the other boys who had been left out. We would stay together as a team for ten years, until we were almost finished with high school. Pai was always our coach.

He called the team *Los Pobres*.

The Poor.

Pai had a lot of rules. Be on time. That was a big one. No shorts or sneakers. Dress for practice in baseball pants and spikes. Team jerseys were for games only, and they had to be clean. Don't miss school. Get good grades. Work hard. Support your teammates. Play selflessly. Don't argue with the umpire. Don't blame anyone else.

All of Pai's rules were about the same thing: respect—for coaches, umpires, teammates, teachers, parents, the game, yourself.

During practices, he took time with each one of us. He'd stand with us in the batter's box, demonstrating how to shift weight from the back foot to the front, how to extend our arms to swing through the ball.

"Great, great!" Pai would say as he threw more pitches. "Again!"

Sometimes Pai would surprise us in practice by throwing a tennis ball instead of a baseball. He'd throw it at our heads so we learned how to get out of the way of an inside pitch. Later he had us swing at a tire skewered on a pole. You had to hit it hard to get it to spin, which trained us to swing with everything we had.

He taught us about strategy. Stealing. Sacrifices. Hitting behind a runner. Mixing up pitches.

He taught us the things that aren't in the rulebooks, too. Failure is part of the game. You're going to strike out, get caught stealing, overthrow the bag. Learn from it and move on. If you don't, the game will crush you. You can't change what you've already done. All you can control is what you do next. What you do now.

Pai didn't yell at us. He wasn't that kind of coach. He spoke to us with respect. As if we were men.

Our field in Kuilan was barely more than dirt, grass, a flimsy backstop, and one stand of wooden bleachers. Pai had to bring home plate. But like all the best baseball parks, it had character. Lumpy pods from the *tamarindo* tree dangled over the left-field fence. When we were bored, we'd toss our gloves at the branches and eat the sweet-and-sour brown fruit from the pods. Beyond center field was a *jobo* tree with pale yellow fruit, juicy as a mango. If a ball hit the *jobo* branches and dropped back onto the field, it was still a home run.

The outfield was an obstacle course. There was a *sanja,* a narrow cement gutter, that ran from the hill above right field all the way through center and left field, carrying rainwater to the street and down into a drain. There was a light pole smack in the middle of left field and another in right field. You had to be ready to jump over a stream of water and scoot around a light pole to catch a fly ball.

Sliding into home was also an adventure. The backstop was unusually close to the plate, and the spiky ends at the bottom of the chain link curled up like old paper. If you didn't stop your slide as soon as you touched home, you risked impaling your legs. Once, when the field was locked, I tried to get in by wriggling beneath the curled-up fence and sliced the front of my right ankle. I still have the scar.

But our strange little field had what every baseball field in the world has: Three bases and home plate. Chalk lines. A pitcher's mound. A batter's box. Two on-deck circles. Two dugouts.

The night before our first game, the new Los Pobres players sat cross-legged on the floor of our living room. Luis. Miguel. Jochy. Steven. Rolando. A dozen of us. Pai stood by the front window next to the table where we ate, now loaded with a pillar of caps and a stack of uniforms that Mai had carefully folded and wrapped in plastic that morning.

A few weeks earlier, Cheo and I had gone with Pai to buy the uniforms at Marco Sportswear, an enormous warehouse and factory with shelf after shelf of gloves, bats, socks, pants, helmets, spikes—whatever you could think of in every size and style. I picked up a perfect, snow-white baseball from an open box. I had never held a brand-new ball. I noticed for the first time how the white covering of the ball was actually made of two hourglass-shaped pieces that fit together like puzzle pieces. It's funny how you can look at something familiar and suddenly feel like you're seeing it for the first time. It was the red stitching that fooled you. It held the pieces together so tightly that they didn't seem like separate parts at all but rather a single thing.

Jesus Rivera "Mambe" Kuilan was our team's *apoderado*—a sort of business manager who handled the team's fees and found sponsors to pay for the uniforms and equipment. Pai and Mambe flipped through a catalog to choose every part of the jersey: collar, buttons, trim, length. They already had decided on colors: yellow and black, like Roberto Clemente and the Pittsburgh Pirates. A lot of teams wore yellow and black for that reason. Many stars have emerged from the ball fields of Puerto Rico since baseball arrived on the island in the late 1800s. There were Hall of Famers Orlando Cepeda, Roberto Alomar, and Clemente. Superstars like Pudge Rodriguez, Javy Lopez, Juan Gonzales, Juan Pizarro, Ruben Gomez, Bernie Williams, José Valentin. More than two hundred players from Puerto Rico have played in the Major Leagues since Hiram Bithorn paved the way in 1942. Puerto Rico was so proud of its baseball stars that schools closed on the day in 1954 when Ruben Gomez—*El Divino Loco*—pitched for the New York Giants in Game 3 of the World Series. He was the first Puerto Rican ever to pitch in a World Series. The Giants won the championship, and when Gomez landed at the San Juan Airport, thousands turned out to greet him. The governor declared the day a national holiday.

But Puerto Rico never had a hero like Clemente. In many houses when I was growing up, including ours, the portraits of two famous men hung in honored spots among the family photos: Jesus, and Roberto Clemente. Most of us knew more about Clemente: signed by the Pittsburgh Pirates in 1954 when he was twenty; won the World Series in 1960; voted National League MVP in 1966; won a second World Series in 1971; hit his 3,000th and final hit of his career on September 30, 1972.

But that's not why he was revered. He grew up in the coastal town of Carolina, east of San Juan. He was eight years old when Bithorn became the first Puerto Rican in the Major Leagues. But Bithorn was white, like the other Latin players who were breaking into the Majors. Clemente was black. No one in the big leagues looked like him. So he turned to the Negro League for role models. As a boy, Clemente rode the bus to San Juan to watch the Negro League stars who played ball every winter in Puerto Rico. He saw Satchel Paige, Josh Gibson, and his favorite, Monte Irvin, an outfielder with the Newark Eagles. Irvin could throw the ball a mile. He could catch anything. He flew around the bases. But he wasn't welcome in the Major Leagues.

The racism in the United States confounded Puerto Ricans. In Puerto Rico, people were all different colors, yet nothing kept them from eating at the same lunch counter, or sleeping in the same hotel, or marrying one another. Clemente's mother came from Loiza, a town founded by slaves who had escaped from the Spanish army. Clemente's father, a foreman in the sugarcane fields, was born just ten years after slavery was abolished on the island in 1873. But there was no societal division between the descendants of slaves and the descendants of the governing Spaniards.

Clemente made his debut with the Pittsburgh Pirates in 1955, just six years after Monte Irvin finally reached the Major Leagues as the first African-American player for the New York Giants. Clemente found that the color barrier might have been broken but it had hardly been destroyed. During spring training in Florida, Clemente had to stay with a black family in another part of town while his white teammates stayed in a hotel. He had to wait in the bus as his teammates ate in roadside diners. He was often quoted by American sportswriters in cartoonish, broken English, feeding into an image of Latinos—especially dark-skinned Latinos—as uneducated and dumb.

But Clemente was so spectacular on the field and so noble off it that he transcended stereotypes. With quiet righteousness, he spoke out on issues of equality and social justice, elevating his stature beyond the sports world. After the Pirates won their second World Series, Clemente pointedly began his postgame press conference in Spanish, speaking directly to the fans watching in Puerto Rico and throughout Latin America.

On New Year's Eve in 1972, Clemente took off in a propeller DC-7 airplane from Puerto Rico to deliver relief supplies to Nicaragua, which had been devastated by an earthquake. The plane crashed into the ocean soon after takeoff, killing everyone on board. When the news spread, people from every corner of Puerto Rico flocked to the beach at Isla Verde, their eyes searching the dark ocean as if expecting Clemente to walk ashore. Only the body of the pilot was recovered. Divers found the briefcase Clemente had been carrying. Three months later the Baseball Writers' Association of America held a special election to vote Clemente into the Hall of Fame, bypassing the required five-year waiting period.

Clemente was all the evidence Pai needed to support his belief that baseball beat out religion six ways to Sunday in turning out strong, decent men.

Inside our living room in Vega Alta, Pai stood at the table while Mai watched from the kitchen, smiling like she always did when she had a house full of people.

"Miguel Lopez!" Pai said as if introducing the starting lineup at the World Series. "Number seven!"

Miguel leapt from the floor. Pai handed him a baseball cap and a uniform. He summoned the boys one at a time to the table with the yellow-and-black uniforms. Finally one uniform remained.

"Bengie Molina!" Pai said. "Number eleven."

I walked up to Pai and he placed the uniform and cap onto my upturned palms. I carried the package with both hands as if it were a fragile plate, stepping over my teammates' legs and hands until I got back to the spot on the floor next to Miguel. He already was wearing his hat, and I put mine on, too. We listened as Pai explained that the uniforms meant we were a family now and we had to think about each other more than about ourselves. We accepted this concept without question, as I would for the rest of my baseball life. My teammates—no matter what team I happened to be on—were my family. I'd do anything for them. And that came from Pai, beginning with Los Pobres.

When the other boys and their parents left, I went into the bathroom and closed the door. I slid the jersey out of the plastic and pulled it over my head. There was a big cursive *P* on the front. I stood on the toilet to examine myself in the mirror. I bent the bill of the cap so it curved just right. To my six-year-old eyes, in my black-and-yellow Los Pobres uniform, I looked just like Pai.

AT THE ENTRANCE of the dugout, Pai clapped and nodded at me in the batter's box.

"C'mon, Bengie," he said. "Eye on the ball."

Mai cheered and hollered from the stands behind me. There was no mistaking her voice. She was a yeller, so different from Pai. She was short and stout with the beefy arms of someone who might, at any moment, deck you with a single blow. She often maintained a running commentary through a game. She yelled at players to slide, questioned the umpires' eyesight, pointed out mistakes, and second-guessed strategy. She'd call me or Cheo and later Yadier to the fence to correct a hitch in our swing or point out a weakness in the opposing pitcher. At home afterward, to Pai and anyone else who happened to be around, she was likely to deliver an in-depth analysis of the game. I told people later that if I were a manager, Mai would be my first hire.

I was ten years old, almost eleven. I looked eight or nine. At the plate, I pawed at the dirt with my back foot, digging into the box. My knees were slightly bent, elbows up, shoulders squared. I watched the first pitch and froze, the bat immobile and useless in my hands.

Strike one.

I could almost feel Pai's hands over mine, adjusting my grip, guiding my arms back, then forward, level across the plate, as if the bat were slicing an apple in midair.

Second pitch. I lunged and missed. Not even close.

Strike two.

A familiar panic began to rise.

Pai had already dropped me down to ninth in the batting order, the spot reserved for the worst hitter.

Third pitch. I could see it was going to sail way over my head. A ridiculous pitch. But the bat was already in motion. I waved at the ball as if swatting flies.

Strike three.

The pitcher slapped his glove, applauding himself.

Hot tears welled in my eyes. I lowered my head so Pai couldn't see me cry. I crumpled into a wet heap at the end of the bench. I hated myself for crying. I hated myself for failing again, no matter what Pai said about letting it go and moving on. My failure felt like a failure for Pai, too. A reflection on him. The embarrassment was almost unbearable.

I looked over at Pai. He was watching the next boy at bat.

"Eye on the ball!" he called. "Be ready!"

I wanted him to look over, to notice I was upset.

I wiped my face and made my way toward him. I stood at his side, leaning lightly into his hip. He looked down at me, startled to find me there. I wanted him to sling his arm around me and tell me, the way fathers do, that everything was all right.

But his eyes were hard. He told me to stop crying.

"There's no room for that here," he said evenly. "Get out there and do your job or go sit with your mother."

My face burned.

Pai turned his attention back to the game.

I knew I was too sensitive. I took things too personally. None of this came easily to me. I wasn't strong like Pai. I knew crying wasn't going to get me very far. But I wasn't at all sure I had it in me to be tough like him.

My darkest fear was that he already knew.

THE BAT WAS too big and heavy for me. Anybody could see that. I was twelve years old but still smaller than my teammates. The bat was new and beautiful, and yellow and black like our uniforms. Everyone else was using it and crushing the ball. I wanted to crush the ball, too. I was the only one on the team who still hadn't hit a ball to the left-field hill at the park in Maysonet where we played some of our games.

I carried the big bat into the on-deck circle.

Behind me, I heard Pai. "Use the lighter one."

"I want to try it," I said, turning toward him.

"Get the lighter one."

"I want to use this one."

"Don't disrespect me."

The worst sin. Pai once kicked the great Pudge Rodriguez off an all-star team for throwing his helmet. Pudge, who went on to become one of the all-time great catchers in the Major Leagues, was about fifteen at the time and by far the best player on the team.

"Take your uniform off," Pai told him.

Pudge started talking back. The other players froze, wondering what would happen. Pai repeated to Pudge that he needed to turn in his uniform and leave the field. "You're off the team."

Pudge stripped off his jersey, tossed it at Pai, and stormed off.

The following week, Pudge arrived at the field with his father. "Benjamín, I'm sorry for what I did," he said. "I want to keep playing with the team. I won't do it again." Pai never had another problem with him.

I knew all that when I ignored Pai's order to use the lighter bat. I didn't care. I didn't want to be the only player too weak to use the new bat. Pai gave me one of his looks. I threw down the heavy bat and retrieved the light one from the dugout. I stepped into the batter's box, fuming. I watched three good pitches go by without the slightest pretense of swinging. I tossed the bat to the ground and brushed past Pai into the dugout.

No sooner had I taken a seat at the end of the bench than, from the corner of my eye, I saw a hand swooping down from behind the fence. Mai grabbed my hair and pulled me the length of the dugout, banging me into my teammates, who scrambled to get out of the way. She pulled me off the field, right in front of everybody. She yelled and whacked my head as she marched me to our car across the street. She shoved me into the backseat and slammed the door. I was furious, but knew better than to talk back to Mai. Through the car window, I watched her return to the bleachers, where she stayed for the rest of the game.

My fury soon died with nothing in the backseat to fuel it. Fear took its place. What would Pai do when the game ended? When the bleachers cleared and my teammates dispersed, I watched Pai walk toward the car. His face told me nothing. When he opened the back door, I braced for the hit, though he wasn't a hitter. Mai was the hitter. Pai had struck me only once in my life. But it had happened recently and was fresh in my mind.

Cheo and I had been fighting all afternoon. Mai kept warning us she was going to tell Pai. We kept fighting. I was supposed to be the man of the house when he wasn't home. I was supposed to look after my brothers and make sure they listened to Mai. When Pai arrived home from work, Mai launched into the story. I shot her an annoyed look, sighing loudly at her complaints, then stomped off to the bathroom. I was sitting on the toilet when my father burst through the door. I reflexively stood up out of respect.

"I need to talk to you," he said.

I started to explain what had happened when I heard Mai yelling from the other room, challenging my version of events.

"Mai, be quiet!" I shouted.

Pai hit me hard across the face.

Stunned, I dropped to the floor and covered my head. I thought he would keep hitting me. I had never seen him so angry. But when I looked up, he was gone. I went straight from the bathroom to bed. I couldn't believe what had just happened. Pai hit me. I felt sick and embarrassed for letting him down. When I woke the next morning, Pai had already left for work. I felt queasy all day. I wondered what he would say when he got home. Would he still be angry? Had he lost respect for me?

That afternoon, he walked into the house without a word. He sat in his chair in the living room and turned on the TV, waiting for *El Chavo* to begin. "Bengie, get me a glass of water," he said.

I leapt up and fetched the water. We went to the field as usual and played baseball. At bedtime, he stopped me in the hallway. "You have to respect your mother," he said. "She is the one who takes care of you. She washes your clothes. She cooks for you. You have to respect her."

"I know, Pai," I said. "I'm sorry."

I became the rules enforcer and the peacemaker, trying to win back Pai's respect. I found that I liked taking charge of my brothers.

They fought about everything. Cheo was more than seven years older than Yadier, and it drove him crazy that Yadier was better at almost everything. When Yadier crushed him in NBA Live on our cousin's PlayStation, Cheo insisted Yadier won because he was the home team and the video game favored the home team. They switched teams, and when Yadier still won—lording the victory over his big brother—they soon were tangling on the floor like feral cats. If I pulled Cheo off first, he'd complain, "Why'd you grab me? Why don't you grab him?" If I grabbed Yadier first, Cheo would still complain: 'Why'd you grab him first? You like him more!"

But the competitiveness stopped at the baselines. We were never jealous of each other or combative on the baseball field. That was unthinkable. Pai and Mai drilled into us that we had to always support each other. That's what families did. I saw how Pai and his brothers and sisters took care of each other. Especially his sisters. They'd hear his car bumping down the dirt driveway of the property where they all grew up, and soon they'd be emerging from their doors. His mother, his sisters Panchita, Graciella, and Pillita, and his brother, whom everybody called Tití, still lived there in various small houses, as did Titi Clara Virgen, Tío Chiquito, Tío Blanco, and Titi Nanita.

"Chino!" they'd cry. Pai visited almost every day, but each time his mother and sisters looked at him as if he were a gift on Christmas morning. They'd beg him to come into their houses for a bite to eat. Pai always said, "No, no, nothing." My aunts fluttered around him, offering to fetch him a beer or a coffee, shoving plates of arroz con pollo at him. No one else received that treatment. He was the prince of the family, the one everyone loved most.

When I went with Pai, my cousin Ivis and my Titi Pillita, who was just four years older than me, would pull me into some game. But

I listened to the adults, smiling at how everybody teased and joked and got each other laughing. When my aunts asked about Mai, Pai would make a big show of rolling his eyes as if to say, "Don't get me started!" His sisters would laugh and slap him on the shoulder. They loved Mai.

When we left, I'd see Pai slip a few dollars into a purse or onto a counter when they weren't looking. Then he'd beat a path back to the car. I'd leap up and run after him, turning to wave at my aunts and grandmother.

I knew we didn't have much money. We had no books in the house except one set of *Encyclopaedia Britannica*. Pai drove a used Toyota Corolla he bought with five thousand dollars he won in the lotto. We hardly ever went to a doctor. If we had a stomachache or headache, Abuelita would rub us with a special oil. She'd stop a bloody nose with a penny carefully placed on our foreheads. I went to the dentist only once during my childhood. (I finally got my cavities filled and the gap in my teeth fixed when I reached the Major Leagues.)

Whenever Pai heard José, Yadier, or me wishing for brand-name spikes or Lee jeans with the button fly or the nice Toyota with a radio that a high school classmate drove, he'd say, "What they have is what they have. What you have is what you have." It was a version of what he said on the baseball field. "This is the team we have. This is the situation we have. So that's what we work with."

Now after my tantrum over the heavy bat, I thought about what a spoiled, disrespectful brat I had been. I was embarrassed. Mai and Pai did everything for us. I was also scared as Pai opened the car door. I braced for his hit. I knew I had earned it. But he just dropped the canvas bag of bats and balls on the floor, closed the door, and got into the driver's seat.

I closed my eyes and exhaled, only to hear the back door fly open again. Mai's hand swooped down on my head, swatting me one last time.

The following weekend, when I walked out of my bedroom in my Los Pobres uniform, Pai shook his head.

"No game for you today."

Mai, Cheo, and Yadier—who was four years old and already built like a tank—went with Pai to the field. I could hear the shouts and cheers through the jalousie windows. When my teammates dashed into the house between innings to use the bathroom, they asked if I was sick.

"If you don't want to be in here like me," I said, "don't disrespect nobody."

WHEN PAI WAS a boy, he and his friends hacked branches off trees in the jungle that ran along the edge of Espinosa. They chose the ones with the hardest woods. They whittled and sanded huge bats, carving out a divot at the top and a knob at the bottom like the real bats they had seen.

Pai had been the smallest of all the boys. The first time he tried to swing the heavy homemade bat, it flopped to the ground. He choked up on the handle. Still not enough. He kept choking up until his hands were halfway up the bat, just below the barrel. Finally he could swing with speed and control, if not power. He looked ridiculous. But he could drive anything thrown his way: beans, bottle caps, grapefruit, taped-up baseballs. The unusual grip drove pitchers crazy. He crowded the plate, a necessity when you have only half a bat to cover the strike zone. If a pitcher threw inside, he risked hitting Benjamín and sending him to first. If he threw over the plate, Benjamín could get the fat part of the bat on the ball and slap it through the infield. So pitchers found themselves throwing outside and falling behind in the count, which forced them to lay one over the plate. Benjamín waited for it and pounced.

"Benjamín was the best," Tío Chiquito told me. "He was tremendous, something incredible. When we were playing in the mountains he would run through those fields like he was a goat and he would catch any ball, it didn't matter where it was. He was incredible, incredible."

Pai's father, Francisco, played some baseball as a kid. Tío Chiquito said he was a catcher for a neighborhood team called Combate. But Francisco worked long hours, and the boys were mostly on their own to learn the game. Pai, Chiquito, their friend Junior Diaz, and some cousins cleared a patch of land behind Mama's house that had once been a guava tree farm. They dug up stumps and cleared rocks, spending hours and days with shovels and rakes and brooms until they had a small field. They cut four pieces of wood for the bases. The guava trees and the mountain oaks served as the outfield fences.

Mama saved paper bags from the grocer for their gloves. But they'd end up playing with their bare hands because the gloves soon disintegrated from sweat and abuse.

When they could, the boys watched the amateur Class A team in Maguayo, a barrio in Dorado not far from Espinosa. They scavenged the team's discards for broken bats and ripped balls. They pounded nails into the split wood. They tore away the balls' tattered covers and wrapped tape around the yarn and cork centers. They practiced every day on their makeshift field, and soon set off to play in their first tournament.

In the first inning of the first game, they were disqualified for the nails in their bats.

Word spread to other neighborhood teams about the kid with the unusual batting grip and lightning-fast speed in the field. When the Guarisco team, in the sector adjoining Kuilan, recruited him to play, Pai was using three pairs of socks as a glove. The other players were bigger and stronger, and most had real gloves. He told his cousin that when the ball hit his hand, he'd feel it in his heart. He learned to block balls with his body. He glided more than darted, getting to the place he needed to be, yet looking as if he'd barely moved a muscle.

Pai and his cousins earned money selling Maria Julia's *alcapurrias* door-to-door. She paid them thirty-five cents for every dollar they collected. The boys also scoured trash bins for copper, which might bring a quarter or two. With the money, they bought five-dollar plastic gloves and six-dollar spikes at Bargain Town in Bayamón.

Soon another sector in Espinosa, Río Nuevo, recruited Pai away from Guarisco. Then Maguayo recruited him from Río Nuevo. He was earning a reputation. People came to see this unconventional player who hit everything thrown and caught everything hit.

ONE DAY A storm rained out our practice. Pai pulled on his jacket, grabbed his keys off the kitchen counter, and headed for the door. I knew he was going to Junior Diaz's.

"Pai, can I go with you?" I asked. I was twelve.

My mother was at the sink washing dishes. She gave my father a look when he said I could go, and I bolted to the car before he changed his mind.

The bar might have had an official name, but all anybody called it was Junior Diaz's, after the man who owned it. It was around the corner from our house, near La Número Dos, the main street through Dorado. I had never been inside, though I'd seen my father there plenty. From outside, you could see a small counter where Junior Diaz sold beer, chips, candy, cigarettes, and on special occasions *asopao,* a rich soup of rice, vegetables, and shrimp. Men sat at tables drinking beer and playing dominoes. Kids wandered in with their quarters to buy soda and chocolate.

Pai and I walked in silence. By then the rain had let up and the low sun threw a shadow across the patio as I followed Pai inside.

"Chino!"

"There he is!"

"Ah, my luck just changed!"

"You bring someone who *knows* how to play?"

Pai laughed and took a Coors Light from Junior Diaz, who had popped the cap before we were two steps in the door.

On the concrete patio were two dominoes tables and a dozen or so mismatched chairs filled with men from the neighborhood, Pai's boyhood friends. I recognized most of them. They looked like Pai: leathery faces, dark eyes, thick arms. But unlike my father, they had round bellies. My father was still broad-shouldered and narrow-waisted. I could see the muscles of his back move beneath his shirt when he walked.

Pai walked the beer over to the low wall of the patio, poured a few drops onto the dirt outside, then took a long swallow. One of the men pushed his dominoes into the center of the table and rose, nodding at Pai to take his seat.

"This your oldest?" the man asked as Pai sat.

"Bengie," Pai said. His face was soft and relaxed.

"Bendición," I said to Junior Diaz's father, who was my *padrino,* my godfather. He was the original owner of the bar.

"Dios te bendiga."

Junior Diaz brought me a Hawaiian Punch in a can. He clapped me on the back and said he hoped I wasn't expecting to learn anything about dominoes from my old man.

Pai smiled, swirling the tiles on the table.

I leaned against the wall and sipped my Hawaiian Punch straight from the can. I knew better than to ask for a straw.

My father was now slapping down tiles and downing one Coors Light after another. The men bet on the games, but they played for beers, not money. With each beer, Pai became more talkative, as he did after our games when my teammates' parents—Pai's coworkers and friends—gathered at our house. He was laughing a lot and telling stories. I laughed at his stories, even the ones I didn't understand. I studied his face, the flat cheekbones, the straight teeth, the short dark hair specked with gray. He caught me looking at him.

"Another Hawaiian Punch?" he asked.

I shook my head. I wanted to show him I wouldn't be a bother.

One of the men asked me if I knew Pai had played Double A baseball when he was only fifteen. I didn't.

"Nobody could figure out how to pitch to him. They throw it here, and he hits it," Junior Diaz was saying, talking about Pai. "They throw it over there, and he hits it. They throw there, and he hits it."

Suddenly everyone was telling a baseball story about Pai. They called him *el bufalo*—the buffalo—and their voices changed when they talked about him. I knew he was famous, though he almost never talked to me about his baseball career. I'd ask him about the trophies in the living room, and he wouldn't even look up from the newspaper. "That was a long time ago," he'd say.

As I listened at Junior Diaz's, I got to wondering. If Pai was so good, why did he work in a factory instead of in baseball? Why didn't he play professionally? What had happened?

"Your boy play like you?" someone asked.

I felt my face flush. The men were looking at me, sizing me up. What was Pai going to say? I was still one of the worst hitters on the team. I had no home runs. Hardly any singles.

"He has *great* hands," Pai said. "The best on the team."

He told the men he liked me to play first base because nothing got by me. "I know I can count on Bengie," he said.

I felt a wave of pure pleasure.

When we returned home, Mai had dinner waiting. I ate my food in silence, replaying my father's words in my head, feeling the same rush of pleasure each time.

In bed that night, I tried to imagine myself in one of the chairs at the dominoes table, listening to the men tell stories about my heroics on the baseball field. But I couldn't make the picture work. It was always my father in the chair.

SOON AFTER THAT day at Junior Diaz's, I had a particularly awful game. I struck out three times. With each missed swing, with each lonely walk back to the dugout, I sank deeper into a funk. Pai never let on that he was disappointed or embarrassed, but I imagined him wondering how a son of his could be so spectacularly weak and ineffectual.

After the game, I went straight to my room and closed the door. Later that afternoon, my cousin Mandy tapped on my window. I cranked open the jalousie window.

"What are you doing?" he asked.

"I feel sick," I said, which was the truth.

When Mai called me for dinner, I told her I wasn't hungry.

"You're eating."

I trudged to the table and fell into a dark silence, not even pretending to eat. Yadier told a story about an argument he had with some kid at school. Yadier never backed down from anyone. He was a tough kid. He attended an elementary school in Vega Alta, like Cheo and I did, because Titi Charo and Titi Yvonne, Mai's sisters, were teachers there and reported back if we skipped class or got into trouble. Cheo and I almost never did. But Yadier had his own ideas about school. He was smart but never worried about what anyone thought. Mai whacked him and yelled at him, but everyone knew she had a soft spot for her youngest son. She liked his warrior spirit. I listened to Yadier's stories and wished I were more like him.

Pai suddenly told me to get up. He said to follow him. My mother, brothers, and I looked up from our plates, wondering what had gotten into him. We never left the table during dinner.

"Come on," he said.

He opened the front door and headed across the street to the field. I jogged after him. Was he going to have me take more batting practice? But he didn't take his equipment bag.

I caught up to Pai at the gate to the field. He went through and stopped near the on-deck circle.

"Look at me," he said. His face was soft.

Then he said the very last thing I expected.

"I love you, *mi hijo*."

My heart pounded. He had never told me. I was surprised and thrilled and frozen. I wanted to say I loved him, too, but nothing came out.

"Good or bad, I love you," he said. "You're going to be fine. God has a plan for you. Do you understand?"

He swept his hand toward the field. "Look at this."

I looked. The bases. The pitcher's mound. The backstop. The dugouts.

"See that?" Pai said. "You know it. You'll be fine. Don't worry."

I didn't know what I was supposed to say.

"Do you understand?"

I nodded. But I didn't understand.

"Okay," he said. Then he walked back through the gate and toward the house.

He turned. "You coming?"

I ran across the street and followed him through the door. My mother and brothers looked up from their plates and studied us silently as we sat back down.

What was he was trying to tell me? That I'd be fine in baseball? That I could always come back there?

The next day at school, I told my cousin Mandy what had happened.

"He said that?" Mandy said, wide-eyed, as if I had told him God Himself had descended from the clouds and personally blessed me. "Man, if he said you'll be okay, then that's it. You'll be okay."

I smiled and nodded.

Pai saw something in me I didn't yet see in myself. I knew then that I'd start hitting. Maybe not that day. But it would happen.

I knew I had to get stronger. My dad's cousin had a son named José Miguel, who had recently signed with the Cubs as a top prospect. He was muscular and strong, and once when I saw him at our field, he told me about lifting weights and doing push-ups and other things that could get my body stronger.

On the way home from high school one day I found just what I needed: a metal pole about four feet long, probably from a chain-link fence. I already had two large tin soda-cracker cans, about the size of Quaker Oats containers. We had half a bag of cement in the *marquesina,* the carport. At that time we were renting a house back in Vega Alta across from the field. I mixed the cement with water on the floor of the *marquesina* then folded in some rocks. I scooped the mixture into one of the soda-cracker cans. I pushed the pole into the cement and positioned it straight up in the center.

The next day, when the cement was dry, I filled the second can. But this time it wasn't so easy positioning the pole. The heavy can at the top kept pulling the pole off center. I held it in place until it seemed set. The next day the pole was leaning slightly, but it was good enough. Now I had a barbell to add to the rest of my carport gym. I had an exercise bike borrowed from my cousin Ramirito, Titi Gorda's son. I had an old tire tied to a rope. I had an ax from my uncle next door. And right outside the *marquesina* was a tree for pull-ups. I'd do regular push-ups and backward push-ups on the cement floor.

I lifted the barbell every day, sometimes before school, sometimes after. One of the soda-cracker cans was heavier than the other, so I had to flip the bar to keep from overworking one arm.

I looped the rope around my waist and ran with the tire behind me through the sand at the ball field. I got the idea from *Rocky.* I ran up our street, which went uphill for about a quarter of a mile and ended at the garbage dump. I ran up and back as many times as I could. Sometimes Tío Felo or one of my cousins would drive me to Breñas Beach or Dorado Beach so I could jog through the sand. I took the ax in the woods behind our house and chopped trees until I couldn't lift my arms. Another idea from *Rocky.*

Over the next year, my body filled out. My shoulders broadened. My arms hardened. My swing got faster and more powerful. My eye was sharpening. I was becoming a steady contact hitter. Pai could count on me to execute a hit-and-run or a sacrifice bunt. I moved up in the lineup from eighth to seventh to fifth. Pai even had me leading off sometimes. And he no longer protested when I picked up the heaviest bat.

One day, at our home field in Kuilan, I got a big fat fastball over the plate. I exploded into it, and the ball rocketed into center field. I rounded first, watching to see if I had a double or a triple. The ball kept going. The center fielder backed up to the fence—and the ball sailed over his glove and out of the park. My first home run. I was fifteen years old.

Pai was coaching third, and he had the biggest smile on his face. As I ran past him, I tried to be cool. He held up his hand for a high five. I slapped it and smiled so wide I almost started to laugh.

That was the year I moved up to American Legion ball—Post 48 in Bayamón—while still playing for Los Pobres. I was playing four games a week and improving quickly. I was a key player, by now one of the best. So was José. Unlike me, he was always a star. Scouts were looking at him even though he still had two more years of high school. So many players from Puerto Rico were signing pro contracts and flying off to the States—Sandy Alomar Jr., Benito Santiago, Carlos Baerga, Pudge, José Hernandez, Ruben Sierra, Edgar Martinez, Roberto Hernandez, Rafy Chavez, Luis DeLeon, Miguel Alicea, Pedro Munoz, Coco Cordero, Julio Valera. They'd return for the winter with better spikes, better gloves, new baseballs, new bats.

I was using an outfield glove that a player I knew in Double A was throwing out. It was ripped in the palm and along the side; a lot of the stuffing had come out. It was thick at the thumb and flat in the palm. I stuffed newspaper into the palm then sealed the rips with Krazy Glue. Every time I caught a ball, I checked the lines of Krazy Glue to see if they held. The newspaper disintegrated quickly from my sweat. But it was the only big outfield glove I had.

Cheo and I talked all the time about what it would be like to play in the pros. But whenever Pai heard us, he told us to think about today's practice, today's game. The rest would take care of itself. But I couldn't help myself. I imagined how proud Pai would be. Could there be a greater gift than to pick up my father's dream and carry it to the finish line? If I made it to the Major Leagues, it would be like we both made it.

One big baseball man.

MY GROWING CONFIDENCE on the baseball field had no effect on the rest of my life. I hated looking in the mirror. My unruly Afro earned me the nickname *fosforo*—matchstick. I was so introverted and self-conscious I barely talked to girls much less dated them. There were times in baseball when I burned to stand up and tell my teammates to keep believing, to keep picking each other up. It was in my head pushing to get out, but I couldn't say it. If I was late for class, I sat on a bench outside rather than bring attention to myself by walking in. In my senior year, we had to read *Don Quixote* and give a talk in front of the class. The guys I hung out with every day persuaded me to practice in front of them. I'd start reading then feel lightheaded and queasy, like I was going to throw up. I couldn't do it.

After class one day, I handed the teacher a written version of my talk.

"I don't know if this counts," I said, "but this is what I'd say."

She said I had to deliver the paper out loud in front of the class. That was the assignment.

"I can't."

The teacher was nice. "Okay, just read it now in front of me."

My voice caught in my throat as it always did. I couldn't do even that.

The teacher said okay and took the paper. She gave me a C. It would have been an A, she said, if I had delivered it out loud. The truth is I would rather have taken an F than speak in front of the class.

EVERY BALLPLAYER IN Puerto Rico raced a ticking clock. Before 1990, Puerto Rican players weren't part of the amateur draft. They were signed as free agents like every other Latin player, usually as teenagers. The youngest were sent to team-run baseball academies on the island until they were mature enough to move on to the farm system in the States. Teams wanted to get you young and develop you themselves. If you weren't signed by eighteen, your chances of signing diminished. Your best hope was to land a spot on a college team in the States and hope you got noticed there. If that didn't work, there was a factory smock with your name on it.

I graduated from high school in 1990, the first year Puerto Rico participated in the June amateur draft. I was sixteen, the age most kids in Puerto Rico graduated from high school. Everyone told me I'd be drafted. I was invited to one or two Major League tryouts a week. Cheo was often invited, too. At fourteen years old, he was already on many scouts' radar. He was a born catcher, with thick legs and a strong arm. So was Yadier.

Not me. I was a pitcher, outfielder, and infielder. I played everywhere *except* catcher. I hoped my versatility would increase my value. The scouts didn't see it that way. They clocked my pitches at 88 mph, but they wanted 90. They timed my speed over 60 yards at 7.1 seconds, but they wanted 6.9. Still they said, "Here, fill out this information. Give us your number." But they never called.

The scouts liked the six-foot-five guys who looked great on paper, whose numbers could be recorded in the appropriate rows, plotted on a graph, fed into a calculator, and ranked accordingly. They didn't like five-nine guys with big hearts and smart baseball minds. They didn't know how to measure that.

The June draft came and went. Nine guys from my American Legion team were drafted. My phone didn't ring.

PAI HAD TURNED pro when he was still in high school. He was fourteen when a scout named Jacinto Camacho first saw him playing Class B ball in Maricao, a sector in Vega Alta. Jacinto had a good eye for talent, and he had ties to the best players and teams in Puerto Rico. He saw something special in the undersized teenager with raw talent and unrefined skills. He swooped and dove at the ball like a bird. At the plate, he slapped one sharp single after another with half a bat. He decided to take the boy under his wing. He threw him in with older players who were hoping to make it to the pros in the States.

"Your father was scared to be with these other guys," Jacinto told me when I sat with him about a year after Pai's death. "He was just a boy of fourteen. But he proved to be better than any of them."

He was more driven, too. Jacinto said he'd never seen a boy as single-minded about baseball. "It was all Benjamín thought about," he said. "He didn't think about anything else."

The following year, when Pai was fifteen, Jacinto took him to practice with players in Double A, the highest amateur league in

Puerto Rico. It was often where the US scouts found their next Major League players. It was crazy that a fifteen-year-old could hold his own in Double A—only one or two new players were chosen from the hundred or so who tried out each season. But not only did Jacinto show up with a fifteen-year-old kid, he announced to everyone there, "This boy will be the batting champion."

Sure enough, the kid from Espinosa made the cut. He signed with Maceteros in Vega Alta for twenty-five dollars per game. (Though the players were classified as amateurs, they were paid to play.) He promptly quit high school, happy to devote himself to baseball practice every afternoon and three games every weekend. Though he wasn't batting champion that first year, he fulfilled Jacinto's prediction a few seasons later, confounding convention with his weird grip.

OUR AMERICAN LEGION team won the Puerto Rican championship in the summer of 1990. We flew to the United States for the national championship. I'd never been off the island. I'd never been on an airplane. Pai and Tío Papo were assistant coaches, so they'd go, too. My cousin Papito loaned me his glove so I wouldn't be embarrassed by my Krazy Glue one.

Before we left, Felix Caro, a family friend, said he might be able to get me on a college baseball team in America. There were supposed to be more scouts at the college games than at tryouts in Puerto Rico. And they were American scouts, who had more pull to sign players. The college would probably be in Florida, Felix Caro said. Good. Not too far from home. I didn't give it much thought. I was too caught up in our trip to the States. I got a seat on the plane by the window and pressed my forehead to the glass. Was that Dorado down there? I knew it so well, yet nothing was familiar from so far away.

In Arkansas for regionals, we stayed four to a room in a hotel that had color TV, an ice machine down the hall, a maid to make our beds, a wrapped bar of soap in the shower, and free breakfast in the lobby. Living large.

When we won in Arkansas, we flew to Oregon to play the other regional winners. Felix Caro called me at the hotel room there. He had found a college in a city called Yuma. There were other Puerto Rican players. I would fly there after I was done playing in Oregon. Pai was happy for me. He said to make sure I studied hard to learn English. It was the language of the Major Leagues. He said to get an American roommate so I could practice every day.

I couldn't think about college yet. The tournament was too exciting. I led the tournament in RBIs and stolen bases—such a long way from my failures of just a few years earlier. ESPN broadcast our championship game against Maryland. We lost, but the sellout crowd and TV cameras gave us a taste of what a life in baseball might be.

The night before we left Oregon, Pai pulled out his wallet and handed me twenty dollars.

"Make it last a month. Then I can send you more."

It didn't seem real until we boarded the team bus to the airport. I began to feel sick. I had never lived away from home. I had never played baseball without Pai. I couldn't picture it. Baseball was my father.

The bus stopped at my terminal first. Everyone else was flying back to Puerto Rico from a different terminal. Pai followed me off the bus. I retrieved my bag from the baggage compartment. Pai gave me a hug.

"God bless you, *mi hijo,*" he said. "Go out and make something of yourself."

"I'm going to miss everyone so much," I said quietly. I was going to miss him especially.

"This isn't the time to think about that. Play baseball. Have fun. Be yourself."

He boarded the bus. I stood at the curb as my teammates slapped the windows and yelled, "Good luck!" Pai didn't look at me as the bus sighed and pulled away. I felt like a piece of me was gone.

The plane made a stop, where I boarded another plane that would take me the rest of the way. This plane looked no bigger than a school bus. It landed again just forty minutes after takeoff. We were in Florida already?

"Yuma?" I asked the man next to me.

"Yuma," he said.

I stepped out of the plane and into a blast of hot air. The land beyond the runway was a moonscape. Flat and desolate as far as you could see. No water anywhere. This didn't look like any pictures I'd seen of Florida. I followed the other passengers to baggage claim. A white man in a baseball cap approached. He was short and thin, in his thirties or forties.

"Bengie Molina?"

"Yes!"

"Welcome," he said, shaking my hand. He continued to talk, but I couldn't understand a thing, though I deciphered that he was the college baseball coach.

"Lo siento, no comprendo," I finally said.

"No problem," he said, smiling. We took a sun-cracked two-lane highway through flat expanses of the driest land I'd ever seen. On the horizon rose craggy mountains without a speck of green. How could anything survive out here? But here and there a lettuce field appeared or a citrus grove. And then, suddenly, buildings.

The sign in front said "Arizona Western College." Arizona? I had never heard of Arizona. I had no idea where it was. I also had no way to ask. We pulled up to a row of three identical two-story buildings with lots of windows. Classrooms, I figured. When the coach parked and pulled out my suitcase from the back, I realized this was where I'd be staying. It looked like a *caserio,* buildings with tiny apartments where poor people lived.

The coach took me inside to a lobby, where I signed some papers and was handed a key and a folder of information. Someone around my own age showed me to Room 116 on the first floor. I was instantly homesick. The room smelled like dirty clothes. Men's smell. There was a bunk bed already made up with sheets, blanket, and small pillow, and a duffel bag on the bottom bunk. There was a little table. The walls and floor were bare.

Behind a door, a bathroom with a shower and a toilet connected to a second dorm room. I dropped my bag into a corner and didn't unpack. I already knew I wasn't staying. I was sixteen, an age when American kids were still in high school. I didn't speak English. I had never been away from my family or, until the American Legion trip, away from Puerto Rico. What was I doing here in this strange, lonely place?

I climbed to the top bunk, sat next to the room's only window, and pushed it open. An oven. I could see the mountains in the distance and a few other buildings. The air had no smell of trees and ocean. No smell of rain or flowers or Mai's home cooking. Just dust and dirt. I stretched my arm out the window and flipped my palm over and back, wondering how long it would take to bake a human hand in this heat.

The room had no TV or radio. I didn't know what I was supposed to do. I walked back to the lobby. A couple of kids sat on couches watching TV. No dominoes. No music. Back in my room, I flipped through the "Welcome" brochure. I could read a few words from taking English in high school, but mostly the sentences were just letters on a page.

I had made a huge mistake. I didn't belong here. I would go back to Puerto Rico and play amateur ball and try to make it to the Major Leagues that way. I returned to the lobby and managed to get someone to show me how to use the pay phone in the hallway: Push zero, say "collect call," push two for Spanish, then give the operator the number.

"This isn't for me," I told Mai, trying to sound businesslike. I knew Pai wasn't home from the American Legion trip yet. I pictured her in the kitchen in her *bata,* and Cheo and Yadier watching TV in the living room. I wanted to be there.

"I don't like it," I said. "The air's too dry. I don't speak the language. I won't understand anything the coach is saying."

"Oh, Bengie, don't start with that! You haven't even been there one day. Give it a chance."

We didn't speak long because collect calls were expensive.

I was hungry, but didn't leave the room. The coach had pointed out the cafeteria on the drive in, but I didn't know how the system worked or when I was supposed to go.

Around ten thirty that night, the door burst open.

"Bengie! *Llegastes!*" You're here!

It was Kenny Marrero from Espinosa. Kenny's dad worked with Pai. He was with four other Puerto Rican guys. I knew Angel "Bambi" Sanchez from Little League; I'd played against him my whole life. I knew Alex Cordoba from school in Vega Alta. I didn't know anyone else, including my roommate, a freshman named Rene Reyes, whom everyone knew as Flaco, which means skinny.

Classes had started, so all those guys except Flaco and me had been on campus for a few days already.

"You know who this guy's father is?" Kenny said. "He's one of the most famous players in Vega Alta. My dad used to tell me he hit like Rod Carew."

He told Flaco and me to meet in the lobby at seven the next morning for breakfast before class. We met up with other ballplayers in the cafeteria, where, following what everybody else did, I showed my food card, got a tray, and, unable to speak English, pointed to the eggs, bacon, potatoes, and something that looked like *avena*, our version of oatmeal. I was so hungry, I took everything. The lady behind the counter spooned each choice onto a plate divided into compartments. I wolfed it down.

"I could eat another plate," I said.

"Go back. You can get as much as you want."

I got eggs and bacon again. Kenny showed me another counter where I could get cereal, juice, fruit, bread, anything I wanted, and all I had to do was give the cashier my food card. There was a soda dispenser like you'd find in a fast-food restaurant. Kenny told me I could fill my cup with Coke or 7-Up as often as I wanted.

Flaco and I were the new students in class. English as a Second Language. Three other Spanish-speaking teammates were also there, along with ten or so adults from the Yuma community. That was our only class, though it lasted all day with a break for lunch. We received credits toward an ESL certificate that prepared us for higher-level college courses.

"Bienvenidos! Me llamo Señora Davene El-Khayyat."

I had taken a seat in the front row, intent on learning as quickly as I could the language of the Major Leagues.

"This is English as a Second Language," Mrs. El-Khayyat told Flaco and me in Spanish. "This is the last time you'll hear me say anything in Spanish. If you have a question, don't be shy to ask in Spanish. But since we're learning English, from now on, it's English."

She was middle-aged with short salt-and-pepper hair and about Mai's height. She wore jeans, a flowered collared shirt, and glasses. Her voice was direct and even. She had an accent, but not a Spanish one. Maybe Middle Eastern.

"You will give presentations to the class," she said.

Presentations. My stomach fluttered. There was no way I was making any kind of presentation. It was nerve-racking enough speaking in front of a class in my own language, much less in English. I had been watching American television in Puerto Rico and in the hotel rooms in Arkansas and Oregon. Everyone said that was a good way to learn English. I picked up almost nothing.

"Everyone participates. This is the only way to learn. Do you understand?"

No one spoke.

"Understand?"

"Sí!" we said.

"No *sí*—yessss!"

"Yessss!"

Mrs. El-Khayyat gave Flaco and me workbooks and told us to stay after class to review what we had missed.

"Ricardo!" she said, looking up from her class binder. "Please come forward and read the first sentence on page seven."

Ricardo was short and round and looked to be in his fifties or sixties. He laughed nervously and shook his head. *"Ay, no, no."*

"Thank you, Ricardo," Mrs. El-Khayyat said, as if Ricardo had agreed. She stepped to the side of her desk to make room for the old man.

Ricardo rose slowly. He held the open book in both hands like a hymnal. At the front of the room, he turned to face us and suddenly burst forth with a string of butchered English words, triggering a ripple of muffled laughter. My heart pounded as if it were me up there. I was embarrassed for him. But he looked up from the workbook when he had finished and smiled.

Mrs. El-Khayyat pronounced the butchered words correctly and told him to try again. The second time was no better.

"Thank you, Ricardo."

Her eyes swept the room. I sank into my chair. She called on one of my teammates, who was as awful as Ricardo. One after another, the students stood and mangled the unfamiliar words. By now, we were laughing out loud, even the speakers and even me. But not Mrs. El-Khayyat. She clapped her hands like a coach. "Come on, come on!" she'd tell the fumbling student. "Slowly!"

Finally she called on me.

My mouth went dry. I would rather run fifty laps in baseball practice than spend one minute up there.

"Page thirteen," Mrs. El-Khayyat said. "Let's go."

There was no escape. I stood, careful not to raise my eyes from the book and see all those people staring at me. I took a breath. The words squeaked out in tortured chirps, like a bird being strangled. But no one laughed. Not even one stifled snigger. I was too pathetic.

"Louder please, Benjamin." She said Benjamín the English way, pronouncing the *j* like a *g* instead of an *h*.

I repeated the sentence, trying to enunciate every syllable.

"Next sentence! Louder!"

She was not going to let up.

I tried to produce some saliva. I read each word carefully. I had no idea what any of the sentences meant. My brain had gone blank.

"Wonderful!" Mrs. El-Khayyat said. "Thank you!"

I sank into my chair as another student took his turn. My heart continued to pound until the bell rang for lunch. We returned for two more hours in the afternoon, then we were done. Baseball practice wouldn't begin for another week or so.

I went straight to the pay phone.

"I have to come home, Mai. This isn't for me."

She told me I wasn't coming home.

The next afternoon I asked for Pai. He wasn't as tough as Mai. He'd understand.

"Mai says you're in Arizona," he said, laughing. "I thought you were going to Florida. Where's Arizona?"

"I don't even know."

He asked about the dorm and the campus and the people.

"Pai, I need a ticket to go home."

"I don't have money for a ticket until my Christmas bonus."

I called every day for a week. Pai kept telling me everything would be okay once baseball started. I was so homesick I could barely sleep. If I couldn't find the other Puerto Rican guys, I didn't eat. I was too insecure to go to the cafeteria by myself. I felt sick every time I had to speak in Mrs. El-Khayyat's class. I wanted to hear the *coqui* frogs outside my window and the rain on the roof and Cheo snoring in the next bed.

Pai finally had enough.

"You're not going anywhere. Be a man. You haven't even started practicing yet. If you talk about coming home one more time, you're on your own. I'm not talking to you anymore."

I didn't call the next day. Or the day after that. Then practice began. I had to get Kenny to ask the coach for a glove. The one I had used for the American Legion tournament belonged to my cousin. Pai had figured the coach would have one I could borrow, and he did. My spikes had so many holes that a teammate gave me his old ASICS, and by the third day of practice someone else gave me an old glove.

I loved practice from almost the first minute. Everything was so organized. We split into groups and rotated from batting to fielding to throwing. We hit off a tee, then soft toss, then normal BP with live pitching. I was playing outfield, and we'd simulate game situations. "Man on second! One out!" We'd whip a throw to the cutoff man, who whipped it home. Bang-bang. It was so cool.

At the end, everyone gathered at the plate to run the bases. The coach said some words and we were done.

The two and a half hours flew by. I had never had a practice like that. Every single minute mattered. This was what baseball was like at the next level. It was amazing. I couldn't wait until practice the next day.

Pai had been right. I needed the grass, the dirt, the lines of chalk. I'd be okay. I knew where I was.

PART 2

THE SUN IN Yuma felt like it had something personal against you. I kept waiting for a good rain. I missed that more than almost anything else about home. In Puerto Rico, you could smell the rain before it arrived. The air turned cool for a few minutes. The breeze rustled through the trees. Then the skies burst. Puerto Rican rain didn't fool around. It came down in big, burly drops, roughhousing with us. I loved the sound of it clattering on our roof.

In Yuma, if it rained at all, it rained wet dust. The first time it rained in Yuma during my first semester, my Puerto Rican teammates and I ran to the basketball court to slide through the puddles. But the heat dried the water before a single puddle could form, leaving only a film of dirt behind. On the baseball field, our spit disappeared the instant it hit the ground. The sun seared our bare necks and arms and hands. Whatever rays got past us on the way down bounced back off the ground for a complete, full-body bake. At the end of practice, our skin was slick with sweat and dirt and dust. Grit coated our teeth as if we'd eaten sand.

I didn't mind, though. I loved baseball practice. It felt like the pros. We ran at a certain time. We took batting at a certain time. Some days I'd take swings in the batting cage until my cheap batting gloves fell apart and my palms turned bloody. The coach was tough and demanding, and I liked that, too. He asked one day who had experience pitching. I said I did, and he had me pitching as well as playing outfield. Then when our shortstop went down with a season-ending injury, he asked who played shortstop. Again I raised my hand, and he tried me out. My teammate Bambi played second, and we turned double plays as if we'd been partners for years. I loved shortstop and pitching, my two favorite positions. I never returned to the outfield.

One of the Puerto Rican guys, Roberto, was our best player. I knew him from home, and he had always been cocky. Now he was worse, exactly the kind of player Pai wouldn't tolerate. I wondered how our coach would handle him.

One day at the end of practice, the coach had us running from the foul pole in left field to the foul pole in right and back again. Twenty-five times. He stood in center field near the warning track. He gave us two rules: Don't run on the warning track and don't touch him when we ran past. We were almost finished when, sure enough, Roberto brushed against the coach.

"Twenty-five more poles," the coach said. "Everybody."

He gave us the choice of running the poles right then, which meant we'd miss dinner, or doing it the following the day, our one day off. We glared at Roberto. It was late and we were hungry. But we ran. We yelled at Roberto as we ran. For most of us, this coach and this college were our last shot at the pros. They kept us in the battle. Maybe we wouldn't make it. But we were squeezing everything we could out of every practice and every game. And Roberto was treating the whole thing like a joke.

"The rest of us are here trying to be better players," I said, running alongside him. "You're here just to have fun and make us run."

"I hate that guy."

"It doesn't matter if you hate him or not. You respect the guy in charge."

"He's an asshole."

I wanted to knock him to the ground. He didn't deserve to be there. He didn't want it enough.

ONE DAY WHEN Pai was sixteen, the scout who discovered him, Jacinto Camacho, had a surprise. They drove to San Juan to watch the Senadores in the winter league. The 20,000-seat baseball stadium was the largest on the island. It had been built four years earlier, in 1962, replacing the old one, which seated about 13,000. The old stadium had been named for the island's first boxing champion, Sixto Escobar. But the new one bore the name of Puerto Rico's first Major Leaguer, Hiram Bithorn—a choice that underscored the shift from boxing to baseball as the island's most popular sport. Bithorn had been a hero, so no one talked much about his tragic end. After achieving his historic milestone, he scuffled around the Majors for a few years before landing an umpiring job in the Class C Pioneer League. Then, nearly penniless, he tried to make a comeback in Mexico. He then disappeared. His family lost track of him only to learn that he had been murdered in El Mante, Mexico, in 1951 and buried like a pauper in an open grave. They had the body returned to Puerto Rico and held a memorial at the San Juan stadium that would later bear his name. Thousands of fans turned out to honor a national hero. They didn't care that most of Bithorn's life had been sad and tragic. All that mattered was that Bithorn had, one day long ago, reached the Major Leagues.

Puerto Rico's passion for baseball attracted the best players to the island's winter league. In the 1960s and '70s, baseball's biggest Puerto Rican stars returned home every October to play a 70-game schedule following their 154-game (later 162-game) schedule in the Major Leagues. (In the mid-1980s, winter league games were pared to between 48 and 60 games.) But not just the great Puerto Ricans played in the winter league. Teams sent their best young prospects to hone their skills. Dozens of future Hall of Famers, from Willie Mays and Hank Aaron to Sandy Koufax, Johnny Bench, and Reggie Jackson, launched their careers from parks in San Juan, Mayaguez, Arecibo, Aguadilla, Ponce, Guayama, Humacao, Santurce, Caguas, Bayamón. Veteran players used the winter league to work their way back from injuries or to resurrect flagging careers. Journeymen came for a working vacation, enjoying the warm weather while earning extra money in the off-season.

On Puerto Rican winter teams, you saw all-star combinations of players you never could in the United States. In the 1954–55 season, the New York Giants' twenty-three-year-old superstar Willie Mays played for the Santurce Crabbers alongside a twenty-year-old Pittsburgh Pirates prospect named Roberto Clemente. The third outfielder for Santurce that season was thirty-seven-year-old Bob Thurman, a Negro League slugger from Oklahoma who would hit more career home runs in the winter league than any player in history. At one point, Mays was hitting .304, Clemente .378, and Thurman .366. On the mound for Santurce was El Divino Loco himself, New York Giants pitcher Ruben Gomez, who was fresh from his triumph as the first Puerto Rican to pitch in the World Series. Two-time National League All-Star Sam Jones, the first African-American to pitch a no-hitter in the Major Leagues (for the Cubs), also was on that team. So was Don Zimmer, the Brooklyn Dodgers shortstop who eventually played for or coached six World Series champions. Even the batboy had star power: Orlando Cepeda, the future Hall of Famer for the Giants and the son of winter league star Pedro "Perucho" Cepeda. No surprise: The Crabbers won the league championship and the Caribbean World Series. And Thurman's great season convinced the Cincinnati Reds to give him a shot at the Major Leagues. (He made his Major League debut in 1955, a month shy of his thirty-eighth birthday. He showed glimpses of the star he had been in his prime, but in 334 Major League games over five seasons, he hit just thirty-five home runs.)

Puerto Rican fans were not like any you saw in the States. They stood on seats, waved banners, jeered players and umpires, broke into song after great plays. They'd pass buckets or baseball caps through the stands to collect money for lower-paid players who made spectacular plays or hit home runs. Players went home with pockets full of nickels and dimes. Paper money flew from hand to hand in the stands, too, as bets were laid on strikes, balls, fouls, errors, who would score first, which pitcher would be yanked first, everything. Even the smell of the park was different. Instead of hot dogs and popcorn, Puerto Rican parks smelled like your mom's kitchen—the deep-fried cod of the *bacalítos,* the meat of the *alcapurrias,* the flaky crusts of the *pastelillos.*

Rivalries ran deep. In Puerto Rico, people take great pride in where they come from. You talk to anyone and they'll tell you they're not just from Puerto Rico, they're from Santa Grande or Santurce or Dorado. You carry that place as close and tight as you carry your family. I was born in Río Piedras. I went to school in Vega Alta. But I am from Dorado. I grew up in Dorado. My struggles were in Dorado. My family's struggles were in Dorado. There was a Puerto Rican poet named Enrique Zorrilla who captured our deep sense of place: "My pride is my land / For I was born here / I don't love it because it is beautiful / I love it because it is mine / Poor or rich, with burning / I want it for my own."

This poet's son, Pedrin, grew up to be the owner of that great Santurce team with Mays and Clemente. He saw the depth of the Puerto Rican connection to their hometowns every week of the winter season. It was said that fans attending a game at a rival ballpark—a San Juan fan visiting Santurce, for example—usually parked a good distance from the stadium; Santurce fans might vandalize a car with San Juan stickers or decorations. Fans lived for winter baseball, huddling around radios when they couldn't get to the parks. I heard that during a game in Caguas one year, a rainstorm hit in the fourth inning. When it stopped, two inches of water covered the field. Players took one look and retreated to the clubhouse to change out of their uniforms. There would be no game. But the fans had other ideas. They already had missed almost a week's worth of games to rain, so those who lived nearby raced home and returned with wheelbarrows, which they filled with soil from a big pile under the stands and spread across the infield. Forty minutes later, the game resumed.

Pai loved the Senadores. He was eight years old when Clemente joined the team during the 1957–58 season. Two years later, after the Pirates won the World Series, Clemente returned to Puerto Rico a national hero. In the winter of 1966, when my father accompanied Jacinto to Hiram

Bithorn Stadium, Clemente had already won three National League batting titles and the NL's Most Valuable Player Award. He was a god, and Pai must have been excited about going to watch him play that day.

But when he and Jacinto arrived at the stadium, instead of climbing the stairs to their seats, Jacinto took Pai straight into the Senadores clubhouse. There among the half-dressed players stood a tall, dark, graceful man in baseball pants and an undershirt. His shoulders and arms looked like they'd been carved from a ceiba tree.

Roberto Clemente. He was thirty-one, in the prime of his career.

I imagined Pai as a sixteen-year-old in that moment, frozen where he stood, his heart thumping against his chest.

"Jacinto!" Clemente said.

Everyone, it seemed, knew Jacinto Camacho.

The two men shook hands. "Who is this?" Clemente asked.

"This one's a special player," Jacinto said. "Benjamín Molina Santana."

Clemente shook the boy's hand and looked him over. Pai was broad-shouldered and fit but hardly imposing at five feet eight. Clemente asked Benjamín what position he played and where he was from and whether he was still in school, chatting as if he were a guy on a street corner in the barrio. I wonder now how much Clemente's humility shaped Pai's belief that it was the most important characteristic of a good man.

When Jacinto and Benjamín were about to leave, Clemente invited Benjamín to sit with him in the dugout. Even Jacinto was surprised. Nonplayers weren't permitted in the dugout during games. But it was Clemente. Who was going to argue? When Clemente returned to his locker to finish dressing, Pai told Jacinto he couldn't possibly sit next to Clemente. He was too nervous.

Jacinto snorted. "Are you kidding?"

He gave the teenager a friendly shove and left the clubhouse to find his seat in the stands. I never found out what Clemente and Pai talked about in the dugout during the game. I never knew that Pai had even *met* Clemente. I didn't understand that about my father. If I had met Clemente, I'd be so proud to tell my kids. But he said nothing. Maybe in his mind it was bragging. Maybe in his mind what mattered was now, not yesterday.

But Jacinto said he saw a lot of Clemente in Pai. Not physically; they had different builds and styles of play. But both were as tough as they come. Pai was small, but he was a bull. He'd get spiked by a runner sliding into second and still turn the double play. He'd plow into a catcher twice his size and pop back up. "You never heard him complain," Jacinto said. "That's what made him who he was."

Like Clemente, Pai never doubted his abilities. He could go 0-for-15 at the plate, and the next time up, he'd dig in to the box as if he couldn't miss. He believed in his own talent, but more than anything he knew no one prepared more than he did. He'd watch every pitcher from the dugout, figuring out patterns, watching for weaknesses he could exploit. He noticed everything—on the field, anyway.

He had no clue about the girl at the Vega Alta ballpark who had been watching him for weeks.

Gladys Matta Rosado was the fiery sister of Pai's teammate, Felo, on the Double A team in Vega Alta. She was funny and outgoing and a savvy student of the game. She liked the look of Pai, his high cheekbones and warm smile. He was not a big man but he seemed to take up more space on the field than anyone else. He had steel and intelligence in his eyes—not that those eyes ever wandered her way. His focus never drifted beyond the baselines. Mai asked her brother about him. Felo laughed. He told his sister that this boy was so quiet and shy he wasn't sure he had ever heard him speak outside the ballpark.

I once asked one of my aunts how my introverted father ever started to court Mai.

"How did *she* court *him,* you mean?" Titi Panchita said, laughing.

Mai wrangled an introduction and, after Pai asked Mai's father for permission, the two started dating. Pai's best friend, Junior Diaz, also had a girlfriend in Vega Alta. Twice a week after baseball practice, they rode the bus from Kuilan to Vega Alta then headed off in separate directions to the houses of their respective girlfriends. Mai's family was as poor as Pai's. Until she was nine years old, the family lived in the woods at the top of a mountain in a cabin with dirt floors and cloth sacks covering the windows. Mai and her six brothers and sisters carried buckets to school and hauled water from the river on the way home. Mai's father got a job at a tractor company as a security guard, and the family moved closer to town, into the house where Gladys lived when Benjamín met her. It had wood floors, running water, and an indoor toilet.

When Pai visited, he sat with Mai and her family in the yard on plastic chairs. Pai left at ten to meet back up with Junior Diaz. The buses didn't run that late, so they made the hourlong walk back to Espinosa in the dark.

Mai was a good fit for Pai. She was lively and gregarious enough to fill Pai's silences. And what luck to find a girl who loved baseball as much as he did.

IN COLLEGE, I was still self-conscious about how I looked. I had yet to go out on a date. But I kept running into the same girl from my dorm. She always looked at me and smiled. No girl had ever really looked at me. She had dark hair and light skin and lived on the girls' side of the dorm. I had seen her around campus holding hands with a boy, so I knew she was off-limits. Not that I knew how to ask a girl for a date anyway. Still, whenever we crossed paths, she smiled at me, and I found myself scanning the campus walkways for her. One day I was with friends outside the dorm, just sitting and talking at a picnic table. And there she was walking by herself and coming my way.

Before I realized what I was doing, I got up and walked toward her. She didn't see me at first. I was twenty feet away when she noticed me. She smiled. Then I was ten feet away. I smiled back. Five feet. Our eyes locked. Time to say something. Hello. Hey. What's up? Anything.

I walked past her without a word. Now what? I continued for a few yards then turned and followed her back toward the dorm. She pushed open the door and disappeared. My friends were laughing when I returned to the picnic table. They had watched the whole thing.

"What was that all about?" Kenny asked.

"I don't know!" I laughed, too. What an idiot. I was sixteen and had never talked to a girl I liked.

A few weeks later, I saw her on a bench by herself. I was returning to the dorm from practice. My throat went dry.

"Hi," I managed.

She looked up from her book. Her face brightened.

"Hi," she said. "I see you around all the time."

I was surprised to hear her speaking in Spanish. I had thought she was American.

"I just wanted to say hi," I said.

"Oh! That's nice."

She closed the book on her lap.

It was my turn to say something. I knew that much. Her eyebrows arched. I sucked in a breath as if to speak. Nothing came out. Her brows arched higher and her chin tilted up, the picture of attentiveness.

I was mute as a stump.

"Okay," she said, reopening her book. "I'll see you around."

"Okay, I'll see you around," I said, echoing her like a toddler learning to speak.

The next time I saw her, she again was alone on the bench outside. I still burned with embarrassment from our last encounter. I wasn't sure I had the nerve to talk to her again. As I drew closer, I saw she was crying.

"Are you okay?" I asked.

She looked up. Her eyes were red. I sat next to her, then thought maybe I shouldn't. "I don't want to get you in trouble with your boyfriend," I said.

"We're not together anymore."

She told me about the breakup and about herself. Her name was Josefa and she was from Mexico, just over the border from Yuma. Her father worked in an orchard in Yuma during the week and went home to Mexico on the weekends. I told her about myself. We talked so long I missed dinner.

SIX WEEKS INTO the semester, Pai's twenty dollars finally ran out. Monday through Thursday, I ate in the cafeteria twice a day. But Friday, Saturday, and Sunday, we were allowed just one meal. So we'd go to the Circle K and buy four cans of soup for a dollar; microwave hamburgers for a dollar; bread, ham, cheese, and mayo for eight dollars. My teammates and I shared shampoo and laundry detergent. Now my cash was gone.

I was trying to figure out what to do for money when a Mexican teammate offered me a job on his uncle's Mexican baseball team. It paid forty-five dollars. The only problem: The games were on Sunday. Sunday was our day off from baseball, and the coach was adamant about using the day to rest. I didn't want to defy him by playing on Sunday. But I didn't want to ask Pai for money, either.

So the following Sunday I climbed into the back of a pickup truck with a few other teammates. Yuma is in the far southwest corner of Arizona, on the border of both California and Mexico. We rode twenty-five miles down Route 95 to San Luis, Arizona, then across the border. The games were fun—lots of families and townspeople in the stands. And we got paid on the spot in cash. I played every week, so suddenly I was flush with money. Instead of just necessities, I splurged on bologna, Fritos, Doritos, Cheetos, 7-Up, fruit juice. Over time, I bought new sliding pants to replace my ripped ones and a new jock strap. I bought a pair of jeans, one T-shirt, and one collared shirt at Kmart. I was making my own way.

TOWARD THE END of the semester, Mrs. El-Khayyat made the announcement I had been dreading.

"On Monday and Tuesday, you'll be making your presentations. So you have the weekend to prepare."

She gave us a two-page story in English, a different story for each of us. For our presentation, we had to read the entire story in front of the class, then explain it in Spanish to make sure we understood. ESL was my only class. Mrs. El-Khayyat was my only teacher. I was with her from seven thirty in the morning until two fifteen in the afternoon. She was kind and encouraging, nothing like the tough taskmaster she seemed the first day. She loved baseball and, after class, she'd ask my teammate Kenny Marrero and me about Puerto Rican baseball and what the fields looked like and how the fans were. She told us that her husband was from the Middle East and that she had a young son and daughter. Kenny and I even went to dinner at her home, a tiny house with lots of overseas newspapers and magazines. She picked us up at the dorm and made us baked chicken. She taught us to put our napkins on our laps and to say, "May I please have the salt?"

She wasn't like any teacher I'd ever had. She taught English the way Pai taught baseball, step by step, little by little, building competence in one small segment before moving on to the next one. She expected us to respect her and our fellow students by arriving on time. She addressed us courteously and trusted we would respond in kind. Like Pai, she drilled into us that failure was the price of progress. I endured the short readings in front of the class with the usual panic and cold sweat but with a growing realization I was improving at a faster clip than most of the other students. Pai's advice to get an American roommate was paying off. Earlier in the semester, I had moved in with one of our pitchers, a big blond kid from Arizona. He'd point to everything in the room and teach me the English word. *Bed. Sheet. Window. Floor.* He taught me to say "Please" and "May I?" and "Excuse me." He told me to listen to Garth Brooks, and I did. I picked through the words in the local newspaper. I watched American television.

But now I had to read *two full pages* out loud. I thought about nothing else the entire weekend. I pictured myself at the front of the classroom. I'd be up there for an eternity, long enough for my self-doubt to slither out from under the floorboards of my brain and wrap itself around my vocal cords, rendering me mute. In my room,

I practiced the story over and over, asking my roommate about pronunciations and definitions.

In class on Monday, when it was my turn, I felt sick. Mrs. El-Khayyat smiled, welcoming me to the front of the class. There was no escaping this the way I did in high school. I read my two pages, then summarized them in Spanish. My voice never cracked. My classmates clapped, which they did after each reading.

Then Mrs. El-Khayyat handed me the *Arizona Republic,* folded to a sports column. "Would you read this to us?"

More? I hadn't practiced these words. I began to protest, but Mrs. El-Khayyat nodded toward the paper, which was now in my hand.

The words flowed, and most of the language made sense. I stumbled a little on the contractions: *don't, weren't, isn't.* But I felt exhilarated. I *spoke* in front of people. And I *liked* it. It was like that movie about Helen Keller when she suddenly understands the word for *water* and the whole world opens up. That's how miraculous it felt. I told Mrs. El-Khayyat after class that I felt like a different person.

"I know," she said. "I could tell. You know, there's no rule you have to be shy just because you've always been shy. Or that you have to be anything just because you've always been that way. You get to decide for yourself what to be."

"I'll be happy if I can be like my father."

I had told her a lot about Pai, about how everyone respected him and how he gave all his time to us.

"He sounds like a great man."

"He's amazing."

"But you're you," she said

I didn't know what she meant.

"You're not your father."

"No, I know. But that's why I work so hard. So I can *try*."

She had a look on her face like she wanted to stay something, but she didn't.

I COULDN'T WAIT to get home for winter break. I inhaled the air when I stepped off the plane in San Juan. I breathed in the *pomerosa* and fell asleep to the *coqui* frogs and the rain dancing on our roof. Yadier had a small bed in Mai and Pai's room. Cheo and I still shared the second room. Mai cooked up shrimp *asopao* and fried steak with onions, my favorites. Pai wanted to know about the baseball. We had talked on the phone every two weeks, but the calls were short and now he wanted details. What were the drills like? What about the other players? How did I understand what the coach was saying? How was my English coming along? Cheo and Yadier wanted to hear everything, too. I told them about the coach and Kenny Marrero and the teammate who always made trouble, Roberto. I told them about Mrs. El-Khayyat.

I wanted to return to Yuma bigger and stronger for the start of the spring college season. I worked out harder than ever. I lifted the soda-cracker barbell in the carport and pulled the tire through the sand on the field. I ran through Kuilan with my new accessory: a cassette-tape Walkman I bought from a guy at college. The headphones bobbed around, so I secured them with a white sanitary sock tied around my head. The neighbors called me *El Caballo Loco*. The Crazy Horse.

I ate everything Mai put in front of me. Rice and beans. Chicken. Pork chops. Fried chicken. Onion steak. Corned beef. Liver. Fried eggs. Chef Boyardee spaghetti. Macaroni with Spam. More food meant more strength. I put on fifteen pounds in a month. My once-wiry body became thick and square. I was happy with the transformation. I was stronger and definitely bigger, if a little slower.

I CALLED JOSEFA from the pay phone at the grocery store near La Número Dos: $1.25 for the initial connection, then twenty-five cents every two minutes. I talked to her for as long as my three dollars lasted.

THE HATILLO TIGRES team in the Double A amateur league—where Pai had made his name—asked me to play outfield during the month I was home. Hatillo was about an hour from Espinosa. I'd hitchhike on La Número Dos. My workouts were having an impact. The league used wooden bats, but still I sent pitches into the outfield stands during batting practice. I ended up leading the team with a .400 average, and we went on to win the league championship.

I didn't mind boarding the plane back to the States. Unlike my arrival on campus in August, now I knew that Yuma was where I was supposed to be. I believed completely that it would deliver me to the pros.

IN A GAME late in my first college season, we botched an easy bunt play. The batter reached first and eventually scored. We were going to lose a crucial game. We were fighting to reach the playoffs. When the inning ended, I was steamed. I ran in from my spot at shortstop and threw my glove on the bench. The words just came out.

"C'mon, we can win this thing!" I said. "Good teams make the routine plays. We have to work hard and pick each other up. We can beat these guys and we're wasting our chance! Let's *go*! All out!"

My teammates had not heard my voice all season. They stared at me for a second then started clapping. "Yeah, c'mon! Let's go!" they said. We rallied to win.

Mrs. El-Khayyat had helped me find my voice.

Pai gave me the words.

BY THIS TIME, Josefa and I were dating. She brought me to Mexico one weekend to meet her parents. They were poorer than we were. The house was mud bricks in a dirt yard on a dirt road. I slept on the sofa in the sitting room and decided I was in love.

I PLAYED WELL enough that first college season to be voted the team's Rookie of the Year from among the team's fourteen freshmen. Scouts had been in the stands for a lot of our games. I was on their radar. I returned to Puerto Rico in late May, ready to find out which team would pick me in the draft the first week of June. In the meantime, I joined the Vega Alta Maceteros for the last few months of the Double A season, which ran from January to June, plus the playoffs in July. The teams counted on the college players to reinforce their rosters. I played shortstop, starting pitcher, and closer, whatever was needed.

The amateur draft came and went again. No call.

"Why isn't anyone signing you?" friends and relatives asked.

"I don't know. I'd sign for a box of Twix bars."

I wondered if this was how it had happened for Pai, one small failure building on another until his hopes disappeared under the pile. It still made no sense that he didn't make it, given everything I had heard about his talent and reputation. I wouldn't ask. I thought it might churn up bad memories that had been safely buried. But maybe I didn't ask because I really didn't want to know. A failure of that magnitude—losing the biggest dream of his life—was too sad to think about.

THE PRO SCOUTS began to take notice my second season at Arizona Western. I had a 2.90 ERA and a .385 batting average. Men in big straw hats and golf shirts ambled down from the bleachers and asked for my contact information. I gave them my grandmother's address in Vega Alta because our neighborhood didn't get mail delivery. The scouts didn't make any promises, but I knew their presence meant I'd get drafted.

"Get ready," I told Mai and Pai. "This is the year." I thought about the example I'd set for Cheo and Yadier, how I would be paving the way for them. I imagined how proud Pai would be sending a son into pro baseball in the States. I had no illusions about being signed for a lot of money. All I needed was a spot on a roster, a chance to prove myself.

On the last day of school, I sat with Mrs. El-Khayyat on a bench outside her classroom. I thanked her for everything.

"If baseball doesn't work out," she said, "you can still go to college and get an education. You're a good student. There are a lot of things you could do."

"Baseball is all I want."

She hugged me, and I thanked her again.

At home in Puerto Rico, Pai came into the bedroom as I unpacked. He noticed a Most Valuable Player plaque on my dresser.

"What's this?" he said. He couldn't read the English words.

"MVP," I said. "The team voted."

"Why didn't you tell us?"

I shrugged. Of course I had wanted to tell him. But it would sound like bragging. There was no bragging in our house. No flaunting of awards. Pai didn't put much stock into trophies and plaques. I learned this early. I was six years old when a flood crashed through our little clapboard house in Vega Alta. Mai and Pai had packed the car with clothes and family photos and whatever furniture would fit. We stayed at Mama's house on higher ground for a few days.

When the rain stopped, Pai maneuvered the car around downed branches and debris to reach our house. The front door was wide open, blasted in by the rushing water. We climbed the three front steps. Mai sucked in her breath. The floor was slick with mud. The back door was open, too. The kitchen table was on its side against the wall. The couch was black and soaked. Almost everything else was gone, out the back door and washed away.

"Pai!" I said, stricken. "Your trophies!"

Kids from all over the neighborhood would come to our house to look at his trophies. Nobody had as many trophies as Pai did.

"We're safe," Pai said, surveying the room, hands on his hips. "That's what matters."

While he and Mai shoveled mud from the sitting room and kitchen, Cheo and I made our way down a slight slope and into an open field, where other kids were already picking through the broken chairs, shower curtains, frying pans, Virgin Mary statues, televisions, T-shirts, baby strollers, trash cans, suitcases, dresser drawers, slippers.

We rooted through the piles.

After a time, Cheo let out a cheer.

"Found one!" He held up a grimy trophy with my father's name on it.

Awhile later, I found one, too.

We wiped the trophies with our shirts and ran home, the treasures cradled in our arms. Pai was unscrewing a bent hinge on the back door.

"Look, Pai!" Cheo said.

"Mmmm," he said, glancing at the trophy. "Anything else?"

I held up mine. "We got two back for you!"

"Hold this," he said, handing me the screwdriver. Pai jiggered the door, trying to line it up in the jamb.

"What was this one for?" I asked, hoping to draw a more enthusiastic response to the rescue of such prized possessions.

"That was so long ago," he said without looking up. "Put those away and go help your mother."

Cheo and I looked at each other. How could he care so little? They were tangible evidence of his success, like medals on an officer's uniform. But he almost never spoke about his honors and awards, so years later when I won the MVP award, I didn't speak of it.

In the bedroom, as I continued to unpack, Pai studied the plaque, then set it back on the dresser. Nothing else was said the rest of the night. The next day, the plaque was gone.

It reappeared when Pai returned from work.

MAI KEPT ME company as I sat by the phone. It was June 1, 1992. Draft Day. The Major League Baseball amateur draft in the early 1990s didn't have a set number of rounds. It lasted as long as teams kept picking players. A draft might go sixty, seventy, eighty rounds over four or five days, with upwards of sixteen hundred players chosen. This was my third draft. I was passed over in 1990 after high school, then again in 1991 after my first year at Arizona Western.

I knew I was a much better hitter now and more versatile in the field than most players. I had played every position except catcher. There couldn't be sixteen hundred young players better than I was. I'd be a late-round pick for sure, chosen on the third or fourth day when teams were taking anyone who could fill a spot on their farm teams. I didn't care how I got on a roster. I could be the very last pick for all I cared.

There was no Internet then, so you waited by the phone. Pai joined Mai and me when he returned from work. Cheo and Yadier popped in and out between school and practice. Cheo would be eligible for the draft the following year, when he finished high school. Already the scouts were fluttering around him in a way they never fluttered around me. Cheo could hit with power, and he was a catcher, a position always in demand. Not everyone had the particular skills and the particular personality required of the position.

Yadier was ten years old and so much better than either Cheo or I was at that age. He was thick and solid and had a cannon for an arm. He could already hit the ball over the fence at the park across the street, a feat I didn't accomplish until well into my teens. He batted cleanup for the Little League team that Pai, of course, coached. Yadier had been kissed by the baseball gods not only with his body and talent but with being born into a baseball family. He had the advantage of three coaches in Pai, Cheo, and me. I helped Pai coach Yadier's Little League team. He soaked up everything we said, even when it looked like he was fooling around and not paying attention.

I stared at the phone for four days, leaving occasionally to watch

José or Yadier. On the fourth day, as I sat in the stands at one of the local fields, one of Pai's friends said the draft was over. A scout had told him. One thousand four hundred ten players had been drafted. The teams stopped picking after fifty rounds.

I couldn't believe it. I was so angry with the Puerto Rican scouts. Why didn't they have my back? They knew how I played. Why didn't they stick up for me? I wasn't worthy of even a fiftieth-round pick? I didn't want to have anything to do with baseball at that moment. I didn't play for two weeks. I didn't pick up a ball or bat. When Mai and Pai asked me why I wasn't going to Maceteros, I said, "What difference does it make? Who's going to notice?"

They let it go. They knew how much pain I was in. I played in one game in three weeks. I needed the seventy-five dollars.

After the Maceteros season ended, Pai and I were at the park, talking with three or four other coaches. No one could understand why I didn't get drafted. There were guys signing for thousands of dollars who weren't as good as I was.

"Listen," Pai said. "You're going to get your chance."

You didn't, I thought. How could he still believe in the fairness and—what was it?—the *beauty* of baseball when it had screwed him over just like it was screwing me? The scouts were morons. They couldn't see my father's talent twenty years ago, and they couldn't see mine now.

"You can play amateur ball here," Pai said. "They pay college kids about a hundred a game."

I thought about giving up, but I was too pissed off.

I hooked on with Hatillo again in the Double A league in early September and talked to Pai about getting a job at the factory.

"Just focus on baseball," he said. He knew I was running out of time. I had just turned eighteen.

My friends were marrying their high school sweethearts. That was how it worked. You dated a girl, and you married her. So over the pay phone at the corner market, I asked Josefa to marry me.

MAI AND PAI got married when she was twenty-four and he was twenty-two. Pai refused to wear a suit. He wore a long-sleeved, white guayabera shirt instead. Mai didn't mind. She wore a white blouse and white slacks. A church wedding was out of the question. They didn't have the money. They were married in Titi Rosalia's living room. Jacinto Camacho was the best man and paid for the cake. No one brought gifts. Mai and Pai didn't expect any.

"What better present than me?" Mai always said when she told the story.

For a honeymoon, they spent two nights at a hotel on the beach in Vega Alta.

Pai already had a job as a machine operator for $1.40 an hour at the Westinghouse factory. His assembly line made electrical circuit breakers. Back then, before I was born, he worked the overnight shift so he could practice baseball in the afternoon and, during the season, play games in the early evening. Mai never missed one.

IN SEPTEMBER, I left the Hatillo team and flew to my fiancée's home in San Luis, Mexico, to ask her father's permission to be married. The wedding was planned for December. I didn't have enough money to return to Puerto Rico then fly back for the wedding, so I stayed in Mexico, sleeping on the family's sofa. I played baseball on Sundays and looked for a job.

A teammate got me on a crew picking cauliflower in Yuma. We set out from San Luis at four thirty in the morning with Tupperware containers of burritos and beans for lunch and crossed into Yuma. My teammate showed me how to grab the crown of the cauliflower, cut the stalk, turn it right side up, cut away the leaves, then quickly place it on the truck bed as it moved alongside us. Workers on the truck washed, wrapped, and packed the cauliflower in boxes. I couldn't cut the cauliflower fast enough. I played catch-up all day. By the second day, the supervisor conceded I was hopeless. I became a washer/wrapper/packer on the truck. Fourteen hours after our day started, we'd arrive back in San Luis. I'd eat, fall dead asleep, and do it all again the next day, rising before the sun.

Pai wasn't happy I was working the fields.

"Is that what you want?" he asked.

"I have to make money."

"If you want baseball, you have to do baseball."

He was right, but I was about to be a husband. I had to think about making a living.

When the cauliflower harvest ended, I got a job at Jack-in-the-Box in Yuma for $4.25 an hour, midnight to eight in the morning. My fiancée drove me to the border, and I walked through customs to a bus stop and rode the bus into Yuma. My fiancée's shift at Jack-in-the-Box began when mine ended. She'd arrive in her family's Chevelle at 8 a.m., and I'd sleep in the car until she punched out at 2 p.m. We'd drive back into Mexico together. Then I'd go to baseball practice.

Mai and Yadier flew in for the wedding in December. There were only about twenty-five people. Pai had to work, and Cheo couldn't afford the plane ticket.

In March, after five months of flipping burgers and wiping tables,

Pai's voice grew louder in my head. *If you want baseball, you have to do baseball.* Scouts didn't go to Mexico. So if I wanted to have a chance, it wasn't going to be in Mexico. My wife agreed we should move in with Mai and Pai so I could play Double A and go to whatever Major League tryouts I was invited to attend. There was still more than two months left until the June draft.

Pai was thrilled to get me back on the field across the street, where he hit me grounders and threw batting practice like he always had. He and Mai divided their time between Cheo's American Legion games, Yadier's Little League games, and my Double A games for Maceteros in Vega Alta. I went to see Cheo and Yadier as often as I could. Cheo was in his last year of high school and had blossomed as a player. He had gotten taller and stronger in the previous year and could throw to second base with such power that runners rarely tried to steal. You could see how well he controlled the game behind the plate.

Yadier at that time pitched and played third base and catcher. He still batted cleanup and hit the ball everywhere. It seemed there wasn't a pitch he couldn't hit. He was more mature than when I coached him as a small boy. Mai always told the story that Yadier was the only five-year-old in the history of Little League to infuriate an umpire enough to get tossed from a game. Little Yadier apparently called the ump a *cabrón,* roughly equivalent to "asshole."

"There's always one bad apple," Mai joked.

Pai would get mad at Yadier, but he also cut him slack that he didn't cut José or me. Once when Yadier threw his helmet after a rare strikeout, Pai upbraided him in the dugout.

"That's the last time you throw a helmet!" Pai said.

"It's because I want to win! I want to hit!" Yadier said.

If José or I had thrown the helmet, Pai would have sent us home.

But he let Yadier stay in the game. He disliked the behavior but loved Yadier's fire, his burning drive to win. I remember Yadier at seven or eight years old tossing his catcher's mitt to the ground and wheeling around to yell at the umpire—who happened to be a close family friend.

"Where do you want the pitch? It's right in the strike zone! What are you looking at?"

Another time he took his catching gear off in the middle of a game because he was angry about something. "I'm not going to be a catcher anymore!" he said. Pai benched him. Cheo and I sat with him and talked kindly to him about respect, about being a leader and a role model. If you wanted Yadier to listen, you couldn't confront him. You just had to talk.

Now, almost a teenager, Yadier was calmer and clearly a leader on the team. Mai, on the other hand, hadn't mellowed a bit. When a fight broke out during one of Yadier's games, Mai rushed onto the field with a baseball bat to protect her boy. I saw Pai explode like that only once, and it happened during the season when I had returned to Puerto Rico for one last push at getting signed. I was playing three games a week for Maceteros—shortstop, outfield, and as the closer out of the bullpen. My teammates called me College Boy and kept asking why I hadn't been signed. Most college guys they knew had gotten contracts. Wasn't that the whole point of going to college in the States? Why go for two years if you don't get signed? I didn't have an answer.

We were facing one of the league's top pitchers in the Double A North championship. Over several games, I had gone 7-for-7 against him. When I came up to bat in the championship game, he threw at my head. I got out of the way. The next pitch hit me on the elbow. I saw Mai in the stands yelling and waving a baseball bat. After the game, I was in the dugout changing out of my spikes and jersey—visiting teams didn't have locker rooms—when I heard a commotion. Pai had waited for the pitcher outside the home team's clubhouse. He and my brothers confronted him, and Pai threw two punches, which the pitcher was nice enough to dodge. He knew Pai, as everybody did. This was out of character.

"Mr. Benjamín! What are you doing?"

Players were holding both men back when I got there. Pai's face was red and his nostrils flared. His jaw muscles twitched. I had never seen him so angry. On the way home, he told me if I pitched in the next game I had to retaliate and throw at one of their players. Not at the head, he said. Go for the butt. Luckily I didn't pitch, because I had no intention of hitting anybody. But I understood Pai's anger. He knew I was working so hard to get signed and that I was running out of time. And here was this pitcher trying to hurt me and ruin whatever chance I had.

When Pai couldn't come to the games, he tried to listen on the radio. Then he'd go over everything with me afterward, inning by inning, analyzing my at-bats and pitching strategy. I never bristled at his comments. I loved those talks with him. I had his full attention. I relished every compliment.

I was in the best shape of my life. I worked out harder than ever, driven almost to obsession by the ticking clock in my head. I ran with my sanitary-sock Walkman, jogged on the beach, lifted my soda-cracker barbells. *El Caballo Loco.* I'd go with my cousin Julito to the field across the street and we'd pitch to each other from Pai's bucket of balls. When we got tired of chasing the balls, we hit them against the flimsy backstop. Cheo would join us if he was around. Yadier, too. We'd take grounders and fly balls. I'd practice throwing from the outfield to Cheo at home. Cheo practiced gunning down base runners. We raced around the bases, trying to make our turns as efficient as possible, hoping to shave a tenth of a second off our times.

There wasn't room in Mai and Pai's house for my wife and I to stay. I couldn't afford rent on the hundred dollars a game I earned from Maceteros. I needed another job. Tío Papo was a supervisor at General Electric, so he got me on the assembly line at the factory in Manatí, twenty minutes from Espinosa.

When I arrived for my first day of work, two of my Los Pobres teammates were on the assembly line. They quickly and emphatically explained, as I did, that the job was absolutely temporary, a stopgap until they got signed, which would definitely happen if the scouts had half a brain.

The Puerto Rican scouts were our favorite topic of conversation on the assembly line. We all agreed they were idiots and scumbags who knew everything about statistics and nothing about baseball. They fell in love with players who *looked* like baseball players. Tall and broad-shouldered. They couldn't see the *real* baseball guys right in front of them. We trashed the latest young superstar, assuring each other we were as good as that kid. He simply had the advantage of being big enough to turn heads. We held fiercely to our hopes of reaching the pros—or as fiercely as any man can as he's building electrical outlets on an assembly line.

My job was to screw three pieces of plastic onto a partially assembled outlet, then hand it on to the guy next to me. He did his part and handed it down the line. We churned out a finished outlet every three to five minutes from 7:30 a.m. until 3:30 p.m. Every day. The same thing. On our feet most of the time.

How had Pai done this for two decades? I never thought about what Pai did when he wasn't at home. All I knew was that he worked at a factory. Now I knew a little more. He calibrated the finished electrical breakers before they were boxed up and shipped. "You do what needs doing, even if it's sweeping the floors," one of his longtime coworkers told me. Pai stood all day except to fill out daily reports. In his fifties, the coworker said, Pai made twelve dollars an hour. Friday was payday. Pai and the other workers cashed their checks during lunch and splurged at a restaurant across from the plant. After work, they'd stop for drinks at Rafy's Place, Barceloneta, El Motivo, or Guacaro. People told me Pai often slapped the bar and announced, "A round for the house!" The cheers went up and the round poured. Soon he'd slap the bar again. More cheers, more beer. But if his Little League team had a baseball practice, the coworker told me, Pai was out the door. "He never failed those kids," he said.

With my $187 weekly paycheck, my wife and I rented a one-room studio for $250 a month on the first floor of a sad, hulking apartment building with drug dealers hustling sales in the stairwells. It wasn't far from Mai and Pai. Espinosa had never been Mayberry, but now it had a criminal undercurrent that had everyone locking their car doors and keeping their children closer to home. We heard gunshots our first night there. I began keeping a baseball bat under the bed. I made sure my wife spent most of her time at Mai and Pai's house when I was at work, at practice, working out, or attending a tryout.

I was playing better than ever. I led the Double A League in RBIs and was among the top five in home runs and batting average. It was late May 1993. The draft was in two weeks. I had been going to tryouts every week since I arrived back in Puerto Rico. There was always some scout who was impressed that I played so many positions. He'd ask for my phone number. Then never call.

One night in late May, on the last Friday of the spring season, I went 4-for-5 with two triples and two doubles.

One of my best nights ever. And it happened in Utuado, where Pai had made his name.

"What a game!" Pai said on the way home. "That triple was a perfect swing."

Instead of lifting my spirits, Pai's compliments depressed me. I couldn't play any better than that. It was my best. And it was never going to be enough. The truth of that hit suddenly and with clear-eyed clarity. I was never going to get signed. I would never be what the scouts wanted. I didn't hit with quite enough power. I didn't pitch with quite enough velocity. I couldn't get down the line with quite enough speed.

How was I going to tell Pai that he had just seen my last game of baseball?

In the car on the way home, we passed baseball parks in every neighborhood. Instead of magical places, the fields now seemed like terrible mirrors showing me who I really was. An also-ran. A wannabe. A young man destined for a factory smock and a time card.

In bed that night, I finally quieted my brain and fell asleep, only to jolt awake from someone pounding on the door. I pulled the bat from under the bed, jumped up, and shouted at my wife to hide in the closet. I positioned myself next to the door. If somebody broke in, they were going to feel it. The knob rattled. I lifted the bat. I heard the scrape of shoes and footsteps moving away.

What kind of life was this? Derelicts and addicts. Crumbling walls. Begging for rides on La Número Dos to get anywhere because I couldn't afford a car. Eating at Mai's because we had nothing left in our cabinets.

"Listen, I know you miss home," I said to my wife, climbing back into bed. "I'm just so tired of this crap. Let's pack up. I'll get a job in Yuma."

I knew I could make a thousand dollars a week picking lettuce; Yuma was the lettuce capital of America. After the harvest, maybe I'd go back to school like Mrs. El-Khayyat had said and do something with computers.

When I opened my eyes in the morning, they fell immediately on my baseball bag on the floor by the bathroom. I pulled it to me and sat on the edge of the bed. I lifted my blue Pony spikes out from under my bats and gloves. I wondered how many miles of base paths these spikes had covered. I tied the shoelaces together.

My wife rolled over. "What are you doing? What time is it?"

"I'll be right back."

The sky was orange-red through the *pomerosa* branches, and the air smelled clean and cool. Even the rotting apartment building looked almost gentle in the morning light. Cars hummed low in the distance along La Número Dos. A rooster screeched. The street was empty. I walked in the direction of the highway to the first set of telephone poles. I looked up at the power wire stretched above me. I assessed distance and angle, taking a step back, then two. Holding one shoe in my right hand, I swung the other shoe. One twirl, another—then whoosh. I let go and the shoes flew toward the wire, spinning and kicking. Their last dash. The laces slammed into the wire and the shoes whipped around it. Tied to the wire now, the spikes swung for a few moments then stopped. They hung above me like something dead.

I told Pai I was done.

"You can't give up," he said. "You need to keep playing."

He still thought things would turn around. He thought I would be fine, like he was always telling me. I wasn't fine. I couldn't live up to his belief in me. I still wanted to play baseball as much as ever. But I couldn't keep waiting and hoping and failing until Pai started feeling sorry for me. I couldn't live with that. It had once seemed unthinkable that I would spend my life on an assembly line. Now it had the stink of inevitability.

"Pai," I said, modulating my quaking voice. "I'll be okay. I'll get more hours at the factory, and I'll help Cheo and Yadier make it."

They could carry Pai's dream forward.

In bed that night, I wondered if this was what Pai felt when he finally had to face facts and give up. Did he really understand what he was letting go? That he was losing the best version of himself? I liked who I was on the field. There was no hesitation, no self-consciousness. Who was I going to be without that, and without the rules and framework of baseball to guide my way?

The next morning, my wife and I were watching television and making plans for Yuma when the door rattled again with fierce pounding. "Coño!" I said, picking up the bat again. "What is this?"

"Get away or I'll smash your skull in!" I shouted.

"Bengie, open up!"

Cheo's voice.

I opened the door, and he threw his arms around me.

"What's wrong with you?" I asked. "You scared us half to death."

"You have a tryout!"

"What are you talking about?"

He explained that he had had a tryout that morning at Parcelas Carmen Field with two California Angels scouts, one Puerto Rican and one American. Mai had gone with him and had waved a fistful of newspaper clippings in the scouts' faces. "You need to see my other son!" She had brought articles about me being the top player in the American Legion tournament, the MVP in college, the RBI leader in Double A. She had the front page of the sports section from that very morning with a big photo of me and a story about my 4-for-5 night with Maceteros.

Cheo said Georgie, a longtime Puerto Rican scout, waved her off, but Mai wouldn't let up

"I can only imagine," I said.

Driven by politeness, exasperation, or fear, the American scout agreed to give me a look at three o'clock.

If a scout had to be badgered into a tryout by somebody's mom, he was not likely to be handing out a contract at the end of it.

"You go have a great career," I said. "It's cool. I'm fine. My time is passed."

"Get your pants. Get your shirt. This could be your chance."

"I'm not going."

"Yes, you are."

"It's a waste of time."

"You tell Mai yourself."

I agreed to show up at Parcelas Carmen Field at three.

"There's one problem," I said.

I took Cheo down the street and pointed up at my spikes. Cheo said I could wear his, though they were a size too big.

Cheo, Mai, and Pai went with me to Parcelas Carmen. My chest was tight. Not about the tryout. I knew I had no chance. But I hated disappointing Mai and Pai. They still thought, after my seventy-five or so tryouts, that someone was going to see something in me that everyone else had missed. Maybe this tryout would convince them baseball was over for me. They needed to witness the rejection for themselves, like having to see the body before accepting the truth of someone's death.

At the field, the American scout sat alone in the stands. Mai immediately plopped herself next to him. I shook his hand and thanked him in English for the opportunity. His name was Ray Poitevint. I nodded to Georgie, the Puerto Rican scout, who was on the field. I didn't like Georgie. He had never given me a fair look. I jogged out to right and played catch with Pai to loosen my arm. He could see how nervous I was. He thought I was worried about not doing well.

"Just take it easy," Pai said. "It's just another tryout. Do your thing and you'll be fine."

"I'm okay."

"I know."

Poitevint yelled out to me. "Hey, come over here! To the backstop!"

I figured he wanted to time my speed from home to first. Okay, I thought, let's get it over with. I knew I'd be too slow to fit their logarithm or whatever they used to weed out players.

When I got to home plate, Poitevint was waiting. "You ready? Your arm loose?" Then he handed me a catcher's mitt.

"Throw to second," Poitevint said, returning behind the backstop. He held a stopwatch. "Let's see how you do."

I looked at Pai. This was crazy. The one position I didn't play, and that was what they wanted to see?

"Hey," Pai said, "you have two brothers who catch. You've watched them. Come on."

I crouched behind the plate. Pai, on the mound, pitched a ball. I caught it and fired to Cheo at second.

Poitevint whistled. "Wow," he said, showing the stopwatch to Georgie. "One-eight."

"Again," he said.

I caught Pai's pitch and threw to Cheo.

"One-nine. You've never caught before?"

"Pitcher, outfield, and infield," I said.

He watched me throw a dozen more.

"Let's see you hit."

I had brought a bat I had gotten from my father's cousin, Carmelo Martinez, who had played for the Padres, Cubs, and Pirates. It was a 35-incher; I usually used a 33. But I wanted to see if it gave me more power. I had nothing to lose. Pai pitched, and I sprayed the ball into the outfield, one line drive after another. Poitevint, standing behind the backstop, called out commands:

"Right field!"

"Pull it!"

"Center!"

Bang! Bang! Bang! I crushed each one.

"Okay, hit then run to first."

Cheo's big shoes made me even slower than usual. I crossed first and turned in time to see Poitevint look at his stopwatch and frown.

"I don't need to see any more," he called out to me.

No surprise there. That's it.

"My son, he's good," I heard Mai saying in Spanish when I joined Poitevint behind the backstop. Felix Caro, who had arranged for me to go to college, had shown up; Mai must have called him. He had the baseball yearbook from Arizona Western College. He opened it to a photo of me receiving the plaque for MVP. Poitevint pulled Felix aside, but I could hear the conversation.

"Why isn't this kid signed?" Poitevint asked.

"I don't know. He should be."

"Is he a bad kid? Is he on drugs? A loose cannon?"

"This is one of the nicest guys you're going to meet. He's a hard worker. I don't know why nobody's given him a shot."

The two men rejoined the rest of us. Or most of us. Pai had walked behind the stands. Maybe he couldn't watch me get shot down one last time.

"Well," Poitevint said to me in English. "I like what you did, man. I can see you come from a baseball family. But I can't sign you to pitch or play third or outfield. You'll never get out of Single A the way you run. But I like your arm and I like your bat.

"So today's Saturday," he continued. "Georgie right here will come to your house on Monday and get you signed. Start packing. You're going to Mesa, Arizona, for rookie ball Tuesday. You're gonna learn how to catch."

Mai grabbed my arm. "What's he saying? Tell me what he said."

"He wants me to play rookie ball," I said in Spanish, barely believing it myself.

"What?" Mai cried.

Suddenly Georgie was arguing with Poitevint. "He's not a catcher. You want a catcher, sign Cheo."

"Hey, shut up, man!" I said in Spanish. "This is my one chance, and you're going to ruin it? What are you doing?" Mai's face darkened in the way it did before she exploded. But Poitevint beat her to the punch.

"If I tell you to sign this player, you sign him." Then he turned to me. "Are you ready to play pro?"

"I've been waiting my whole life."

Mai grabbed my arm again.

"Is he going to sign you? How much?"

I asked Poitevint straight up. "How much, sir?"

"Twenty-five thousand."

I translated for Mai, and she started crying. "Benjamín, did you hear?"

Pai emerged from behind the stands. He had missed the whole conversation. "What?"

"Bengie's going to rookie ball! He's going to the Angels!"

"Oh man!" Pai said, lighting up like he had just won the lottery. He hugged me and hung on for a beat longer than usual. "You deserve this."

Poitevint told me to keep the catcher's mitt, a Lance Parrish model. I was happy to have it, if only as evidence that what just happened had really happened.

I burst through the door of the apartment waving my new glove.

"We're out of this dump!" I told my wife. "We leave Tuesday!"

We celebrated that night at Mai and Pai's. Mai had called all the aunts and uncles and cousins. Pai squeezed grapefruits from the tree and mixed up vodka cocktails. Mai cooked onion steak, rice, beans, and *tostones,* fried plantains. It seemed like a dream.

On Monday, Georgie brought the contract to Mai and Pai's house. We sat at the kitchen table: Mai, Pai, Cheo, Yadier, my wife, and me. The contract was in English and didn't have my name or the amount of money. Only that day's date.

"Don't worry about it," Georgie said. "I'll take care of it and fill out the rest." I didn't trust him, but I signed. He said I'd get my check at rookie camp.

Poitevint called in the afternoon.

"You ready for tomorrow?"

"Yes, sir. What should I bring with me?"

"They'll give you everything you need."

I thanked him again and told him I'd work hard to show him he made the right decision.

My wife and I packed everything we owned into one suitcase and one carry-on. "Well, you're a pro now," Pai said, hugging me at the airline gate. "It's official."

"Thank you for everything. I'm going because of you. I love you, Pai."

"Work hard. Play all out all the time. Leave everything out there. This is the chance you've been waiting for. Take advantage of it. Make it work."

On the plane, I said a prayer. I knew it was childish for a grown man to think God would grant wishes like some genie in a bottle. But I said it anyway.

Please let me measure up. Please let me make Pai's dream come true.

PART 3

THE PLAYERS IN camp looked as if they had stepped out of a baseball magazine: square-jawed, broad-shouldered, long-limbed. They had such a shine of confidence in their eyes. They walked through the clubhouse as if all this minor-league business were just a formality, that their names were already being sewn onto the backs of Major League uniforms.

I was in way over my head.

I knew what Pai would say: Don't worry. Everything will be proven on the field.

My locker at the Angels' minor-league complex in Mesa was alongside five other catchers. In camp was a range of young players. We were all part of what is called the farm system. This is where Major League organizations "grow" their next stars. Every team's farm system has five levels of competition: rookie ball, Low A, Single A, Double A, and Triple A. However, Single A has three levels of its own: Short A, Low A, and High A. They play in different parts of the country against other minor-league teams. Most minor leaguers had already been dispatched to teams in Boise, Idaho, and Lake Elsinore, California, and Midland, Texas; their seasons began in April.

The ones left in camp now, in May, fell into three categories: rookies like me, experienced players rehabbing from injuries, and players discarded by other teams. The rookies would stay in Mesa to play in a rookie league from mid-June to the end of August. The others would be sent to a minor-league team, put on the disabled list, or released.

I unpacked the small baseball bag I brought from home—an infield glove, the catcher's mitt from Poitevint, deodorant, comb, razor. In my locker hung two uniform jerseys with bright red "Angels" on the front.

Then I unpacked the larger Angels bag from Eric, the clubbie who had picked me up at the Phoenix airport. Two pairs of uniform pants, sliding shorts, practice T-shirts with the Angels logo, sanitary socks, athletic socks, and full catcher's gear—shin guards, mask, and chest protector. All brand-new.

I felt around inside the bag.

Empty. No spikes.

I glanced at the lockers on either side of me. Shoot. They all had their own spikes. I also noticed their catchers' gloves. They were magnificent, meaty things. The pockets were nearly black from repeated poundings, and the rest of the leather was velvety brown, the color of infield dirt, and impressively scuffed and scarred. The thick laces corkscrewed along the edges like ripped muscles. If I ever had to smother a grenade, these mitts were what I'd use.

I noticed the catcher at the adjoining locker eying my mitt on the bench between us. He looked from the mitt to me then back again, as if trying to figure out if this was really what I was going to use. My glove, compared to his, was a plastic beach toy. I realized it wasn't real leather. The stitching looked cheap. But I didn't care. I was happy. Still, I swiped it from the bench and stashed it on the shelf in my locker.

I headed off to find someone with an extra pair of spikes. I took a few steps before turning back. I grabbed my mitt. I was envisioning a crowd around my locker, gawking at it.

I looked for the Latin players I had met in the hotel lobby that morning. Latin players were more comfortable leaning on each other than American players. Maybe it's because most of us grew up poor. We shared each other's toys. We invented games together. We were never really alone. When I was home in Dorado, neighbors spilled into each other's kitchens and yards to celebrate births, grieve deaths, fix leaks, ride herd on wayward sons and daughters. When one person struggled, everyone carried a piece of the burden. We played baseball the same way.

But none of the Latin players had extra spikes, of course. They had no more money than I did.

I found Eric, the clubbie, in the laundry room folding towels.

"You didn't bring *spikes*?" he said.

I told him I forgot, which sounded less stupid than saying I tossed them over a power wire.

"Give me a few minutes and I'll see what we have."

I returned to my locker and realized I didn't have batting gloves, either.

Back to the laundry room.

Eric told me to wait and disappeared down the hall. He returned with spikes left behind by another player and two pairs of used batting gloves.

Borrowed shoes, borrowed gloves, borrowed mitt. Almost nothing was mine, not even the position I was supposed to play.

THE ANGELS' ROOKIE ball manager was a white-haired, leather-faced former catcher named Bill Lachemann. He was built a little like me: kind of short, with a thick waist and strong legs. The clubhouse fell silent when he emerged from his office and stood at the front of the room. He smiled and rubbed his hands together as his eyes swept over us.

"Welcome to the California Angels," he said. I sucked in a breath. Four days earlier I was making plans to pick lettuce in Yuma.

Lachemann introduced his coaches. I recognized the catching coach, Orlando Mercado, who was well-known in Puerto Rico. He was from Arecibo and had played for eight Major League teams. Lachemann explained that we'd be split into groups and dispersed among the complex's four fields, two batting cages and about twenty pitchers' mounds. Each group had its own daily schedule of drills, which would be posted every morning. A horn would sound to prompt us to move on to the next drill and location.

All six catchers were in a single group. When it was my turn behind the plate that first day, I caught one pitch and Mercado stopped me.

"B-mo! Turn your hand the other way! Thumb up!"

If you picture the mitt as a clock, my thumb was supposed to be at two or three o'clock. But I'd raise my elbow when the pitch came in, which turned my thumb down to six o'clock. It dangled there just waiting to be broken. Plus, trying to catch an inside pitch that way, you're twisting your arm and hand inside out. You need to stay centered, elbow down, thumb up, allowing yourself a wider reach and greater flexibility to react to the pitches.

I did it right for several pitches, but then my thumb started turning down again. Mercado corrected me. *Up, up, up,* I told myself. I was by far the worst catcher in camp.

"B-mo, knee down and turn this way!" Mercado said, showing me how to turn my left knee in and down so it didn't interfere when I went to catch pitches to my left. Mercado, Lachemann, and another catching coach, John McNamara, worked really hard with me. McNamara taught me more about the mental part of the game—how to control the tempo, how to stay focused, how to stay tough. Mercado was the technician. He taught me literally how to catch pitches.

Soon, my hand throbbed from the impact of the pitches. My cheap mitt had started to split across the palm. The padding inside, what little there was, had also torn and was shriveling up. I knew better than to blame my bungling on the glove. No excuses. It was one of Pai's rules. I learned it the day we checked the baseball field a few days after the flood that washed away most of Pai's trophies.

We had loaded rakes and shovels into the trunk of Pai's car. The field didn't look too bad. We filled ruts and swept puddles. Kids from the neighborhood showed up with plastic cups and bowls and got to work scooping up drier dirt along the baselines and sprinkling it over the mud at first and third.

There was a little daylight left when Pai pulled his bag of balls and bats from the car. The other kids raced home to get their gloves. Pai hit grounders to me at shortstop while Cheo took my throws at home. Pai directed the neighborhood boys to various positions and hit all of us fly balls and line drives and grounders. I could barely stop a dribbler. One after another the balls slipped beneath my glove or bounced past me. I was only six, but still expected more of myself.

"Bend!" Pai said. "Get in front of it!"

When the sun dropped below the tops of the tamarind trees, he called us in. Five-year-old Cheo began loading the balls and bats into Pai's bag. I didn't move from my spot at shortstop.

"A few more," I said. In the pink-gray light, I had to squint to see Pai at the plate.

He hit me a grounder. Then another. Ten. Twenty. Thirty. I missed about half. With each flub, my frustration grew. I could feel the sting of pent-up tears in my nose and eyes. Pai kept hitting and I kept fielding until it was too dark to see.

On the way home, I hunched in the front seat next to Pai.

"You have to get in front of the ball," Pai said. "Stay with it. You have good hands."

I made a show of pounding my glove and bending the fingers toward the palm. "Glove's too small," I said.

"Glove's fine."

In the backseat, Cheo was picking a knot from his wet shoelace.

"The field was really muddy," I said.

"Field was fine."

I turned away, arms crossed. In the window, I could see my face twisted up like an old sock. Pai wasn't trying to make me feel better. Whose side was he on?

"*Mi hijo,*" he said, "listen to me."

I turned back.

"You play with what you've got," Pai said. "You figure out how to make it enough."

In Mesa, among the stars and studs in the Angels' rookie camp, my ripped catcher's mitt would have to be enough. When we got back to the hotel late that afternoon, I walked to 7-Eleven and bought Krazy Glue.

ERIC DELIVERED AN envelope to me in the clubhouse. It was a $770 check from the Angels. I knocked on Bill Lachemann's door and asked him about the rest of my $25,000 signing bonus.

"All I know is that's what you got," he said. "I'm sorry if you were told different."

"Georgie knows the American scout said $25,000!" Pai said over the phone, his voice rising. "If the Angels send you home, Georgie better watch out!"

Pai knew, as I did, that the less money a team invested in you, the less committed it was to your success. A team will give up on a $1,000 player more quickly than a $25,000 player—or a $300,000 player. My roommate, a seventeen-year-old Puerto Rican pitcher named José, was a $300,000 player. He looked like Dwight Gooden and threw a 95-mph fastball. He'd have to screw up royally for the Angels to give up on him. I could be cut without a second thought.

I heard Pai take a take deep breath.

"Listen," he said. "Forget about it. It's done. Nothing you can do. Focus on baseball."

I wired $700 to a Western Union office in Yuma. My wife would drive over from Mexico, where she was staying with her parents, to pick it up. Part of the money would pay back her father for loaning us money for her plane ticket from Puerto Rico to Arizona. I was making just $333 a month as a minor leaguer, but it was enough for my wife and me. I spent almost nothing on food. I ate as much as I could in the clubhouse and at a cafeteria at the mall, where the Angels paid for a second meal every day. I'd stuff what I could in my baseball bag for later.

Two weeks after I signed with the Angels, Cheo was drafted in the fourteenth round by the Cubs and signed for $31,000.

Unlike me, he had an agent, who made sure he received exactly what was promised. He bought a Mitsubishi Mirage and surprised Mai by putting a $13,000 down payment on the house next door to their rental in Kuilan. It was a little bigger, and Mai had always admired it. For the first time, Mai and Pai would pay a mortgage instead of rent.

Like the Angels, the Cubs trained in Mesa, so Cheo and I would be close to each other. I knew his experience at rookie camp would be different than mine. One, he knew how to play his position. And two, his agent would get him free equipment, as all agents did. He wouldn't be begging the clubbies for discards and hand-me-downs.

With Cheo and me in the States, only Yadier was waiting for Pai when he came home from work. Actually, Yadier probably was already at the field. He was too restless to sit on the floor like Cheo and I did, waiting for Pai to finish watching *El Chavo.*

A month into the rookie-league season, I was still catching the ball with my thumb down. Sure enough, just as Mercado has warned me, a foul tip sprained my thumb and I couldn't catch for the last six weeks of camp. I DHed the rest of the way.

At the end of rookie camp, Lachemann gathered us in the clubhouse. He told us to work hard, to keep learning, to realize we'd have our ups and downs. Then he said something I never forgot.

"Of everyone in this room, maybe three of you will make it to the Majors. Those are the numbers. So you can't let up for a second."

Three?

I looked around me. There was the guy with the million-dollar signing bonus. The guy over there already had earned all-star honors in the minor leagues. José, my talented roommate, was a sure thing.

That was three right there.

A select few of the top prospects—including my roommate, the hotshot pitcher—went on to play in the Arizona Fall League. The rest of us were on our own from September until spring training began in February.

I joined my wife in Mexico and worked with my father-in-law in the citrus groves in Yuma, digging irrigation ditches and laying pipe. And I played ball in San Luis, Mexico. My mitt, a disfigured mess of Krazy Glue scars, finally fell apart. The San Luis manager gave me an old one of his. It was a no-name brand but real leather. I had no agent to get me a glove and no extra money to spend. Even if I did have money, it was hard to find a decent glove in Mexico.

In February, I returned to Mesa for spring training with the Angels.

"What's this?" I asked José, my roommate, the hotshot young pitcher. "You're drinking now?" There was a six-pack of beer in the mini-fridge. He had begun staying out late with the other big-money players, the guys with the Mustangs and the pickup trucks with monster wheels.

"I don't get drunk. It's fine. No big deal," he said.

I looked at him as if he were a dense child. "Do you *see* the competition here?"

There were about two hundred players from every level of the Angels' minor-league system. Locker assignments reflected the hierarchy. Triple A players occupied the first two rows in the clubhouse, then the Double A players, then all Single A guys, and in the last rows, the rookies. Walking past the rows of lockers every morning was a reminder of the mountain I was climbing to reach the Major Leagues. I'd have to beat out every catcher in every row.

One night I returned to the hotel to find my roommate and another player smoking weed. I exploded. What if a coach found me with them? There'd be no reason to keep around a marginal player like me if they thought I might be a troublemaker.

"I only have one shot!" I yelled at them. "This is it for me. I'm not going to let you screw it up. Don't ever bring that in here again."

José stomped out of the room, insisting I was overreacting. He moved out a week later, into a room with another partying player. He was a good kid. I had met his parents. When I tried talking with him, he'd say he knew he had to work hard and be serious. Then after dinner, when I headed to my room, I'd see him peel out of the hotel parking lot with the other fools.

I didn't have money to go out. And I didn't drink. Plus, at the end of the day, my legs ached from crouching, my head hurt from so much new information, and my arm hurt from throwing. I'd see other catchers pace themselves, but I didn't know any way to throw to second except 100 percent. Rookies weren't supposed to seek treatment from the trainer. People might think you're soft. So you didn't let on how much you were hurting. At night at the hotel, I retrieved ice from the machine down the hall and scooped handfuls into a towel and wrapped it around my throwing arm. I rubbed lotion into my muscles to keep the arm loose.

When the ice melted, I'd squat in front of the TV and work on my transfer—switching the ball from my mitt to my throwing hand. You're not supposed to reach over and pluck the ball from the mitt. You're supposed to move the mitt to your throwing hand. I'd toss a ball in the air, catch it, and transfer. Toss, catch, transfer. I'd do it a hundred, two hundred times a night as I watched sports on television. I'd give myself pep talks: You don't know your position yet, but you know baseball. No player in camp knows the game better than you. No one else had Pai as his coach.

At practice, I studied the more experienced players as if they were textbooks. I wrung everything I could out of my bullpen sessions. I scared a pitcher one day when I caught a pitch, popped to my feet, and cocked my arm as if I were going to fire it past his head to an imaginary second base. I didn't throw it, of course; I was just working on my moves, trying to make myself quicker. The startled pitcher threw his arms in front of his face.

"What the hell are you doing?"

"Sorry," I said. But I wasn't. How else was I going to get better at throwing to second when, as the lowest of the lowest catchers in camp, I had so few chances to play in real games?

Spring training was almost over when my wife drove the three hours from her parents' home in Mexico to Mesa to spend the weekend with me. She had news: She was two months pregnant. I'd be twenty when the baby was born. I was thrilled and crazy nervous. It wasn't just about the pressure to make enough money for everything a kid needs. Pai was twenty-four when I was born. Was I mature enough to do this? Could I sacrifice the way he did for my brothers and me?

"Congratulations," Pai said when I called home. "Now you'll see what life is about. It's family. When you have a baby, you find out that it's all about family. Nothing else matters."

On the last day of spring training, the Angels gave us our team assignments—Triple A, Double A, High A, Low A, or the lowest of the low, extended spring training. That's what I got. I drew the "Do Not Pass

Go" card. I'd be back where I had been the previous year, with the new signees, the injured, the discards, and the not-ready-for-anything-else.

Midway through extended spring training, the Angels promoted me to the Low A team in Cedar Rapids, Iowa. They needed a bullpen catcher. But once I got there, the manager, Tom Lawless, began putting me into games as a DH and then gave me some starts behind the plate. One day I went 4-for-5 and coaxed a young pitcher through a shaky inning. Lawless called me into his office.

"Don't let anyone tell you you can't play this game."

He made me the regular starter.

My body wasn't prepared for what that meant. I was about to find out that being a catcher was as much about stamina and pain tolerance as about skill and strategy.

I squatted 120 to 170 times a game. I took dozens of pitches every day to my hands, toes, fingers, legs, arms, neck, head. I ran up the line on every grounder to back up first base. I leaped from my crouch to field bunts and to throw out runners trying to steal. Late in a game one night, a runner barreled toward me, trying to score from second on a base hit to right. The throw home came in high. I stretched. I figured the runner would slide. He didn't. Just as the ball hit my glove, he leveled me, his shoulder spearing my ribs. Somehow the ball stayed in the glove. My body felt as if it had been cracked in two. But I stayed in the game. That's what you do. Afterward, I submerged myself in an ice-water bath in the trainer's room. It was supposed to ease the pain and reduce swelling. But afterward I could barely walk to my friend's car. The next morning, I couldn't move enough body parts to get out of bed. The trainer didn't let me back on the field for two weeks.

Even in that short season, my catching hand became swollen and discolored. (I had learned to keep my bare hand behind my glove when

I caught. Always.) My arms and legs bore ripe-banana bruises in shades of yellow, black, and purple. The pitches hurt and left marks despite the chest protector, mask, and pads. Catchers, I quickly learned, don't complain. And they don't wear their beatings like badges of courage, either. You don't expect a parade for doing what you're supposed to do.

Cheo was playing for the Cubs' Low A team in Des Moines, which was in the same Midwest League as the Angels'. Cedar Rapids had already played Cheo's team by the time I joined, but we ended up facing them in the first round of the playoffs. It was weird. We had always been each other's biggest cheerleaders, and now we were in opposing dugouts.

"Please," I told Cheo before the game, "try to get me out. Because I'm going to try to get you out."

We had to be professionals on the field. We owed it to our teams, and we owed it to ourselves. Those games ended up being tough for Cheo. Des Moines was up one game to nothing in the best-of-three playoff. We won the next game in the ninth inning on a wild pitch that got past Cheo. In the third game, we took the lead in the top of the ninth on yet another wild pitch that skipped past Cheo. Cheo's team had a chance to tie it in the bottom of the ninth with two outs, two strikes, and a runner on third. Our closer bounced a split-finger fastball. I blocked it with my chest then inadvertently kicked it up the third-base line. I scrambled after it, turned the wrong way around the ball, slipped, picked the ball up as I fell, and from flat on my back flung it to first base. Somehow it beat the runner, and we won.

As we celebrated, I saw Cheo walk off the field with his head down. I felt horrible for him. He and his teammates boarded their bus quickly after the game, so I didn't get a chance to tell him to forget the loss. No one could have caught those wild pitches.

Our Cedar Rapids club went on to win the league championship. We would each receive a championship ring with our names on it. All I thought about was showing it to Pai. When I received mine the following year and brought it to Puerto Rico with me, Pai said simply, "Great accomplishment." He was pleased, but didn't want to make a fuss: My success had come at the expense of Cheo's.

PAI INSISTED I take his car.

"No, you need it for work. I'll get myself there."

After the season in Cedar Rapids, my pregnant wife and I had moved in with Mai and Pai. They were living in the three-bedroom house that Cheo had helped buy. We were in one bedroom, Mai and Pai were in another, and Cheo and Yadier shared the third. Cheo had landed a winter-league spot with the San Juan Senadores. The park was only twenty minutes away, and he had his new Mitsubishi.

I was with the Indios de Mayaguez, the Mayaguez Indians, as a bullpen catcher. I was an inactive player, meaning I wouldn't play in any games. I wouldn't get to hit. But I'd make six hundred dollars a month, and I'd catch a million pitches. I was happy. I needed to accelerate my learning curve by catching as much as possible. I had to close the gap between me and the guys who had been catching all their lives.

But Mayaguez was across the island, a two-and-a-half-hour drive from Dorado. I didn't have a car.

"Take the Nova," Pai said. The Toyota had finally died, and he'd been driving an old Nova for the last few years. He said he'd go with his coworker Lee Perez, who lived a minute away in Fortuna. Or, he said, he'd catch a ride on La Número Dos. The factory in Toa Baja was a twenty-minute ride. I argued, but there was no changing his mind.

The morning of my first game, I rose when I heard Pai in the kitchen around five.

"What are you doing up so early, *mi hijo*?"

"Driving you to work."

The darkness was starting to dissolve when we turned onto La Número Dos. The Nova chugged and shivered when I picked up speed. It convulsed when I hit fifty.

"*Suave*," Pai said, laughing. "Easy."

Later that morning, I set out for Mayaguez, babying the old car across the Cordillera Central—the Central Mountain Range—through Vega Baja, Arecibo, Aguadilla, Rincón, passing homemade crosses scattered along the hairpin curves. About ninety minutes into the drive, the skies opened. Pai had warned me that the windshield-wiper motor was burned out. I turned the knob anyway. Nothing. I slowed the car and rolled down the window.

I held the steering wheel with my right hand and grabbed the wiper with my left, trying to pull it back and forth. To get a better grip, I leaned farther out the window. Rain pelted my face. I couldn't see a thing. With my hand still on the wiper, I crooked my neck to keep my head inside the car. When it rained at night, driving was hopeless. I couldn't manipulate the wipers nearly fast enough to see the road. Even if I fixed the wipers, I still couldn't drive safely in the rain. The tires were bald. I found myself hydroplaning even in a light shower, praying to God to save me from sliding off the road or hitting another car. The two-and-a-half-hour commute often took three and a half hours at night.

I wasn't nervous about joining the Mayaguez team. I knew a few players, including one of their stars, José Hernandez, a Major League infielder from Vega Alta.

"Oye, cabrones!" José hollered in the clubhouse when I arrived. "This is Bengie Molina. He's my brother, and I don't want any of you guys trying to mess with him. If I see it, you'll have to deal with me."

José knew I was quiet and shy on top of being the only Single A guy in there. He knew I could be a target for pranks and other funny business. I was a little embarrassed by José's declaration but also appreciative. I'd work my butt off to make him look good.

The bullpen was behind a fence along the right-field line. During the day, it was like any other bullpen. But once the sun dropped, it was a cave. There were no lights, just the spillover from the ones in right field and first base. I got into the habit of widening my eyes before each pitch, like opening the lens on a camera. I had to focus completely on the pitcher's hand, following the ball from the point of release into my glove—an elapsed time of half a second. I don't know if the human eye can actually track an object as small as a baseball traveling that fast. Maybe our eyes pick up the trajectory and extrapolate from there. Now factor in the movement of the ball, especially on breaking pitches. The only hope I had of catching pitches that broke and dipped was to train myself to see how the ball was actually moving instead of how I expected it to move.

I got plenty of practice. I caught about three hundred pitches while warming up five or six pitchers before games. I warmed up two or three relievers during the game. Sometimes I'd catch guys who weren't even on the team. They were aspiring pitchers who were friends of the Mayaguez players. I tried to compensate for my lack of real playing time by creating scenarios in my head the way Pai did at practices.

"Runner on third, batter bunts!" I'd tell myself. I'd catch the pitch then leap to my feet as if scrambling for the bunt and swipe at an imaginary runner trying to score. I lunged at every off-target pitch as if the deciding run of the World Series was at stake. I blocked balls with my arms and legs, my chest and shoulders, experimenting to see what worked.

"What are you doing?" a pitcher barked at me one day in the bullpen.

I didn't know what he was talking about.

"Why are you doing that?"

I stood. "What?"

"Your butt up in the air."

"My butt?"

"Let me tell you, the really good catchers sit down and relax when there's no one on. You're always catching like there's somebody on. Makes me nervous. Makes me think I have to throw a strike. Sit down. Low."

I caught from the higher crouch because I could more easily leap up to throw a runner out or field a bunt. But I lowered my rear so it was almost resting on my heels. I spread out my knees.

"There you go," the pitcher said.

I put down two fingers for a curveball.

He nodded and went into his windup.

I rose into the higher crouch.

"No! No! Sit down! Just make me throw the pitch."

"This is the only way I know."

I felt more able to block pitches from the higher crouch.

He dropped his glove, came back to the plate, and actually showed me how to squat low and give him a big, steady target.

It felt weird, but I understood that catchers do whatever makes their pitchers comfortable. I eventually became more relaxed in the lower crouch, and over the long haul, it put less pressure on my legs.

But during those early seasons, while I was still learning, I ached from head to toe. I'd arrive home from Mayaguez around one thirty in the morning, fill a couple of socks with ice, and lay them on my battered arms and legs.

I savored the off days, not just for the rest but for the time I could spend with my family. I missed them when I was in the States. I still felt like my real life was going on without me. My favorite place in the world was Mai and Pai's house, with Mai and Pai's bickering and the smell of Mai's cooking.

"*Arroz con gandules* again?!" Pai would moan when he lifted the lid off a pot on the stove. "Good for Pinky. He's going to love eating this." Pinky was the dog.

Mai would hustle him out of the kitchen. "Oh, go sit down!"

I especially loved the evenings when the house filled with neighbors and friends and Pai got tipsy enough to be silly. Mai would put a pot of soup on the stove. Pai fired up the hibachi in the carport. Everyone pulled up lawn chairs and drank beer or poured a shot of Finlandia into plastic cups of Pai's grapefruit juice. They played dominoes. Babies were passed from lap to lap. Toddlers waddled around. After Mai bought Pai a karaoke machine for his birthday, there was lots of singing. Once Pai had enough Coors Light or vodka in him, he'd belt out songs by Marc Anthony and José José and Tito Nieves. He'd make hilarious attempts to dance to reggaeton and bachata, pulling the neighbor ladies up from their chairs to dance with him.

On Mai and Pai's anniversary that winter, the house was packed as usual. The concrete floor of the carport, where everyone danced, was slick from rain. Our neighbor Lourdes slipped and fell on her backside. Pai tried to help her up, but when he fell too, he had such a laughing fit he kept falling with every attempt to lift Lourdes and himself, which threw them both into convulsions and got everyone else laughing.

Later in the evening, Vitin made a toast and called for Pai to give his bride a kiss, well aware of Pai's discomfort with public affection. Pai made a face, and everyone hooted at him to kiss Mai. Mai puckered her lips. She was having a great time. Pai laughed and finally kissed her full on the mouth to thunderous cheers. For the rest of the night, Mai was all over him, kissing him at every turn, making everyone laugh.

The next day, when Pai saw Lourdes at the field, he teased her. "You left such a hole in the floor that I have to go get cement to patch it up!"

Increasingly, though, I noticed Pai getting angry over little things I did. Late one night when I was sitting with ice on my arms and legs, Mai padded into the kitchen.

"You eat?" she asked.

I was tired and sore after long bullpen sessions and the two-and-a-half-hour drive in the cranky Nova.

"How would I eat? I have no money and nothing's open this late anyway."

Pai's voice suddenly boomed from the bedroom.

"Why do you say that to your mom?"

"I just said I hadn't eaten," I called back.

"You're making her feel bad because she didn't cook for you. Don't talk to her like that!"

Mai shook her head and waved her hand, indicating I should ignore Pai. I wasn't sure why he was snapping at me. Maybe it was his way of letting me know he was still the man of the house. As if there could ever be any question on that front.

But those were small things. I still got up to drive Pai if I was using the Nova. I hated getting up; I needed the sleep. But I liked having Pai to myself. He talked to me about the special relationship catchers had to have with pitchers. A catcher was like a coach on the field. The one guy who always had to be a grown-up. He had to know his pitcher better than the pitcher knew himself. When a pitcher struggled, a catcher had to get him on track. Maybe slow down the pace. Or quicken it. Maybe call only breaking balls. Maybe kick him in the butt. Maybe tell him he's a stud and the whole team is behind him. Whatever worked for that particular pitcher.

But I wasn't playing in any games, so I couldn't put Pai's advice into practice. Sometimes I was just trying to survive. One night late in a game, the bullpen coach summoned me to warm up a relief pitcher named Roberto Hernandez. "This should be entertaining," I heard one of the other pitchers say.

I knew about Hernandez. He was a beast. He was said to throw 100 mph and had a crazy split-finger fastball that moved all over the place. It would be tough enough to catch Hernandez during the day, but in the murky nighttime bullpen I was a dead man. Guys in the bullpen settled into their seats as if for a performance. They crossed their arms and smiled.

Hernandez went into his windup. He threw. The ball hit my mitt like a bullet. *Thwap!* Oh my God. That was what 100 mph looked like. I never moved my glove. If the ball had been a little higher or lower, it might have blown right through me like a cartoon missile.

I tossed the ball back. I couldn't believe anybody could throw that hard. I had been a catcher for all of a year. I didn't know how to catch this guy. I stretched my eyes as wide as I could. Focus. Watch the hand. Lock in.

Windup. Throw. *Thwap!*

Windup. Throw. *Thwap!*

One after another. Right into my mitt.

I didn't miss a pitch.

When I finished, I could barely straighten from my crouch. My heart was pounding and my mouth was dry.

"Good job, kid," the bullpen coach said.

I smiled all the way home. I'd have a good story to tell Pai in the morning.

KYSHLY WAS BORN on November 25 at the Bayamón hospital where Cheo and Yadier had been born. I couldn't take my eyes off her. The way her tiny hands closed around my finger. Her chubby legs kicking. Her eyebrows bunching up like a worried old lady.

"Becoming a father changes everything," Pai told me. "Now you have something to live for."

My love for her was unlike anything I'd ever felt. It was thrilling and terrifying. I hovered over Yadier and Cheo when they cradled her.

"Her head! Hold her head!"

Kyshly slept in a secondhand crib in our room in Mai and Pai's house. There was no baby shower, though my aunts and uncles gave what gifts they could: blankets, bottles, rattles. I earned six hundred dollars a month with Mayaguez, not enough to cover doctor bills and everything else the baby needed. We applied for welfare and began receiving food and milk every two weeks.

Two months after Kyshly was born, three of my Mayaguez teammates intercepted me when I arrived at the clubhouse. Doug Brocail, Robin Jennings, and Kerry Taylor were all Major Leaguers.

"We want to give you something," Brocail said. He pointed to Jennings and Taylor. "He's got two daughters. He's got three. I got two." They handed me three huge bags of baby clothes and toys. I couldn't believe it. My wife cried when I arrived home with the gifts.

By the end of the Mayaguez season, I calculated I had caught about twenty-two thousand pitches. We made the playoffs. But I wasn't eligible for the playoff bonus. As I was packing up my belongings in the clubhouse on the last day, a bunch of players appeared at my locker with a thick envelope.

"An appreciation from everybody," one of the players said. "You worked your butt off."

Inside was $1,500. A fortune. We'd have plenty for food and Pampers. We wouldn't have to borrow money again from my father-in-law for plane tickets back to Arizona. I could buy a battery, spark plugs, and a windshield wiper motor for Pai's Nova. The motor burned out again before I even left for Arizona.

THE BUZZ IN the Angels' farm system the spring and summer of 1995 was about a twenty-four-year-old out of Georgia named Todd Greene. He had been drafted two years earlier. Now he was on his way to hitting forty home runs, the most by a minor leaguer in a decade. He had already been promoted to Triple A, the highest level in the minors.

And he was a catcher.

"Catcher of the Future," the newspapers said.

I spent the 1995 season with the Angels' High A team in Lake Elsinore, California, putting up solid numbers. Mayaguez invited me back for winter ball, this time as the backup catcher. I'd finally catch in actual games. But three days before the start of the season, Mayaguez signed San Diego Padres catcher Brian Johnson. He'd be the team's starter. The domino effect knocked the previous starter to the backup spot—and me back to the bullpen.

For the second winter, I didn't catch a single pitch in a real game. But I caught another twenty-two thousand pitches in the bullpen.

The following spring and summer, I was promoted to Double A. Todd Greene was again tearing up Triple A. By midseason, right on schedule, he got the call: He was going to The Show. He had earned it, no question. But what were my chances of cracking the Major Leagues with the Second Coming of Johnny Bench already behind the plate?

As soon as I mentioned Greene's promotion on the phone to Pai, he shut me down. All you can control is you. Work hard. Keep learning. Talent carries you only so far. You carry yourself the rest of the way. I knew he was right. I had seen my old rookie-ball roommate, José, during the most recent spring training. He was no longer the sure thing with the rocket arm. He was out of shape, probably from too many beers and too much weed. He had lost the snap on his fastball. The Angels had demoted him to Single A. He had been such a natural. Baseball had looked so easy when he played it, the way I imagined Pai must have looked as a young man. I knew by then that even for naturals, nothing was guaranteed. So much can get in the way. Laziness. Injury. Attitude. Bad luck.

Which had it been for Pai?

IN THE WINTER of 1996, the Mayaguez dugout became my classroom, the best since Mrs. El-Khayyat's. My teacher was a catcher named Sal Fasano.

I was on the actual roster for the first time. Sal was the No. 2 catcher and I was No. 3. He was only a few years older than I was and had made his Major League debut just a few months earlier with the Kansas City Royals. But he had been catching all his life.

"What would you call here?" Sal asked me. We were in the dugout in Mayaguez. The batter had chased three sliders away, fouling off one. Clearly he was struggling with the slider away.

"Another slider away," I said.

"That's not a good pitch here. The more he goes out there, the better he's going to get at reaching it. Go fastball in. Straighten him up. *Then* go slider away again."

It was how you set a trap for a batter.

That winter with Sal Fasano was like graduate school.

He showed me how to be quiet in my body behind the plate. Move nothing but the glove, and even that as little as possible. When the pitch is slightly out of the strike zone, shift the glove back into the strike zone and hold it still so the umpire can register its location.

"You'll get more strike calls. Your pitchers will love you," Sal said.

He told me never to face the umpire when you're questioning a call. If you argue face-to-face, he'll think you're showing him up and he'll make you pay.

Sal showed me how to position myself behind the plate to provide the biggest target for the pitcher. Never lean forward. It diminishes the target. Keep your back straight so your entire torso is visible.

He told me to look confident when I called a pitch so the pitcher felt confident, too. The catcher has to project calm and confidence to all his teammates. He's the conductor. He initiates the action and sets the rhythm. He is the focal point of the field, where every run begins and ends. A good catcher sees all eight teammates, plus the batter and base runners, as a single entity, an ensemble, and he adjusts to the shifting circumstances.

Before games, Sal took me through reports on every opposing hitter. A guy with a slower swing wants sliders and curves. So you throw hard and in. A quick-bat guy likes fastballs in. Pitch him away. Notice who chases high and who chases low; who'll take a pitch to the opposite field; who's a hit-and-run threat; who's a base stealer. Put yourself inside the batter's head.

"But let's say you know everything there is to know about a hitter," Fasano said. "Let's say you know he can't hit a slider, so you want to call the slider. But say your pitcher's slider isn't working. What's Plan B? You have to have a second option in your head at all times."

I was the No. 3 catcher but played in a lot of games with different pitchers. I had caught all of them in the bullpen. But games were a different story. It wasn't just about strategy and mechanics. Fasano taught me to watch the pitcher's face and body language. Was he still thinking about the double he gave up? Was he annoyed with the second baseman's throwing error? Was he losing his nerve? Did he need a pep talk? You had to know the styles and personalities of each pitcher, and you learned that only on the field. Did a pitcher respond to failure with productive anger? Did it make him even more competitive and determined? Or did it plunge him into a funk? A catcher had to manage the pitcher's mood, coaxing and cajoling like a patient father. The catcher had to be the steadying influence, the soothing advisor who knows what the pitcher needs before the pitcher does.

The best catchers squat inside their pitchers' brains.

As we watched together from the bench, Sal pointed out pitchers' "tells"—small indications that a pitcher was fatigued or distracted or upset.

"See this guy? He's creeping up in the zone. He's tired. The catcher should be checking on him. See how much more he has."

Fasano said he didn't have a body part that hadn't been hit by a pitch or foul tip. Toes, inside ankle, top of foot, inside part of heel, inside part of calf, inside part of knee, the knee itself, top of knee, quadriceps muscle, inside quad, biceps, belly, ribs, chest, neck, face, shoulder, arms. He said you could expect to get hit about five times a game. That doesn't count the foul tips that glance off your glove and bend your thumb back. Sometimes, Sal said, you get hit so hard you'll go to the mound to confer with your pitcher, or call for meaningless throws to hold a runner at first, just to buy a few seconds for the pain to subside. But if your pitcher's on a roll, you don't do anything. You ignore your own pain. You don't want to disrupt his rhythm. A catcher is a warrior, strapping on his gear as if for battle. He keeps his back to the crowd. His eyes are on his teammates, watching out for them, protecting their turf.

Catching so many pitches in Mayaguez and in the minors had a side benefit: My hitting improved. I knew the grips and motions for different pitches, so I was beginning to recognize pitches before the pitcher even released the ball. A slider was more sideways in his hand. A fastball was all up-and-down motion. A curve came over the top. A change-up showed more of the ball.

I also had a better idea of what the pitcher was likely to throw. I'd think, If I was pitching against me, what would I call? I tried to think along with the pitcher. If he threw two curves in the dirt for balls, I could be pretty certain he wasn't going to risk going down 3–0 by throwing another curve. I'd look for a fastball. I don't know if I became a more athletic hitter, but catching had made me a smarter one.

THE ANGELS BUSTED me back to Single A to start the 1997 season. It was a numbers game, they said. Too many catchers, not enough spots.

They wanted to promote Bret Hemphill from Single A to Double A. So that left me with Single A. I was furious. I'd had a good year in Double A. Done everything they had asked. And I get demoted?

All my underdog rage spewed through the phone lines to Puerto Rico.

"Pai, what else do I have to do? This is ridiculous."

Pai didn't answer.

"Pai?"

I wanted him to say something.

"Do you want come back to the factory?" he said.

"What?"

"Tío Papo can get you your old job back."

Halfway through the season, Bret Hemphill went down with a shoulder injury. I returned to Double A. Todd Greene, meanwhile, had been demoted from his job as the backup catcher in the Major Leagues back to Triple A for more seasoning. He tore up Triple A pitchers like he always did, and soon he was back in the big leagues. Angels manager Terry Collins reiterated to reporters: "Todd Greene is the future."

When the season was over, Greene had shoulder surgery. The Angels quickly signed veteran catcher Matt Walbeck. The message was clear: If Greene couldn't play, Walbeck was their Plan B, not me or Hemphill.

Mayaguez won the Caribbean World Series that winter, which meant a $5,000 bonus plus $2,000 in extra pay for playing in the post-season. It was the most money I'd ever had. The championship was in Hermosillo, Mexico, so afterward my wife and I rode seven hours by bus with Kyshly on our laps to my in-laws' house. We still didn't own a car, and in Mexico we looked at a used Mustang at a local car lot for

$3,000. We could make a down payment then pay it off in monthly installments. My wife wanted it. She saw the cars the other players on the Mayaguez team drove. She saw me still hitching rides or chugging along in Pai's Nova. She saw the clothes the other wives wore. This had become an ongoing argument. Why aren't you in the Major Leagues yet? Why are those guys passing you by? Why are you still in the minors making nothing?

"Let's do something for ourselves for once," she said at the car lot.

I looked at Kyshly in the stroller. She'd need clothes, checkups, who knew what else? I couldn't justify the $3,000. We left the lot, bought a TV for our bedroom, and put the rest of the money in the bank.

As I packed for spring training in February 1998, I wished I could take Kyshly with me. I hated leaving her. She was a perfect little soul. I felt guilty that I couldn't give her more. I couldn't be there for her every day like Pai was for me. I told myself I'd earn enough money someday to make up for it. She would have everything. She would know how much I loved her.

At the end of spring training, I saw Troy Percival handing out something to each of the clubbies and batboys.

"Hey, Percy, is that a tip?"

He explained about tips. You tipped the clubbies for washing your uniform and scrubbing your spikes, ordering bats and gloves, delivering mail, shipping luggage. He said when you played on the road, you tip the visitors' clubhouse attendants at the end of each series.

"First couple years, don't worry about it. You're making minimum. No one expects you to tip. When you make Major League money, you take care of the guys."

When. Not if. A matter of time.

My wife was pregnant again. Due in October. Soon I'd be making Major League money. I could buy a nice house with lots of room for the children. I'd send them to the best schools. I was sure a second child and a bigger paycheck would bring my wife and me closer. The marriage had the feel of make-believe, like kids playing house. Or at least that's what it had once felt like—superficial but pleasant. Now we were easily irritated. We picked at each other over stupid things.

I began the 1998 season in Triple A in Vancouver, British Columbia. I had made the leap. The next step was the Major Leagues. I had paid my dues. If something happened to Matt Walbeck or Phil Nevin, I was next in line. One night in late May my Triple A manager summoned me to his office.

"B-Mo, the Angels are making some moves."

Finally! I was hitting .293, the highest of any catcher in the Angels' entire organization. I knew I was the best defensive catcher, too.

"They need you in Double A."

"What?"

"They have some pitchers down there they want you to—"

"Are you kidding me? This is insane!"

I was twenty-three years old. I was running out of time. A couple more years in the minor leagues and they'd be telling me I was too old for the Majors. Clearly, I couldn't stay in this organization. I'd rot in Vancouver and Midland and Lake Elsinore forever. Maybe another team would give me a fair chance.

"Call them right now and tell them I want my release. I'm not going back to Double A. That's insane."

The manager stood and raised his hands to calm me. "Take it easy. You don't want your release. You have an opportunity here."

I flung open the door, letting the knob bang against the wall.

I stormed to my locker, where my teammates had gathered, wondering why I was so upset.

"They're crazy if they think I'm going to Double A," I said, shoving clothes and equipment into my duffel bag. I slung it over my shoulder and huffed toward the door, spewing every vulgar, hateful word I knew.

"B-Mo!"

I kept walking. Screw everyone.

Suddenly I was hurtling backward. Jovino Carvajal, a veteran minor leaguer from the Dominican Republic, had grabbed the back of my collar. He shoved me into a chair in the hallway.

"You want to play baseball?" he yelled at me.

"This isn't fair!"

"I said do you want to play baseball?"

We were yelling in Spanish. The Latin players were bunched in the doorway, listening.

"They're screwing with my career!"

"Everybody here knows you belong in the Major Leagues," Jovino said. "You're throwing it away."

"It's not fair."

"You want not fair? I'm twenty-nine years old. *Nine years* in the minors. Four years in Triple A. You want me to get you my numbers? You want me to show you? I'm the best outfielder here four years in a row. I still haven't gotten the call. That's the game, bro. This ain't Little League."

"It's screwed. I'm not going to Double A."

"You gotta grow up, B-Mo. You got a daughter."

And another on the way, I thought. But I didn't answer. I was fuming. Carvajal returned to the clubhouse. I didn't move. After a time, players walked by in twos and threes, heading home. "Good luck, B-Mo," they said. Carvajal emerged and smacked me on the shoulder as he passed.

"Go and show these guys who you are."

I called Pai from the clubbie's office.

"You got to go," he said.

He didn't remind me that Cheo was still in Double A, the league I felt was now beneath me. He didn't ask what made me more deserving than Cheo. He didn't tell me I was a grown man with a wife and a child to provide for. He didn't have to. It was all there: *You got to go.*

You think baseball is all about numbers, rankings, concrete measures. Cut and dried. I put up the numbers they wanted. It didn't make any difference. They had a way of measuring that I didn't understand.

I flew to Texas to join the Midland team.

One night, I was watching ESPN and there in the highlights was a benches-clearing fight between the Angels and Kansas City. Five Angels players had been suspended for four games. One was Phil Nevin.

The next day in the Midland clubhouse after BP, our manager, Mario Mendoza, called for everyone to gather up. He called me to the front.

"I have something to say," he said, pacing slowly with his hands clasped behind his back like a lawyer. "I feel so sorry for one of us. That's Bengie Molina. This is a very tough thing for him, I want to make sure you give him a hug. He's going back to Lake Elsinore."

My mind was racing. This couldn't be happening.

"I don't think he's going to take it very well," Mendoza said. But now I could see he was smiling. Something was up.

"Okay, everybody please stand up and give Bengie a hug. He's going to the Major Leagues!"

Everybody cheered and congratulated me. I knew I'd be up there for a short time, just until the suspensions were over. I didn't care. I had made it to the Major Leagues.

I found a phone to call Pai.

"I'm going. They called me up. Just as a fill-in. I'm meeting them in Dallas."

Silence. Then, "Wow, *mi hijo.* I'm so happy for you! Congratulations!"

I could hear my mother in the background: "What, Benja? What?"

"Thank you, Pai. Where I am now is because of you," I said.

I wanted to make sure he knew that I didn't think for one second I had done this on my own.

"If you didn't put me in my place when I needed it, if you didn't pick up the phone and talk when I needed it, I'd have quit. You kept me going. I won't let you down."

"Don't worry. You'll be fine. Baseball's baseball. Same in Dallas as Dorado. Ball's no bigger or smaller. They still have to throw it over the plate for a strike."

"I wish you could be there. I know it's too far."

"I'm always with you."

Then Mai was on the phone. "What the heck did you tell him? What's going on?"

I gave her the news. I said it was only for four days until the suspensions were over and Nevin returned to the lineup.

"You show them you should stay! You're better than any of them!"

I laughed. I'd have paid money to see Mai in the stands, ragging Angels manager Terry Collins to put me in.

• • •

I DROPPED MY bags at the hotel and headed straight for the park, a short walk away. The Rangers' ballpark looked like a fortress, all red brick and stone with huge Lone Stars and steer heads looming high above arched entrances. The game wouldn't start for another six hours. I circled the building, pulling on locked doors until a security guard walked me to the players' gate, down the elevator, and into a wide concrete concourse that led to the visitors' clubhouse. The guard's name was Noel Saldivar, and from that moment we were friends. Over the years, we'd talk whenever the Angels played the Rangers, eventually exchanging phone numbers and playing fantasy football together.

The clubhouse wasn't like any I had ever seen. There were TVs everywhere and sofas in the middle of the room. The lockers and benches were dark wood polished to a gleam. The carpet looked as if it had been installed that morning. The room even smelled good, like fresh laundry. Clubhouses in the minors had one or two toilets and at most three showers. This one had seven showers and six toilets. The cafeteria was bigger than most minor-league clubhouses. Inside was an actual cook. In refrigerators and freezers, in bowls and baskets, were heaps of food—candy bars, ice cream, crackers, cookies, fruit, sandwiches, soft drinks. All of it free. It was like our own personal Circle K. In the minors, you made your own sandwich from the cold cuts or the peanut butter and jelly on a counter in the clubhouse.

My eyes fell on a locker across the room with a nameplate.

MOLINA.

Inside hung two practice jerseys and two road jerseys with the Angels' red, white, and blue logo on the front and MOLINA sewn across the back. There were also undershirts for the jerseys, T-shirts, socks, hats, pants, and a belt. I brought spikes and bats.

"B-Mo!"

It was Kenny Higdon, the Angels' clubhouse manager. He had been one of the first people I met in rookie ball six years earlier. He showed me the trainers' room, the weight room, and the batting tunnel. Everything was bigger and better and shinier than I had imagined. It made me even hungrier to make it.

Players began arriving. I knew them, of course, from spring training, and they hugged me and greeted me like I was a big deal. Coaches stopped by, too, and gave me a warm welcome. Then manager Terry Collins.

"Congratulations, boy," he said.

The rare times he had addressed me in spring training the last two years, he called me "boy." I couldn't help but hear the condescension.

The first game was close; I knew I wouldn't go in. So I relaxed and took in the beauty of the park. The stripes mowed into the grass. The flags of every Major League team flapping from the outfield roof. The old-timey tiered decks and out-of-town scoreboard. The enormous video screen in right-center flashing gargantuan photos of every batter. Everything was so monumental and majestic, even the neon ads for Coke and Budweiser. Pai was right about baseball being baseball no matter where you played. But the game looked and felt different in a place like this. It was like holding Mass in a cathedral instead of a school basement.

When the second game turned into a blowout, reliever Troy Percival told me to be ready. The innings passed. Collins never put me in.

The third game, another blowout. "You'll get your shot," Percy said. Again no call.

The fourth game we were losing badly late in the game, the seventh or eighth inning. Percy was more certain than ever I would make my Major League debut. When the inning passed without a call, Percy picked up the bullpen phone.

"Put Terry on the phone!"

Then: "What are you waiting for? Put the rookie in!"

But Collins didn't.

Nevin returned from suspension. My Major League stint was over. When I arrived back at Double A, everyone gave me a hard time about not getting a single minute of playing time.

On September 1, when the minor-league season was over, Major League teams could add a certain number of minor leaguers to their rosters, a practice referred to as September call-ups. It gave minor leaguers a taste of the big leagues, and it gave managers and general managers an opportunity to see their minor leaguers in person against top competition. I was sure I'd get called up. But September 1 came and went. No call.

So on September 3, I flew to Yuma and drove to Mexico to join my wife and daughter. The tendons in my knees had become increasingly painful. A local Mexican doctor injected both knees with cortisone. I wanted to get it done quickly so I'd be ready for winter ball. The shots were so painful I could barely walk out of his office. He said I'd be good as new in two weeks. In the meantime, I had to stay in bed; I wasn't supposed to bend or put weight on my knees.

Three days later, as I watched TV on the couch, the phone rang. Charlie O'Brien, one of the Angels' catchers, had gotten hurt. The team had booked a flight for me that left the following day. I was in pain but I didn't care. I wasn't going to say anything about the shots or my pain. In the back of my mind, I thought I probably wouldn't even play. I didn't care how painful it was. I was in the Major Leagues. The Mexican doctor had given me strong pain pills, and that was enough.

There were ten days left in the season. I mostly caught bullpens, wincing behind the mask every time I crouched. I didn't tell anyone about the shots.

Technically I made my Major League debut: I got in twice as a defensive replacement. But both times Collins took me out before I could get an official at-bat.

Soon it was the last game. We were in Oakland. The game was meaningless for us. We were too far behind in the standings to make the playoffs. The veteran players, tired and battered from a long season, were happy to sit on the bench and let the rookies play.

"Hey, rook, get ready. You're gonna catch," Matt Walbeck said in the clubhouse before the game. I saw him go into Collins's office. Then he spoke briefly to each of the other catchers—Nevin, Greene, Chad Kreuter. I knew they were conspiring to get me into the game.

Kreuter started. Inning after inning, Collins kept him in. "Put B-Mo in!" several pitchers shouted from the bullpen, where I sat next to Troy Percival. "What the hell is he doing?" Percy fumed.

I said nothing and showed nothing on my face. But I was seething. Every other call-up had gotten an at-bat. What was Collins's problem with me? Six years in the minors working my butt off and he couldn't give me one lousy at-bat?

We were up 4–1 in the eighth inning when Kreuter stepped into the on-deck circle. Suddenly he turned around, walked into the dugout, and slid his bat into the rack. Percy elbowed me. "He's trying to get you into the game."

We watched Collins go to Walbeck, who waved him off. Collins moved on to Nevin, who also waved him off, too. Even Todd Greene waved him off.

The phone rang in the bullpen. I was going to hit.

Buddy Groom was pitching. Good. I had faced him in winter ball. I worked him to a hitter's count then crushed a sharp grounder to the left side. Third baseman Eric Chavez made a great play and threw me out.

I caught the bottom of the eighth and ninth, and we shut down the A's pretty easily. The season was over. I had made my Major League batting debut. I lingered in the dugout, breathing in the moment. Darin Erstad, our center fielder, stopped in front of me. I didn't know him well. I stood out of respect. He put his hands on my shoulders.

"Hey, now you have an at-bat in the Majors. You're a Major Leaguer," he said. "Nobody can take that from you."

KELSSY WAS BORN in Yuma three weeks after the end of the season. When my wife's water broke, we drove from her parents' home across the border to an American hospital. We flew to Puerto Rico soon afterward so I could play winter ball. My family of four crammed into the guest bedroom at Mai and Pai's. Kyshly slept in the bed with us and Kelssy in the crib. I loved my two babies, but more and more I was realizing the marriage was crumbling.

All my wife and I seemed to talk about was money. I earned a little more in winter ball than the previous year—$1,300 a month—and received food from the government. I gave money to Mai and Pai for groceries, gas, and rent. I saved for our plane fares back to Arizona in January. There was nothing left at the end of each month. I was working as hard as I could. But every discussion seemed to spin off into a fight about money. Neither of us knew how to talk to the other. We were too immature and inexperienced. Our fights had none of the underlying affection that smoothed the edges of Mai and Pai's arguments. Whatever affection we once felt was all but gone. I'm sure my absences didn't help. But it was deeper than that. We didn't seem to like each other. I wasn't happy, and she sure didn't seem to be happy. But I couldn't leave my daughters. I would be there for them no matter what, the way a father should be, just as Pai was for my brothers and me.

One day in Puerto Rico, the rain drummed the roof so hard we could barely hear the television. Then it knocked the reception out altogether. My game in Mayaguez had been canceled. My wife was in the bedroom taking a nap with Kyshly and Kelssy. Mai was in the kitchen. Cheo and Yadier were out. It was just Pai and me in the living room. I mentioned how many trophies used to be crammed onto every shelf when I was growing up. Now there were only a half dozen or so.

"Mmm." Pai folded back a page in the newspaper.

"I remember the one with the wood base and big cup," I said. "I looked for it all day after the flood."

Pai lifted his eyes and scanned the shelves, as if only now realizing the trophy had been missing all these years.

"That was for the batting title," he said.

"It was always my favorite."

Pai laughed. "You don't know what I had to go through to win that thing."

I waited for him to elaborate. But he rose and fiddled with the rabbit ears on the TV.

"Did scouts ever talk to you?" I asked.

"Oh, yeah. They were around."

He walked into the kitchen and asked Mai what was for dinner. The conversation was over.

AS SOON AS I saw her, I couldn't pull my eyes away.

It was the first week of spring training in 1999. We were jogging backward in a running drill. Leaning against the railing just beyond first base stood the most beautiful woman I had ever seen.

"Who's that?" I asked my teammate Omar Olivares.

"If you want to get shot down, go ahead and ask her out," he said. He told me her name was Jamie, and she was a stage manager and feature producer for KCAL, the TV station that carried the Angels' games. "She's really nice, but she doesn't date players. Believe me, guys have tried."

I had no intention of asking her out. I was married. But I couldn't deny I was mesmerized. I found myself weaving through the ragged line of jogging players to get a better look. I stared at her as I jogged backward into center field, then sprinted forward with the rest of my teammates toward the right-field line. Back and forth we jogged, and I never took my eyes off her. There was such a sense of familiarity about her that I almost expected her to wave at me. Instead she turned away.

Throughout spring training, I watched her interview players. She was comfortable among the guys, like she was everybody's sister, like she didn't know she was beautiful. She didn't interview me because I was a nobody, a minor leaguer. But I plotted in great detail what I'd say to her and what she'd say back, as if I were in seventh grade. But I couldn't bring myself to even say hello.

At the end of camp, I was summoned into Terry Collins's office. I knew what he was going to say. And he said it.

"We're sending you to Triple A Edmonton."

Back to the minors for the seventh straight season. I was disappointed—you always held out hope—but I wasn't surprised. Todd Greene was still Collins's golden boy, even though he had barely been behind the plate all spring because of his troublesome shoulder. Matt Walbeck was named the Opening Day starter, and Greene was the backup, at least until his shoulder was back to 100 percent.

I rose to leave, stepping toward Collins's desk to shake his hand. But the manager wasn't finished.

"I don't think we're going to see you at all this year. Maybe next year, if you work hard."

I wasn't sure I had heard him right. He didn't expect to see me this season? What if Greene's shoulder never got better? What if Walbeck got hurt?

And *if I work hard*? Who worked harder?

I felt my jaw tighten. I wanted to lunge over the desk. Whatever shred of respect I still had for Collins disappeared in that moment. The words registered for what they were: a bully's playground taunt meant to diminish his target.

Now Collins stood, indicating the conversation was over. I kept my arms at my side. I couldn't shake this jerk's hand, I didn't care what Pai taught me. I turned without a word, walked out, and sat at my locker, my back to the clubhouse. I wanted to punch a wall. Kick a chair. That guy, for whatever mysterious reason, was going to keep me in the minors until I was considered too old to get a shot.

"Did you talk to the man?" Pai asked when I called him that night.

"I was right in front of him."

"I don't understand."

"He's an idiot."

"Listen, you got to keep battling. Your chance will come."

Right, I thought, like yours did?

During the 1999 season when I played in Edmonton, rumors circulated that Collins was in trouble. The newspapers carried stories about the infighting and splintered factions in the clubhouse. Collins had lost control. The players, led by veteran star Mo Vaughn, reportedly had signed a petition calling for Collins's ouster. General manager Bill Bavasi told reporters Collins was staying put.

Greene's shoulder continued to be a problem. And Walbeck was struggling. Collins brought in Steve Decker, Charlie O'Brien, and Hemphill, and all had fallen short of expectations.

Late one night in August, there was a pounding on my door. I tiptoed up to the eye-hole. It was my Triple A manager Carney Lansford and first-base coach Leon Durham. Were they there to send me down? I got back into bed, hoping they'd go away.

"Hey, you idiot, open the freakin' door! You're going to the big leagues!"

I waited a second or two, then opened the door, trying to make it look like I hadn't heard them.

"You're going to Anaheim," Carney said. "Congratulations!"

This was the real thing. Not a fill-in for a suspension. Not a September call-up.

Of course, I called Pai.

"I'm going to The Show, Pai. For real this time."

"You worked hard for this."

He didn't say he was proud of me. He didn't say it when I went to college and learned English. He didn't say it when I signed with the

Angels. He didn't say it when I won a championship ring in Single A or when my winter team in Mayaguez won the Caribbean World Series.

I had mentioned this once to Mai awhile back.

"Oh, he says it to me. He tells me how proud he is and how happy he is for you."

"Why can't he say it to me?"

"That's just the way he is."

So I didn't expect him to say it now. But I waited anyway. I was going to the Majors, probably as a starter—accomplishing something he had dreamed of all his life.

"You better get some sleep," he said.

COLLINS BARELY SPOKE to me even though I was his starting catcher, at least for the moment. As much as I disliked him, I knew my fate was in his hands. I stayed away from the clubhouse drama, careful never to say a negative word about Collins. I didn't know if Troy Percival was trying to make up for Collins's treatment of me, but he became my cheerleader. "He's not afraid," he told reporters soon after my arrival. "And there's no hiding that arm."

With my promotion to the Majors, I began earning the league minimum, which was $109,000 a season, prorated for the weeks I was there. With each paycheck, I sent gifts home for the girls: dresses, shoes, a toy xylophone, a doll house, a *Dora the Explorer* doll, Woody from *Toy Story.* I called five days a week. I sent money to my wife through Western Union. I wanted to buy a car, but I didn't know how long I'd stay in the Majors, given Collins's opinion of me. I didn't want to spend money I didn't yet have.

On September 3, with less than a month remaining in the 1999 season, GM Bill Bavasi walked into the clubhouse before a game. We knew there had to be big news. Collins had resigned. Who would have thought, back in spring, that by season's end I'd be on the team and Collins wouldn't?

In December, I was back with Mayaguez. Mai and Pai were in the stands. I saw the ball coming in. A fastball. I couldn't get out of the way. The pitch hit my batting helmet on the left temple. My head snapped back. A piece of the helmet went flying, which I later found out Mai thought was my ear. "His ear! His ear! Get his ear!" Mai had screamed. I don't remember falling. I know I tried to get up but couldn't. The catcher for Caguas, Javier Valentin, whom I knew from Little League, cradled my head and neck in his arms. He told me to stay calm and not move. They're coming, he said. Then there was a crowd around me.

"Get me up, man. Get me up," I kept saying.

At some point they got me on my feet and walked me to the clubhouse. One of the clubhouse boys carried the helmet, and I saw the hole. The trainer didn't want me to lie down. He asked me what year it was and questions like that. My head and neck hurt. Someone drove me to the hospital for X-rays. Everything looked fine. Pai and Mai drove me home.

Forty-eight hours later, I was back on the field. We were playing in San Juan, so Mai and Pai came to that game, too.

The first pitch to me was a curve. I flinched. A curve looks like it's coming right at you then breaks toward the plate. Strike. Another curveball. Flinch. Strike two. Yet another curve. Flinch. Strike three. I struck out without ever swinging the bat.

Two innings later, I was in the on-deck circle when I heard Pai's voice behind me.

"Hey! Hey! Bengie!"

Pai was leaning over the front-row railing.

"Hey, are you scared?"

"What?"

People in the lower rows were now watching and listening.

"Do you want to play baseball or do you want to go to the house? What do you want to do?"

"What are you talking about?"

"You looked scared. They know you got hit. So they're going to keep throwing curves. You know it's coming. So wait for it. No way they're going to throw you fastballs. Just sit on the curve."

He was right on both counts: I had been flinching without realizing it, and I could now use that to my advantage. I sat on the curve and got two hits in my next two at-bats.

It didn't bother me one bit that he yelled at me in front of other people. He said what I needed to hear. He had my back. I thought later about how harsh he had been when I cried after striking out in Little League. I remembered longing for his arm around my shoulders. But he had my back then, too. Benjamín Molina would raise strong sons. He knew the world chewed up the soft ones.

"WHY DON'T YOU come?" Pai asked.

It was late afternoon. I was watching TV in the living room with Kyshly on my lap. Mayaguez had an off day. Pai was heading to Junior Diaz's. Mai offered to help my wife watch the girls. Money had loosened up a little with my two months in the Major Leagues. We could have afforded to pay for our own place during the winter season this time, but Mai and Pai wanted us with them. I was certain they weren't pleased about the constant bickering between my wife and me, but they loved us, and they adored their granddaughters.

When Pai and I walked into Junior Diaz's, men looked up from their dominoes games and broke into big smiles. I thought they were for Pai. But the smiles were for me.

"Big leaguer!" one of the men said, standing to shake my hand.

Junior Diaz emerged from behind the counter. "Congratulations!" He shook my hand, too. "What'll it be? On the house."

Junior Diaz clapped Pai on the shoulder.

"Your boy!"

Then he turned back to me and squeezed my bicep.

"What are they feeding you over there?"

Pai allowed himself the slightest smile, as if a full smile might give someone the wrong idea, like he had a big head. When neighbors had stopped me on the street or in the market since I had returned home that winter, almost every one said the same thing: "I had to see it in the paper for myself. Your father said nothing!"

Junior Diaz left and returned with two cans of Coors Light. Pai was already at the dominoes table, where, over his objections, someone vacated a chair for him. One of the neighborhood men offered me his seat.

"No, no," I said, embarrassed.

I leaned against the low wall behind the table, the way I did as a kid. Everyone wanted to know what it was like in the big leagues. How much money did I make? How were the fields? How did I deal with the fans? How big were the stadiums? How was my English? How was the food? Did I go to a restaurant every day? How were the people? Were they racist? What kinds of cars did the players drive? Did I see movie stars in California? How was the game different?

I told them the big leagues were even better than I imagined. Every ballpark was like a jewel. They cut the grass every single day. The dirt was so smooth and clean. The clubhouses were huge, twice as big as in the minor leagues. There were TVs everywhere. You got fresh towels every day. Every clubhouse had a dining room, so you didn't have to worry about food. There were freezers filled with ice cream and shelves lined with candy. You could take handfuls, as much as you wanted. I patted my belly. "I have to watch it!"

A few neighborhood boys wandered in and bought Cokes at the counter. They hung by the entrance, far enough away to avoid attention, close enough to hear.

I described the different states and cities I visited. Mostly they knew just about New York and Florida. I said I hadn't seen a movie star yet. I said the people were educated but humble and friendly. They weren't racist. I said big stars like Mo Vaughn were nice; he had even taken me out to dinner. I said the game was a lot faster than it looked on television. But at the same time, it's not so different from playing on our field. I told them about the chartered planes and how every player pretty much had a row to himself. I said on my off days I got to go to Disneyland and Knott's Berry Farm with my daughters. It was like a dream, I said. Better than anything.

The dominoes were scattered on the tables untouched. I kept talking. I had never talked so much. It was exhilarating to command the attention of the men at Junior Diaz's.

Then I caught a glimpse of Pai. He was listening, too, but his face was closed. His look suggested it was time to dial it down, that I might have a fancy job in California but I should be humble, remember who I was and where I was from.

It occurred to me for the first time that maybe his feelings about me making it to the Major Leagues were complicated. I wondered if he truly was okay with me surpassing him in baseball and money. Was he mad at me in some way?

I was still figuring out the rules to Pai's world.

I wrapped up my story as Pai slid the tiles around the table with both hands, mixing them for a new game. No sooner had I uttered my last word than Pai was asking one of the men about his children. Wasn't one of them working at Kmart? Didn't another just have a baby?

Pai drank a half dozen Coors Lights. He talked and laughed more as the cans piled up. He told stories I had never heard. He told of calling Mai from the police station late one evening. He had been arrested for driving drunk after a night out with Vitin.

"So I told her, 'I just wanted to let you know where I am and I'm fine. Whatever you do, don't tell Vitin, Joel, and especially Eliu. He's the mother of gossip.'"

In Pai's telling, Mai promptly called Vitin, who called Eliu, who called his brother Miguelito, who was a police sergeant. Miguelito and Vitin went to the station, where they found Pai laughing and chatting with the police officers. Miguelito brokered a deal. Pai could go home as long as Vitin drove.

At Junior Diaz's, Pai leaned forward to deliver the punch line.

"So I say to Miguelito. 'What? I'm not driving home with Vitin! He's drunker than I am!'"

Everyone howled.

I watched Pai slapping domino tiles with the other leather-faced men who worked hard and drank hard, whose lives began in Dorado and likely would end there, too. Was that enough for Pai, who by all accounts had had big dreams? With two of his sons playing baseball in the States, and another sure to follow, I wondered if his beloved Dorado suddenly seemed small.

I BEGAN TO dread going home after games. My girls were asleep by the time I drove across the island. My wife was awake. Every conversation became a battle and an indictment. I had failed her again in some way. She was suspicious of every female fan who spoke to me. She became more possessive, wanting me to account for my time. Among family and friends, I barely talked to her. She retaliated by contradicting everything I said with snide remarks, jumping into conversations to say I didn't know what I was talking about and retelling my version of a story. In private, I told her it embarrassed me to be upbraided in front of other people. She said it embarrassed her to be ignored. Soon we'd be yelling.

In retrospect, I should have been more sensitive and tried to understand how difficult it must have been for her. I was gone all the time. I came home exhausted, often in pain. I wasn't great company. For her part, she couldn't put herself in my shoes and see that I was doing the best I could.

My $109,000 salary wasn't exactly lotto money, but it meant that soon I could move my family out of my in-laws' house and buy a home of our own. Not that I expected this would stop the arguments. I'd beat myself up for being drawn into these fights. I hated yelling in front of the girls—and I hated being yelled at in front of the girls. I felt weak and petty, the opposite of my father. I didn't like who I had become. I worried about the effect on our daughters. What were they learning about how to treat people when they saw their mother and father behaving with such disrespect for each other?

We tried to put up a good front with Mai and Pai. But the marriage disintegrated day by day, word by word. My wife and I were combatants in a war we couldn't remember starting and had no clue how to end.

Mayaguez won the winter league championship for the third year in a row, and Mai, Pai, and my brothers were waiting when I emerged from the clubhouse after the deciding game. Among the well-wishers was a Puerto Rican scout who had dismissed me every time I tried out. I still resented him.

"I want to congratulate you," the scout said, reaching out to shake my hand. I brushed past him, leaving his hand hanging in the air.

When we got into the car, Pai exploded. He was angrier with me than I had ever seen.

"You do that in front of *me*? Act like a man!"

"He tried to keep me out of professional baseball, and you want me to be nice?"

"He's an older man and you disrespected him! I taught you better than that."

"Okay, Pai. I'm sorry. You're right."

I felt terrible that I had embarrassed him. But I didn't feel bad about snubbing the scout. That felt good.

Mayaguez made it to another Caribbean World Series, and it was held at Bithorn Stadium in San Juan. I hit a grand slam to help us win the first game against Mexico. I was whisked to a press tent for the first time. Yadier tagged along and advised me to wear my hat backward. "Cooler that way," he said. (I've worn my hats that way ever since.) There were more cameras and microphones than I had ever seen. All the Caribbean media was there. My legs shook. I took a breath and thought about all the times Mrs. El-Khayyat made me speak in class.

"Well, first I give thanks to God," I said. "And second to my father, who taught me everything."

In the morning Mai and Pai bought three copies of Puerto Rico's two main papers, which had photos of me hitting the grand slam. At the kitchen table, I watched Pai's eyes move down the pages. Then he folded the papers and smoothed the wrinkles.

"Next season is yours," he said. I knew he meant the Angels.

I'd had all of two months as a starter in the big leagues. Todd Greene's shoulder could be healed. The Angels could sign a starting catcher. There were no guarantees for me.

But I couldn't help thinking about what my cousin Mandy told me about Pai when I was a kid: "If he says it, it must be true."

All these years later, I still believed it.

PART 4

WHEN I PULLED into the lot of Tempe Diablo Stadium in Tempe, Arizona, for the start of spring training, my eyes went straight to the gigantic, wide-stanced *A* on the roof. I loved that *A*. The first time I saw it, it kind of reminded me of the Statue of Liberty because it was a symbol, at least for me, of arriving in a new world. I remember relatives from Puerto Rico who had moved to New York saying they felt like they loved their new city more than people who had been born there did. Pro baseball was still a new world for me, and I felt an immigrant's love for everything about it. I loved the Angels' training complex—the brick walls of the park, the uniform with my name on the back, the craggy buttes beyond the left-field fence. I loved the moment on the first day every spring when I walked from the clubhouse into the dim underground hallway and then emerged into the bright morning sunlight at first base. If I were a poet I might have made something of winter giving way to spring, dark opening to light. As a ballplayer, the field was symbol enough. Not a footprint on the dirt, not a divot in the grass. You felt like it was waiting for you to leave your mark.

Todd Greene was in camp. So were Walbeck and Hemphill, all of us again after the same job. Terry Collins was gone, however. Mike Scioscia—a forty-two-year-old former catcher—was getting his first shot at managing. He set a new tone immediately with morning team meetings, where in addition to talking about baseball stuff, he dispatched players on crazy assignments. He sent several Latin players to dinner with a young American pitcher from the Deep South. No one was allowed to speak his native language. They had us crying the next day recounting each side of the butchered conversation. Another day he sent players out to report back on a local ostrich festival. During the team meeting the following morning, an ostrich suddenly galloped into the clubhouse, sending us scrambling for cover. A saucer-eyed Ramon Ortiz dove into his locker. *"Mire el pollo grande!"* (Look at the giant chicken!) Another day, Scioscia showed up with two Arizona State University mathematics professors who proceeded to make pitcher John Lackey retake an algebra test he had flunked nine years earlier. In Scioscia's meetings you could count on two things: You'd learn something, and you'd laugh.

During games, however, Scioscia was like an operative assessing his target—considering variables, noting patterns, anticipating moves and countermoves. He pounced on the smallest opportunity to gain the upper hand. He played to win every inning of every game, even in spring training. Everyone knew we didn't have the talent to compete against the top teams. But apparently no one had told Scioscia. He reminded me of Pai with Los Pobres.

With a week left of camp, Scioscia called me into his office.

"Have a seat."

I had been in that chair before. I knew the drill. I was being sent down.

"I want to be straightforward here," he said. "You got nothing to worry about. You made the team. We believe you can do the job."

I was stunned. Camp wasn't over, and he was giving me the job. I was on the Opening Day roster. Not a fill-in, a call-up, a disposable part.

"I want you to understand something," he said. "The reason you're here is defense. The way you handle your pitchers. I want you to take care of these guys like they're your own family."

"Thank you," I finally said, rising to pump his hand. "I won't let you down. I'll take care of those guys."

"I know you will."

It was early morning, an hour before practice. I walked onto the empty field in my shower shoes. All those years. The bus rides from Cedar Rapids to Peoria, Midland to Shreveport. The broken wipers on the Nova. The dozens of failed tryouts. The soda-cracker barbells. El Caballo Loco. The spikes on the phone wire. The dark Mayaguez bullpen. And of course, all those afternoons with Pai on the field across the street.

I called him that afternoon when I got back to the hotel.

"I'm on the team."

"Which team?"

He thought I meant one of the farm teams.

"Opening Day roster, Pai."

"For real?" He laughed. "Opening Day? Oh, *mi hijo*, I'm so happy for you."

"Thank you for everything, Pai."

Mai got on the phone and whooped it up. Then Pai got back on.

"Don't waste this opportunity."

What? After all I had I been through to get this far? Did he really think I'd do something to blow it now?

I called Cheo at the Cubs hotel in Mesa to give him the news. Later, after Cheo and I went out for our usual Panda Express dinner at the mall, I was still thinking about Pai's comment about wasting my opportunity. Maybe his warning was meant not for me but for his younger self.

When camp broke, Todd Greene was sent to Triple A. I was named the starter.

After I packed up my locker, I tipped the clubbies.

THE ANGELS STUNK. We sank in the standings every week. But every day we showed up at the park utterly convinced we would turn the season around. Scioscia's team meetings and nutty assignments in spring training were paying off. Our inside jokes and stories had the effect of bonding us like a family. They reminded us we were in this together. Us against the world.

Scioscia continued to hit the same themes he did in spring training: Play smart, play hard, pay attention to everything, outwork your opponent, think more about the name on the front of the jersey than the name on the back. And win today.

I caught almost every day and learned the nuances of each pitcher. With high-strung, talkative Ramon Ortiz, I was hard-nosed and blunt; he wouldn't listen otherwise. With Scott Schoeneweis, I spoke more gently; a kick in the butt only got him rattled. I talked to Jarrod Washburn more like a friend. With Tim Belcher, a veteran and Cy Young contender, I just listened; he knew what he wanted to do.

Pai having fun in the bleachers with Mai after a game at the field across the street from our Espinosa house.

Mai puckering up for Pai, making a show to embarrass him at a party.

Pai's grandma, Mama, with me in her house in Espinosa.

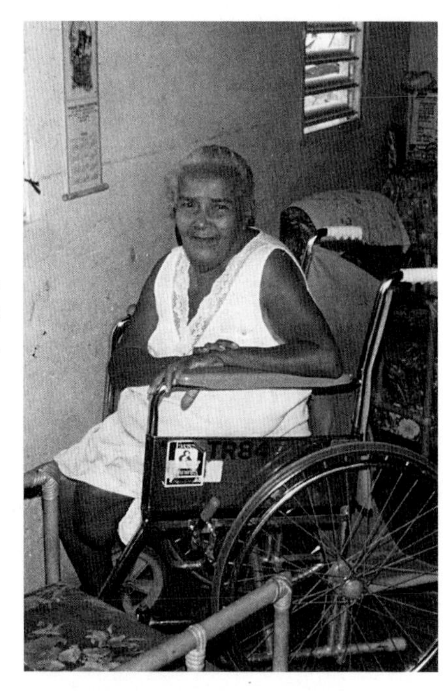

Abuelita Luz Maria, Pai's mother, in her house.

Pai (middle) representing Puerto Rico in Nicaragua.

Pai (middle row, first on the left) at age fifteen. He played second base and outfield for the Vega Alta Maceteros, an amateur Double A team. He made $25 a game and was the league's batting champion a few seasons after making the team.

The field across the street.

Our house in Ponderosa (pictured here in 2008) that was flooded. You can still see where it is sitting on bricks.

Me holding a bat with Pai's grip in front
of Mami's house in Vega Alta.

Cheo outside Mami's house in Vega Alta, 1977.

Yadier, two, in the yard of our Espinosa house
in front of the stadium, 1984.

Me (eleven), Cheo (ten), and Yadier (three) at our home in Ponderosa after the flood.

Me (twelve), Cheo (eleven), and Yadier (four) at the opening day ceremony for Dorado in Río Nuevo.

Los Pobres fifteen-to-sixteen-year-olds team. Our first and only Puerto Rican championship, in our final year as Los Pobres on the field across the street. Me (bottom row, far right), Yadier the bat boy (not in uniform, bottom row, second from left), and Cheo (top row, fifth from left, no cap).

The first Los Pobres team. Benjamín (back row, left)
and me (top row, third from the left).

My All-Star baseball card with the 1996
AA Texas League Midland Angels.

The first time Pai and Mai saw Cheo and me in our Major League uniforms, Tropicana Field, Tampa Bay, 2001. Yadier was just finishing his season with the Johnson City Cardinals.

Cheo and me in Anaheim in 2001. One of the first photos we have together in the same Major League uniform.

During Game 2 of the 2002 ALDS.

Beating the Yankees in the 2002 ALDS.

Me in the Rangers' clubhouse after the 2010 ALDS, holding Pai's framed photo that I carried with me to every game since he passed away in 2008.

Celebrating in the Rangers' clubhouse after beating the Yankees to earn a trip to the 2010 World Series.

Me with my brothers after the final game
of my career, November 1, 2010.

Me with my daughters and Jamie at AT&T Park in June 2008, after the Giants' Wives vs. A's Wives Charity Softball Game.

Me, Jamie, and Jayda during spring training, 2010.

The most important thing, Scioscia often reminded me, was to build trust and respect. You want your pitcher to know you've done your homework, that you know which hitters are hot, which are scrapping. A pitcher has to have complete confidence in what you're calling. He can't hold anything back on his pitches. Doubt is a killer.

I remember one game coaxing our erratic twenty-two-year-old pitcher through the first few innings. Then I took back-to-back foul tips to my fingers and lost feeling in my hand. The numbness gave way to prickly pain, like when you put heat on freezing hands. Then the hand swelled and stiffened. But I wasn't leaving the game. The kid's focus and confidence might crack if he suddenly had to switch to a different catcher. With a ballooning hand, I hit a home run to win the game. In the clubhouse afterward, I was a ragged, sweaty heap of black-and-blue—a great kind of ragged, sweaty heap. It was the best feeling because I knew I'd given everything I had. I'd gone all out. The papers the next day played up my home run. They didn't understand that the home run contributed less to the win than the work behind the plate.

Scioscia was a gifted teacher, following in the footsteps of Mrs. El-Khayyat, Bill Lachemann, Sal Fasano, and, of course, Pai. He'd call me into the office to ask why I called for this pitch instead of that one. He pointed out flaws in my thinking. Late in the game, he told me, don't give a hitter anything in his comfort zone, even if you think you're outsmarting him. Go with your pitcher's best pitch. Respect the hitter's strengths. Respect your pitcher's strengths.

On the days I wasn't catching, I watched the game closely, the way I did with Sal. Against the Toronto Blue Jays one day, I noticed a pattern with one of their players, Carlos Delgado. When he was on base, he alternated taking big leads and short leads. The next day I was back behind the plate, and Delgado was at second. I waited until I knew he would take a big lead and called for a half pitchout—far enough outside so the batter wouldn't swing but easy for me to catch and throw. I whipped a bullet to second and nailed Delgado. Inning over. I got Delgado at second base again the next day when, on a throw home from the outfield, he tried to stretch a single into a double.

My defense was attracting attention. "Have the Angels Found a Catcher?" one newspaper story asked. I was described in another story as "the ponderous rookie who runs like a catering truck and plays like a Porsche." There was no question I had gotten slower since becoming a catcher. All that squatting and hunching. I had gotten thicker, but I actually didn't weigh much more than I did in college.

JAMIE WORKED ON the TV crew at about half our home games. I had to find a way to meet her. During batting practice one day, I saw her in the dugout chatting with Kenny Higdon. Here was my chance. I clattered down the steps to retrieve a bat I didn't need. I looked directly into her eyes as I approached. I nodded, passed by, took a bat from the rack, and clattered back up the steps and onto the field.

During our next series I almost ran smack into Jamie in the hallway outside the clubhouse.

I felt my face burn.

"Hola!" I said. Jeez, really—*hola*?

"How're you doing?" she said.

"How are you doing?" I parroted back.

"Good!"

I couldn't think of a single other thing to say. She smiled, waiting.

"Okay," she said. "Good luck today."

Not exactly how I had played it out in my head.

I concocted scenarios in which she and I could be together. It was childish, magical thinking. Even if I weren't married, I had no chance with her. I was nothing to look at and obviously no conversationalist. She was actress-beautiful. Yet there was something about her that made me feel as if I knew her. Maybe it was true that there was one perfect person for each of us, that one-in-a-billion you are lucky enough to find. I began to think of her as my black pearl. It was rare enough for a diver to find a white pearl. To find a black one was like being kissed by God.

I badgered José Tolentino to get me her phone number. José was a Spanish-language broadcaster for the Angels. I often saw him and Jamie talking.

"Sorry, B-Mo," he said. "She doesn't go out with athletes. She doesn't go out with married guys. She doesn't go out with guys with kids. You're oh-for-three."

I just wanted to get to know her, I told him. She was amazing.

"Not gonna happen."

"Just ask her."

"She's not interested," he said.

"Ask again."

I pestered him for weeks until one evening my phone rang in my hotel room in Baltimore.

"Hey, it's Jamie. You've got five minutes to tell me what's so important you can't tell me on the field."

I didn't recognize the voice. "I'm sorry, who?"

"Uh, Jamie from KCAL? José told me I should call and put you out of your misery."

"*My* Jamie? My black pearl?"

"Black pearl?"

I told her about the rarity of black pearls and how she was my black pearl. As soon as the words escaped my mouth I knew how insane and cheesy they sounded.

Jamie laughed. "You don't even know me."

"I feel like I do."

But her story was not at all what I expected. She was a lot like me. She told me she grew up on an island, too, a place called Whidbey Island in Washington State, and that her family didn't have a lot of money either. She always loved sports. She recorded games on ESPN and watched them after her parents went to bed. She was twelve when she saw a woman working as a sports reporter on television and knew that was what she wanted to do. She made a map that day of every bed-and-breakfast within ten miles of her house and applied as a maid to earn money for college. By age fifteen, she was managing one of the B&Bs. And at sixteen, she set up her own housecleaning business.

I told her about my wife and two daughters, about Dorado and Mai and Pai and my brothers, about the field across the street with the spiky backstop and light poles and tamarind trees, about pulling a tire on the sand and lifting homemade weights.

She said she had earned a bachelor's degree at Washington State University, worked freelance for ESPN, ABC, and Fox, then landed at KCAL as an associate producer and stage manager for Angels games. She was nominated for an Emmy when she was twenty-two. She told me about the advice she received early on from former ESPN anchor Robin Roberts.

"In this industry," Roberts told her, "you can never put yourself in a position where someone can misunderstand what you're about. It takes a lifetime to build your reputation, and five seconds to lose it. And your reputation is everything in this industry, especially for women."

Jamie said that's why she didn't date athletes.

I told her I didn't expect to date her. But I just had the greatest conversation of my life. I had never talked so much or so easily with anyone. Couldn't we talk again? Wouldn't she give me her number? She was hesitant. She didn't want anyone, including me, to get any ideas. I told her I understood. She gave me the number.

We began talking once a week. Then twice a week. We talked a lot about baseball and the Angels but also about our families and childhoods. Jamie told me her father had separated from her mother when she and her sister were young.

"Don't do that to your daughters. It is very painful for young girls when their father leaves."

"I would never leave my daughters. I'd always be there for them even if I wasn't married to their mother."

"It's not the same thing," Jamie said.

AROUND MIDSEASON, I sank into a batting slump. I could barely sleep at night. When I managed to get on base against the Rangers one day, All-Star first baseman Rafael Palmeiro started chatting during a time-out. Was he talking to me? This big star?

"You know," he said, "it doesn't matter how bad you're going, every time you step to the plate you have to tell yourself you're the best guy out there."

"What?" I asked. I still wasn't sure he was speaking to me.

"You have to show the pitcher you're confident. If you go up there defeated, you have no chance."

I felt my face grow hot. Could he see I was still the thin-skinned boy crying in the Pobres dugout after striking out? Palmeiro was telling me now what Pai had told me back then: Grow up. Do your job. Or go sit with your mother in the stands. I knew Palmeiro wasn't trying to embarrass me. For whatever reason, he was trying to help.

"Thank you," I said. "Thank you so much."

Soon afterward, I began listening to "Can't Be Touched" on my headphones before every game, channeling the fearless confidence of boxer Roy Jones Jr. by blaring his song.

"Can't be touched / Can't be stopped / Can't be moved / Can't be rocked."

It became my walk-up song for every at-bat. I worked my way out of my slump.

In June, the St. Louis Cardinals picked Yadier in the fourth round of the 2000 amateur draft. We knew that meant pretty good money, not the $770 I got or even the $31,000 Cheo got. He was sure to get a signing bonus that would be more than I made in a year in the Major Leagues. We were all thrilled for him. His success was our success, just as ours was his. While his agent negotiated with the Cardinals, Yadier stayed in Puerto Rico, working out and living with Mai and Pai.

Around the All-Star Break, Kyshly and Kelssy flew to Anaheim with my wife for a visit. They didn't live with me during the season. The team was on the road so much, and my wife would have been alone with two babies. She preferred staying in Mexico with her family and friends. Also, I still wasn't making a lot of money. I lived during the season at the inexpensive Candlewood Suites instead of renting a house or apartment.

It seemed like years since I had seen my girls. We watched fireworks at the ballpark after a game. I tossed them balls in the batting tunnel when all my teammates had gone home, teaching them the way Pai taught me. We went to Disneyland and Knott's Berry Farm.

I cradled Kelssy in our bed at the hotel and understood why Pai took my brothers and me to the ball field every day no matter how tired he was. I would do anything for my girls, even stay in a loveless marriage. If keeping my daughters happy meant I had to be unhappy, that was the way it would be.

My thick catcher's legs carried me through the long season. I caught 130 games during that 2000 season, the most by an Angels catcher in ten years. I hit fourteen home runs.

Scioscia told me to skip winter ball. He wanted me to rest. It would be the first year since college I didn't play winter baseball in Puerto Rico. I went instead to Mexico with my wife and daughters. Mai and Pai wanted us in Puerto Rico. Cheo and Yadier were there. The whole family. But my wife's family was in Mexico. Kyshly was starting school there.

My phone conversations with Jamie ended. We didn't have cell phones yet, and I could hardly use my in-laws' landline.

A month after the season ended, I was watching TV when my agent called.

"We have an offer," he said.

The Angels wanted to sign me to a multiyear deal. Four years with an option. He'd know the dollar amount tomorrow, he said.

Four years! I needed ten to qualify for a full pension, which was my goal. Lifelong security for my family. I already had one year. Now I was guaranteed at least four more. Halfway there.

I told my wife and her parents and Kyshly and Kelssy, who had no idea why we were all so excited. I called my parents, and Mai screamed.

"Benjamín! The Angels want to sign Bengie for four years! He'll find out about the money tomorrow!"

"Tell him to take it!" Pai hollered back. I could hear him as clearly as if he were on the phone himself. "Tell him don't be dumb enough not to take it. Don't think about the money. Tell him he had nothing before. Just take the years and be happy."

"Tell him I know that!"

I couldn't sleep that night wondering about the money. Real Major League money. I paced the living room floor all the next morning, staring at the phone, willing it to ring. My wife suggested we take the girls to the movies. I was driving them all crazy.

"You go," I said. They left.

The phone finally rang around three.

"Four point two five million for four years plus a five-hundred-thousand-dollar signing bonus," my agent said.

Almost $5 million guaranteed. *Five million.*

Pai couldn't make that in a lifetime. In ten lifetimes.

My agent said he thought the Angels would go higher if we pushed. "We can get more," he said.

"No, no, no. I don't care, Miguel. This is good for me. I just want to play. If I get hurt, now I have security. They still have to pay me. Just say yes, we want it."

I'd earn $350,000 in 2001 and 2002; $1.425 million in 2003; $2.025 million in 2004; and $3 million in 2005 if the team picked up my option. The Angels announced my new contract the next day and arranged a conference call with Los Angeles reporters.

"This is the greatest day of my life," I told them.

Money bought more than houses and cars. It bought stature and respect, security and freedom. Anyone who said money wasn't important never lived without it. When you have enough zeros on your paycheck, no one can say you're too small or too slow or too much of a risk. The paycheck proved otherwise.

Cheo and Yadier called me and said the Angels were getting me cheap. You're worth way more, they said. My loyal brothers.

My wife and I made wish lists. A house in Yuma, for sure. She wanted an Escalade and an additional bedroom in her parents' house. I wanted to buy my parents a bigger house in a safer barrio. I wanted Pai to quit the factory; I had enough to support them.

"What do we need with a new house?" he said when I presented my plan. "The family is here. Our friends. Everyone we know."

"At least stop working. Enjoy your life."

"I got to take care of my *gorda,*" he said, referring to Mai. He teased her about being fat. "I have to get all her medicines. If I don't keep working, I don't have insurance."

"I'll put you on my insurance."

"I'm not leaving my job. I'm taking care of my family myself."

"Let me buy you a car."

"I can buy myself a car. You use that money for your daughters. I don't need your money."

There was an edge to Pai's voice. I wasn't sure what he was thinking. Was he worried that he'd lose his stature as head of the house if he took money from his son? I wished he understood that the money was as much his as mine, that he was the reason for all of it.

It occurred to me that I had never heard my father talk about wanting money or about what he had or didn't have. He and Mai lived paycheck to paycheck. He'd get paid on Friday and the money was gone in two or three days. They never had a bank account and paid everything in cash: groceries, utilities, gas, clothes, the mortgage. He was proud to work hard week after week without ever getting ahead. To live where he lived, among his family and friends, to have food on his table every day, that was success enough.

In my baseball life, money seemed to be the subtext of every conversation. Houses, cars, clothes, gadgets. Contracts, bats, gloves, gear. First class or business? Town car or limo? Suite or superior king? Private school or public? In amateur baseball and the minor leagues, guys measured their worth in performance: RBIs, batting average, fielding percentage, ERA. In the Majors, worth was measured in dollars.

The next day, my cousin Rolando called from Southern California to share reports from the Los Angeles newspapers. Scioscia said I was "a guy who pushed through the cobwebs of not playing every day in the minor leagues, who was not considered a top prospect, but emerged as one of the top catchers in the American League."

Soon after my deal was completed, Yadier came to terms with the Cardinals for $325,000. He would report to spring training in January and play rookie ball during the upcoming 2001 season.

Then Cheo got a call from his agent with devastating news. The Cubs had released him.

Cheo had been in the minors for eight years with a few brief stints in the Majors. Now he was out of a job. His agent was working the phones and said several teams were interested but there were no contract offers yet. I called Cheo every day from Mexico. He was as low as I had ever heard him—yet he was genuinely happy for me when it was announced I finished third in Rookie of the Year voting and had been invited to play in Japan on an American All-Star team.

The team—which included Barry Bonds, Randy Johnson, Sandy Alomar, and Omar Vizquel—was to gather in Los Angeles and depart for Japan from there. When I landed at LAX on a Monday afternoon, I called Jamie at her office. She wanted to hear everything about the new contract and the All-Star team. What was new with my Angels teammates? How was my family?

I told her I needed a shirt and tie to go with the suit I had bought in Mexico, and she offered to drive me to the mall. We had never been in each other's company off the field. Even on the field we barely spoke. Our friendship had played out over the phone. But the conversation flowed in the car, in the food court, and in the men's department at Macy's as easily as it did on the phone. We hung out all day and decided to watch *Monday Night Football* together at the hotel. She invited two friends to join us. We ordered pizza.

"You know how to tie a tie, right?" Jamie asked while we waited for her friends and the pizza.

"Yeah, of course."

I had no idea. I never learned. Pai didn't wear ties.

Jamie raised a skeptical eyebrow. I laughed.

"Okay," I said. "Show me."

She draped the new tie around my neck and crossed and tucked until she had a lopsided mess. She laughed and unraveled the knot and started again. Her face was inches from mine.

Her second attempt was no better. Now we were both laughing. "No, no, I think I got it this time!" she said.

"There!" She pushed the knot up to my neck and tugged softly to tighten it.

I looked in the mirror. "I'll never be able to do this."

"You look great."

I believed it. I didn't feel ugly around her. She had that effect. No matter what lousy thing happened in a game, or what kind of crazy argument I had with my wife, Jamie's voice took me to a place where I was this other, better person. I knew I was falling in love. And I knew there was nothing I could do about it.

I carefully loosened the knot, lifted the loop over my head, and laid it on the desk, praying it would still be intact in the morning. Jamie and her friends watched the game from the little sofa. I took the chair by the desk. All three women hugged me when they left. In the morning, I slipped on the tie for the flight to Japan. I was a rookie among superstars. I said little and copied what they did. One day some of the Spanish-speaking guys—Sandy Alomar, Omar Vizquel, Livan Hernandez, Javier Vazquez—invited me out shopping. I had $1,500 in my pocket from the per diem we were given for the trip. I could splurge if I wanted. They stopped first at an electronics store to find computers compatible with American systems. One player bought five computers. Another bought ten. Christmas gifts, they said. Holy crap. I found myself spending $1,200 on a laptop with a big screen. And another hundred on a phone I never figured out how to use.

Then came the jewelry store. Livan found a watch he liked. He asked for the price. I was figuring $1,500, maybe $2,500, though I couldn't fathom anyone spending that much on a watch.

"Fifty thousand," the jeweler said.

Fifty thousand? Five-oh? There was no way Livan was going to spend $50,000 on a watch. You could buy a house in Dorado for that.

"I'll take it," Livan said.

I realized I was shaking. In what kind of crazy universe did a watch cost $50,000? And how do you pay for that on the spot? Do you just hand over $50,000? Livan handed over his credit card.

The jeweler returned a few minutes later.

"Sir, this card has a limit of twenty-five thousand dollars."

Livan turned and looked at the rest of us, as if we were going to loan him the rest. I looked out the window to avoid making eye contact.

"Here," Sandy said, handing over a credit card. Livan would pay him back when they got home. Livan showed off the watch as we left the store. It looked no different to me than a gas station watch. But I said, "It's pretty, bro. Really nice."

It was like dropping into somebody else's life for a week.

CHEO SOUNDED EXCITED over the phone. It was mid-January. I was back in Mexico. With spring training around the corner, Cheo still hadn't signed with a team.

"Angels called," Cheo said.

I swung my legs off the bed and onto the floor, sitting bolt upright. "For real? What'd they say?"

"I'm going to spring training. Nonroster invitee."

I howled. "Yes!"

Cheo laughed. "You sure you're okay with this? I don't want you feeling like I'm trying to take your job or anything."

"Listen, Cheo, if you take my job, I'd be the happiest person in the world for you." I had meant it. I said the same thing to Angels general manager Bill Stoneman when he called me a few days earlier to see how I felt about it.

Days later, I received more good news. I was the winner of the Big Brothers Big Sisters of Los Angeles "Rising Star Award," beating out Kobe Bryant. My wife didn't want to fly with me to Los Angeles for the banquet. I gave my complimentary tickets to Jamie, her friend, and her friend's fifteen-year-old daughter. Jamie and I didn't sit at the same table—I barely saw her that night—but I loved that she wanted to be there for me.

• • •

WHEN I ARRIVED at spring training in 2001, a small stack of fan mail waited in my locker. I had never received fan mail. I opened the first envelope, and a baseball card slipped out. I picked it up off the floor. Fleer. Angels. Me. *Ben Molina,* it read. My rookie card. A genuine Major League Baseball card.

I turned it over to check out the number on the top right-hand corner: 40. I wondered if kids still played the baseball-card betting game that filled so many hours of my childhood. Would this card ever be worth keeping safe inside a metal lunch box?

The letter writer asked me to sign the card and send it back in the enclosed stamped and addressed envelope. I opened the next letter and out fell another card. Every letter had a card to sign and return. The Angels' media relations director, Tim Mead, asked if Ben was correct or if I preferred Bengie. I said Bengie. He said he'd have it corrected for the following year's card.

I signed and mailed all the cards back to their owners. Except one. I said a quick apology in my head to the kid who sent it, then put it in an envelope addressed to Pai. I pictured him lifting the card and reading the name across the top. My name, yes. But his, too.

I officially signed my new contract a few days later in the general manager's office at the Angels' spring training complex. I knew the big numbers typed on the pages belonged to me, but the money didn't feel real. Before I left Mexico, my wife and I had bought our first car, a Yukon Denali, which she kept with her there. I didn't have a car yet for myself. I didn't have a cell phone. I still planned on living at the Candlewood Suites in Anaheim during the regular season.

As I was signing, Bill Lachemann stuck his head in the door. "Congratulations, B-Mo!"

I rose and shook his hand. "Do you remember what you told us in rookie camp?" I asked. "You said only three of us would make it to the Majors."

"I say a lot of things," he said.

"Know how many of those guys made it?"

"How many?"

I smiled. "One."

During the first week of camp, Jamie arrived with the KCAL crew one morning. I hadn't seen or talked with her since the awards banquet in Los Angeles four weeks earlier. She was chatting with her crew near first base when I emerged from the tunnel. Her face lit up. I'm sure mine did, too. Our friendship still wasn't known among our colleagues at the Angels and KCAL. I waited until the guys walked away before greeting her.

"Bengie!" She wrapped her arms around me, the first time she had ever shown me any sign of affection in public except at the end of our *Monday Night Football* evening. I had seen her give the same kind of hug to other baseball pals—warm, but nothing more. Still, it was new for us.

The clubbies put Cheo's locker next to mine at Tempe Diablo Stadium. Two "Molina" nameplates side by side. I wanted to take a picture and send it home. Your two boys, Pai. Reporters asked Cheo what it would mean to make the team as my backup. "That would be the greatest thing that could happen," he said.

After practice one day, I asked Cheo to teach me his pickoff move. "Show me what you do with your feet."

Cheo was much better than I was at nailing runners. He could catch a pitch and snap the ball to a base in one explosive burst. Yadier had the strongest arm, but Cheo had the quickest release. They were more graceful and natural than I was. I was the mechanic and the technician, the factory worker mastering the assembly of electrical outlets. I had to learn everything step by step.

Cheo crouched behind the plate as if receiving a pitch. Then he leaped to his feet and shifted forward in a single motion, firing an imaginary ball to second base. The whole thing was so fast I couldn't follow what he did. He showed me again, more slowly. I could see this time he was leaping up before the ball hit his glove. His feet were already jumping forward.

I got behind the plate. I couldn't push myself forward the way he did. I couldn't jump to my feet until after the ball touched my glove. But I worked on it every day.

In spring games, Cheo played great, as I knew he would. The pitchers loved him. But his hitting wasn't coming around. When camp broke, Cheo went to Triple A in Salt Lake City. Yadier was in rookie camp in Jupiter, Florida. And I was in Anaheim.

Mai and Pai took turns calling each of us every day. Pai called in the late afternoon after he got home from work and before he changed his shoes to go to the field. He still coached every day, hauling his bag of bats and balls across the street. Instead of three sons, he now had dozens. All the boys in Kuilan seemed to find their way sooner or later onto Pai's field. Long after they moved on to higher-level teams or into factory jobs or professional ball, they continued to stop by the house to introduce their girlfriends or to ask his advice. Pai would tell them to grab a soda inside, from the same little fridge he and Mai kept in their bedroom, near the only available electrical outlet. That fridge was just for his players.

I would picture all this when I heard Pai's voice on the phone. I'd tell him about losing my feel at the plate or calling the wrong pitch in a crucial moment. I still needed to hear Pai tell me I'd be okay.

"Calm down," he'd say. "If they punch you out today, you have another opportunity tomorrow. It's going to be fine. Did you play all-out?"

"Yes."

"Okay, then. Tomorrow you play all-out again."

Mai was less diplomatic. "Why are you chasing balls up in the zone?" And: "Every single time there was a man on second, the first pitch they threw was a slider. Didn't you notice? You had to notice!"

If I told her I called just to say hello, she didn't care. "You're going to hear me."

"Okay, Mai, okay," I'd say, laughing. "I hear you."

With all three of us in the States, Mai wanted to visit more often. She wanted to spend a week with each of us. Pai said he couldn't be away from the factory that long.

"You don't have to work!" I said. How many times had I told him to stop working? Yadier and Cheo told him, too. "We will take care of you! You've worked hard enough."

"Your money is yours," he said.

With one of his first paychecks, Yadier bought fancy rims for Pai's Toyota Matrix. Pai promptly hit a pothole on Kuilan's ruddy streets; one of the rims split and punctured the tire.

"I told you I didn't want that crap!" Pai barked at Yadier over the phone. "I'm on foot now because of those rims!"

Yadier also got Pai a cell phone. "I don't like talking," Pai said.

So Yadier recorded a greeting for Pai's voice mail: "This is Benjamín's phone. Leave a message, and he won't call you back. So don't leave a message. This is his favorite son."

When I bought Pai an expensive watch, he stashed it in his dresser drawer. I never saw him wear it. I bought him a necklace chain. He never wore it. If we bought him clothes, they had to be simple: jeans, solid-color shirts, nothing that would attract attention. The only gifts he happily took were gloves, bats, helmets, and catching gear, because they went to the kids. My brothers and I always sent whatever we had.

Mai, on the other hand, reveled in all our gifts. She loved the bracelets and chains, earrings, clothes, furniture. Like Pai, she wasn't flashy, but she enjoyed having her sons spoil her. "I battled for you guys, I'm taking it!"

During one visit, I asked Tío Chiquito to talk some sense into Pai. Get him to retire, I said. Tell him to take it easy for once. We want to take care of him.

"When he cannot work anymore, then help him, but if he's still working, let him be," Tío Chiquito said. "Let him be a man while he is still a man."

A MONTH INTO the season, the Angels' Triple A manager told Cheo to get on a plane to Anaheim. The Angels needed him. He was thrilled until he found out why: I had partially torn my right hamstring rounding second base. The doctor said I'd be out for two months. I told Cheo his promotion was the only thing that made the injury tolerable, which was true, but just barely. I was devastated. I started worrying that my career might be over. When I was a kid, Pai told me the story of Wally Pipp, who sat out with an injury and lost his job forever to a backup first baseman named Lou Gehrig. I didn't trust my good fortune yet. I was still afraid it was all going to be taken away.

I pushed myself so hard during rehab that the trainer ordered me to slow down. During games, I sat with Cheo in the dugout and talked about how he might handle this batter or that one, or what he could do to get the most out of the pitcher.

In June, Mai called in tears. Mami, her mother, had died. When Cheo and I were babies, Mami took care of him every morning while I was with Pai's mother. In elementary school, my brothers, cousins, and I went to Mami's house every day for lunch. She was in her eighties, but her death was a blow. Cheo and I flew to Puerto Rico for the funeral. I had never seen Mai so quiet. Her loss was so great that there were no words. Mami was buried in the old cemetery behind the junior high school in Vega Alta. Cheo, Yadier, my cousins, and I carried the casket.

When my hamstring healed and I returned to the lineup in late June, we were already eighteen games out of first place. Cheo returned to Salt Lake City. He returned two months later with the September call-ups. We became the first brothers to catch for the same Major League team since Amos and Lave Cross of the Louisville Colonels in 1887. Pretty amazing.

Mai and Pai flew to Tampa to watch us against the Devil Rays. It was their first time seeing either one of us in the Major Leagues. By then, Yadier was finished with his rookie league in Johnson City, Tennessee, so he joined Mai and Pai on the trip.

When I saw Pai in the stands, I couldn't shake my nerves. What was he going to think? Why did I still feel I had something to prove to him? I went 0-for-3 with an RBI sacrifice fly. But we won, 2–1, and my pitchers gave up only four hits.

Afterward at dinner, I expected Pai to say something about my 0-for-3. I knew he was itching to help, to suggest a tweak, to remind me what I had learned on his field. *Let the ball come to you. Keep your body straight, straight, straight.* But he didn't say a word. Maybe as a gesture of respect? Maybe he wanted me to ask?

The next day, Cheo started instead of me and struck out twice. As I drove the rental car to dinner, I whispered to Mai, "I'm going to get Pai fired up."

"Hey, Cheo," I said, "what happened today? You were swinging at balls in the dirt."

Pai, in the backseat with Cheo, erupted.

"How many times do I tell you about swinging at balls in the dirt? You don't learn!"

Cheo kicked my seat hard. "What are you *doing*?"

Mai and I laughed while Pai lectured Cheo for being too aggressive sometimes and not aggressive enough other times. "You have to have a *plan* up there!"

Okay, we were back to normal. Pai was always hard on Cheo and me. He was gentler with Yadier. The worst he'd say to Yadier after a bad at-bat was, *"Yo bateo a ese pitcher hasta con los puños!"* That pitcher's so bad I could get a hit with my fists!

Maybe it was because Yadier was the baby. But I think he understood that criticism didn't motivate Yadier. Cheo and I, on the other hand, seemed to have a perverse need to hear it, as if listening to Pai's critique was a kind of absolution for our mistakes and we could let go of them and move on.

The Angels finished the 2001 season forty-one games out of first place, the worst showing in franchise history. Cheo had played in fifteen games, most of them when I was out with my hamstring injury. He was sent back down soon after Mai and Pai saw us in Florida. We didn't get much time together as teammates.

In the off-season, my wife, the girls, and I moved into our new $240,000 house in Yuma: two stories, four bedrooms, big yard, pool. I slept in the guest room most nights. My wife and I were unhappy strangers who shared two beautiful daughters and little else.

WE WERE ALREADY ten games behind the first-place Mariners before the first month of the 2002 season had passed. The Mariners had swept us at our own ballpark. It was humiliating, like watching someone steal from your house. You want to go out and get your stuff back, and you want to inflict as much pain as possible on the thieves who took it. So when we flew into Seattle two weeks later, we were looking for payback. We wanted to show that their sweep was a fluke, that we were, in fact, the better team.

We lost the first game of the series 16–5.

Usually the clubhouse was a refuge, the place where you could be furious or idiotic and no one outside would ever know. You could let down your guard. You could rage, cry, dance, fight, belch, confront, console, and walk around naked. You could stay there as long as you needed after a game to turn yourself from an angry, frustrated, self-doubting baseball player into someone fit for normal society. The Code of the Clubhouse was the pro baseball version of the code drilled into me by Pai. Respect your team as you would your family. What happens among the players stays among the players. Don't embarrass a teammate in public. Watch each other's backs.

But every now and then the clubhouse was the opposite of a sanctuary. You wanted to get away from everything and everybody that reminded you of the humiliation you just endured.

We were slumped in front of our lockers, yanking off our

uniforms as if they reeked from the stink of the game, when Scioscia charged in, swearing and kicking over trash cans and laundry bins. He picked up a chair and tossed it across the floor. He grabbed clothes from random lockers and flung them. No one moved a muscle. We had never seen him like this.

He upended a basket of dirty laundry. "This is what we are now!" he said, kicking the clothes. "Everything's the pits! This team is the pits!"

Scioscia's coaches were scattered behind him, arms folded across their chests, their eyes traveling from him to us, gauging the impact.

"Damn it! We're embarrassing ourselves!" Scioscia raged.

I had seen managers in the minor leagues hurl bats across the floor and kick over chairs. Sometimes it seemed like a show, as if the guy had watched *Bull Durham* and figured that's what he was supposed to do. But this was the real deal. Scioscia was pissed.

Then he stopped. He dragged his hand over his head. He took a deep breath. Every eye was on him.

"Okay, listen, this is where we are now," he said, nodding toward the clumps of laundry. His voice was even. "We're playing like garbage. We're not playing together. We're not picking each other up. We look like the team everybody out there thought we'd be. We're better than that. You know we're better than that. If we're going to win, we've got to find a way to do it together. Nobody else is going to fix this for us. Nobody's going to feel sorry for us."

He scanned the room, looking at each guy as if sizing him up.

"I believe this team can win. Every coach in here believes this team can win. If we keep working hard and stick together, I promise you we'll be fine."

When the coaches left, All-Star outfielder Darin Erstad stood.

"We have to leave our egos at home. We have to play for the team. When you come to the park, you leave your egos outside."

The next day we lost, 1–0.

Then we started winning. We beat Seattle in the third game of the series and won the next eight games in a row. We were finally playing our game: getting on base, working the count, hitting guys over, playing for each other. We were a little like Los Pobres, with a lot of long shots and underdogs. Five-foot-seven-inch shortstop David Eckstein got on base twenty-seven times by getting hit by pitches, leading the league in that category. We were generous in sharing info after our at-bats, telling the next guy what to look for. The camaraderie Scioscia had fostered over two seasons was finally translating into wins. In May, we were the hottest team in the Major Leagues.

I talked to Cheo every few days. He was in Triple A. Jorge Fabregas was still with the Angels as my backup. I was coming into my own as a catcher. I dug pitches out of the dirt and leaped into a throwing position in one motion. I lunged backhanded for wild pitches and used the momentum to pull me to my feet, ready to throw. Almost nothing got past me. I might have slowed down on the base paths but my reflexes behind the plate were quicker than they'd ever been. I wished Cheo had been there to see how much his lessons in spring training had helped me. I was throwing out 52 percent of runners trying to steal, best in the league.

In late July, we were back in Seattle for a three-game series. Jamie had moved to Washington earlier in the season to help a friend get through a tough divorce. She was freelancing for Fox Sports Northwest. I missed seeing her in Anaheim, but we talked on the phone several times a week. Sometimes every day. It didn't matter where we lived. I left tickets for her, her roommate, and her parents at Safeco Field then took them to dinner after the game. When I dropped Jamie and her roommate at their house, Jamie lingered by the door.

"I wish we saw each other more," she said.

"Then let's see each other more."

"I mean I wish I still saw you at the park."

"Come back to Anaheim."

She laughed. "You should get back to the hotel and get some sleep."

"Why do I feel you're always pushing me away?"

Jamie let out a deep breath.

"I'm not. It's just—" She stopped.

"What?" I asked.

"Listen, everything's fine. Ignore me. Thanks for dinner." She gave me a friendly hug. "Talk tomorrow?"

In August, the Angels traded Fabregas to the Brewers. Cheo was promoted to fill his spot. His name went back up on the locker one over from mine. He was a boost of energy for me in the dog days of August. We sat together on the plane and in the dugout. We shared cabs to the stadium. We talked baseball at the field. We talked baseball in the clubhouse. We talked baseball at P. F. Chang's and Benihana. We talked baseball at the mall when we were killing time on the road. It was like being back in our bedroom in Espinosa, talking in low voices in the dark. After games, we separately called Mai and Pai from our hotel rooms.

"Now all I have to worry about is Yadier," Pai said. Yadier was in Peoria, playing Single A ball for the Cardinals. Cheo and I talked to him as much as our schedules and his allowed.

"Hey, wait for me!" he'd say. "I'm going to get up there."

We told him we had no doubt. He was better than both of us.

By season's end, our pitching staff had allowed the fewest runs in the league. I got a fair amount of the credit, but much of that praise belonged to Cheo. He taught me and pushed me, and I did the same with him. He picked up on things I missed. Everything I did—calling pickoff plays, calling pitches, everything—was smarter and sharper because Cheo was with me.

We finished second in the AL West, good enough to get us into the American League Division Series for the first time in a generation. The bad news was we had to play the Yankees, American League champions four years running. Their roster was like a future Hall of Fame ballot: Derek Jeter, Roger Clemens, Andy Pettitte, Mariano Rivera, David Wells, Jason Giambi, Alfonso Soriano, Robin Ventura, Bernie Williams, Jorge Posada, Mike Mussina.

Pai couldn't get off work, my daughters were in school in Yuma, and Jamie was in Seattle, so none of them (including Mai) came to New York. In one of the most stunning playoff upsets in years, we beat the Yankees, three games to one.

We faced the Minnesota Twins in the American League Championship Series. Mai and Pai still couldn't come. But Cheo and I wrangled Yadier a pass so he could be on the field for batting practice. He traded in his Cardinals jersey for an Angels shirt and cap. "This is my team right now," he said.

The Twins took the first game and we took the next two. In the fourth game, we were up 4–0 in the bottom of the seventh. I hit a screamer to center field. I rounded first and headed to second. I looked toward the third-base coach. He was waving me to third. Seriously? Me? Was he out of his mind?

So I kept chugging, running as fast as I could, praying to beat the throw. I slid into the bag. Safe! A completely improbable triple. In the dugout, my teammates were hooting and clapping and going crazy.

In his postgame press conference, Scioscia—no gazelle himself during his playing days—had some fun. "Triples and Bengie Molina are like going sixty miles an hour on the Hollywood Freeway. It doesn't happen too often. Hey, my wife *pregnant* beats Bengie in a race."

We won that game and the next to win the American League pennant. We poured out of the dugout, screaming and hugging one another. I ran straight for Cheo and we looked at each other for a moment in stunned disbelief.

"We're going to the frickin' World Series!" he yelled. His face was so nakedly open and alive. We clutched each other and jumped like little boys.

As champagne sprayed and music blared, Cheo and I ducked under the plastic sheet covering my locker and called home. We could barely hear Mai over the clubhouse noise, and Mai said she could barely hear us over the cheering at their house. Half the neighborhood was there, she said.

"Where's Pai?" I asked.

"He's out on the street yelling with the rest of the crazies!"

Soon, though, he came to the phone talking in his happy, Coors Light voice.

"Wow, the World Series!" he kept saying. "Wow! That's amazing!"

Mai took the phone away.

"Go celebrate!" she told us. "We'll talk to you tomorrow."

In the morning, I drove from one gas station to another looking for a newspaper. Every store was sold out. I finally found one in Anaheim Hills.

I looked for my name and Cheo's in the box score.

There they were. In black and white. It was real.

The team had the day off, so Cheo and I went to breakfast at Denny's. Fans kept congratulating us and taking pictures and asking for autographs. In the car afterward, we talked about how as kids we had fantasized about playing in the World Series. But we never dreamed we'd be together.

The press took hold of the unusual story. One story was headlined "City of Brotherly Glove." It recalled how Pai took us to the field every day after work and described Pai's unorthodox batting grip. "My dad was short," I was quoted as saying, "but he could *hit*."

The reporter wrote: "Bengie, the proud son, talks about his father like a kid whose dad can beat up yours."

I laughed, because that was exactly how I felt.

Mai and Pai couldn't come to the Series. Pai was being inducted into the Puerto Rican Amateur Baseball Hall of Fame on the same day as Game 7, if the Series went that long. My wife and daughters couldn't come for Game 1, either, so I asked Jamie to fly down and use one of the tickets.

I saw her before the game in the hallway outside the clubhouse. She gave me a hug and told me how proud she was of me. That was the only game I could invite her to; my wife, daughters, in-laws, and friends used my tickets for the rest of the games. But Jamie and I talked by phone before and after every game. She settled me. She lifted my spirits when I allowed a passed ball or failed, yet again, to get on base. To her I could admit that I was worn out from the long season. Probably every player was toast by that point. But catchers took a particularly brutal beating. In addition to the usual swelling and bruising, I had developed tendonitis in both knees. I arrived at the park early for my knee-survival routine with the team trainer: ultrasound therapy, ice, hot pad. That was enough to get me through batting practice. Thirty minutes before the game, I took a Voltaren, an anti-inflammatory drug. That got me through most of the game. By the ninth inning, the pain and swelling had returned. I iced again at the ballpark then once more at my apartment or hotel room. Before bed I took another Voltaren to stave off the pain so I could sleep.

I downplayed the pain among my teammates and coaches. I never wanted them to doubt I could answer the bell. Only Jamie knew what I was going through. She was the person I was closest to, who truly knew and accepted everything about me—and she couldn't be with me at the most important event in my career. I knew she felt hurt and frustrated. She obviously was more than a friend but just as obviously not a girlfriend or a wife. She had no clear or comfortable role in my life. And I had none in hers. It was totally screwed up.

Still I was surprised when, after Game 5, she wouldn't come to the phone. We lost the game in part because of a pitch that got past me. Now we were behind three games to two. If we lost the next one, we were done. Jamie always found a way to make me feel okay. I knew she'd tell me to stop obsessing on what I did wrong and focus instead on everything I did that helped the team. I should have been able to tell myself this. But I needed to hear it from her, with that gentle certainty in her voice.

I called a half dozen times. She didn't answer. I called her roommate.

"Jamie doesn't want to talk with you right now."

"Why? What's going on?"

"That's between the two of you."

"Please put her on the phone."

Jamie wouldn't come.

The Giants' Game 6 starter, Russ Ortiz, shut us down inning after frustrating inning. We fell behind 5–0 in the seventh inning, eight outs away from losing it all. When we finally got a couple of hard hits, Giants manager Dusty Baker walked to the mound and took the ball from Ortiz, signaling he was taking him out.

Great, we thought. Ortiz had been giving us fits. We'd much rather face their relievers. Then as Ortiz was about to leave the mound, Dusty Baker did something that ignited a firestorm on our bench. He handed the ball back to Ortiz, like he was giving him the game ball. Like the game was already over.

"Did you see that?" someone in the dugout said.

We had all seen it. If we needed a kick in the butt, Dusty Baker had just delivered it.

In came reliever Felix Rodriguez to face Scott Spiezio. Two men on base. One out. Speeze fought off one pitch after another, fouling, fouling, fouling. Then he laid into one. It sailed toward right field. The right fielder leaped. He hit the wall, impeding his jump. The ball cleared the top of his glove, and the wall, by a fraction of an inch.

Three-run homer!

Now it was 5–3.

In the eighth, Erstad hit a solo home run: 5–4.

It was the bottom of the ninth. Still 5–4. On the mound for the Giants was Robb Nen, who had more saves than any closer in Giants history. We put two guys on. Up came Troy Glaus. A single would tie the game. Troy hit a double. Two runs scored. We won 6–5! The stadium erupted. We flooded out of the dugout to tackle Troy. It was one of the greatest comebacks in World Series history.

Young John Lackey took the mound for us in Game 7. He'd been in the Major Leagues for all of 125 days, and he was starting Game 7 of the World Series. Cheo had caught him several times in the minors earlier in the season and huddled with me before the game. His inside fastball worked as a cutter, Cheo told me, so you should use it to your advantage against lefties.

"And use the changeup," he said, "even though it's not a great pitch for him."

Lackey gave up a run in the first inning. In the second, I hit a run-scoring double to tie the score at 1–1. Garret Anderson hit a three-run double in the third inning to put us ahead, 4–1. Now it was up to our pitchers and me to hold the lead. Lackey gave up nothing for the next three innings. Brendan Donnelly, another rookie, replaced Lackey in the sixth. Cheo kept me relaxed. "One inning at a time," he said when I came into the dugout. "Get each pitcher through one inning." He sounded just like Pai.

Donnelly got through the sixth and seventh.

In the eighth, Scioscia brought in K-Rod, Francisco Rodriguez—another rookie, just twenty years old, fresh out of Double A. These were not exactly your typical World Series pitchers. But over eight innings, they gave up just one run and five hits.

When I returned to the dugout for the bottom of the eighth, I looked Cheo square in the face.

"I don't want to cry on TV," I said. "So when we win, don't come to me because you'll make me cry."

"Okay," he said. "Three more outs."

"I'm serious, man. Don't come to me."

We were holding a 4–1 lead when Troy Percival came in to pitch the ninth. He got two outs. We were one out away. Kenny Lofton was at the plate for the Giants. I called for a fastball up and away. Lofton swung. The ball sailed into center field. Darin Erstad positioned himself under it. I pushed my mask up over my forehead to watch.

"Fall down already!" I yelled, my heart pounding.

The ball dropped safely into Erstad's glove. Oh my goodness. I hurled my mitt into the air, ripped off my mask, and bolted to the mound. Erstad was racing in, holding the ball over his head. I leaped onto Percival as everyone from the dugout swarmed us, jumping and screaming and hugging. In the jostling, I fell to the ground and suddenly found myself on my knees as if in prayer, my eyes closed and my arms in the air, thanking God. This was beyond dreams. Beyond anything.

When I opened my eyes, there was Cheo.

"I told you!" I said, climbing to my feet to hug him. We held on to each other and cried.

"We won a frickin' World Series ring!" Cheo shouted into my ear.

The pain in my legs and back was gone. The sickly nervousness was gone. I couldn't feel anything. It was like my body was no longer a physical thing but just weightless energy. Pure emotion. Joy, disbelief, gratitude, relief.

Cheo and I stood with our arms over each other's shoulders and let the roar of the crowd roll over us.

"This is amazing!" Cheo said. "Listen to that. Look at all these people." Tens of thousands of clapping, cheering people in red-and-white rows rising into the night sky.

"I wish we could give this to Pai," I said.

As families came into the clubhouse, I thought about how much I wanted Jamie to walk through that door. Instead there was my wife. Kyshly and Kelssy jumped on me and squealed when I doused them with water instead of champagne.

When they left, I ducked into my locker.

"Mai?"

"*Ay Dios mío, mi hijo!* What a special moment for my two special sons!" I could hear people yelling and laughing. "It's Bengie!" she yelled.

She said the house was packed, and the carport and the street were packed. Pai had set up a television in the driveway, and the whole neighborhood had gathered to watch. Pai was out there now, Mai said, watching the clubhouse celebration on TV. Yadier was driving through the streets in a caravan of honking cars. People were going crazy, she said. I asked about the Hall of Fame banquet earlier in the day. They had a great time, she said. They chartered a bus for the two-hour drive to the event, and Pai wore a suit!

Suddenly he was on the phone.

"Hey, *mi hijo*, congratulations! You stuck together! That's how you're supposed to play the game."

He asked for Cheo, but I had no idea where he was. The clubhouse was bedlam.

"We'll talk tomorrow, Pai. Congratulations on the Hall of Fame. We really wished we could be there. Mai said it was great."

"Thanks, I'm so proud of you boys."

Ah. Maybe the beer had loosened his tongue. But he said it. I knew that no matter what else I did in my life, I had earned Pai's respect. By any yardstick, I had measured up. More than measured up.

When we hung up, I called Jamie. I wanted her to know how much she had helped me. This time she answered. She sounded as if she'd been crying. "I'm so happy for you," she said.

"You should be here."

She said to go enjoy the party, that we'd talk later, and she hung up.

I drank more that night than I ever had in my life. I was celebrating, for sure. But I was also numbing myself. From the outside, I had hit the jackpot, won the lotto. The happiest moment of my career and, besides my little girls, I had no one to truly share it with—someone who understood what this unlikely success meant to me, who knew the hard road I walked to get there. In the crowded clubhouse, I felt as lonely as I ever had.

I had to have Jamie in my life. The decision was made before I realized I was making it.

I WON THE Gold Glove that year. It was the first time in eleven years any American League catcher had wrested the honor from Pai's former player, Pudge Rodriguez.

PAI WAS WAITING for us at the airport when my wife, daughters, and I flew in for Christmas. His face was open and happy. His belly was round and soft. When a few people recognized me in the terminal and asked for my autograph, I saw Pai watching and smiling. In their dining room, he showed me photos from the Hall of Fame banquet. He wore a dark suit and white shirt. Mai wore a flowered blouse and dark slacks.

On the wall behind Pai hung a team photo of Los Pobres. I was eight or nine. I was small and worried-looking. I couldn't remember if I was happy. Did I like playing baseball, the game itself? Or did I play because baseball allowed me to be with Pai every day? Because that's how I could gain his approval?

I wanted to tell that serious little kid not to worry so much. You'll someday play better than you ever imagined. You'll make Pai proud.

That's what I thought on that December day, that Pai's respect was like a win in the record books. Once earned, it was there forever. I was wrong.

I TOLD MY wife I wanted a divorce.

She said no. No decent man left his children.

I said I'd be there for the girls. I would always take care of them.

"What do you think your father would say?" she asked.

A knife in soft flesh. She knew Pai would disapprove, and that it would kill me. But I believed that when I explained the situation, he would come to accept it. He had to know I wouldn't make such an important decision without careful thought. And he had to know my daughters meant more to me than anything.

I wasn't going to tell Mai and Pai, or the girls, until my wife and I had reached an agreement and I had found a place of my own. It wouldn't happen overnight.

Jamie and I hadn't talked much during the off-season and hadn't seen each other since Game 1 of the World Series. She had continued to be distant in our conversations. I told her I was moving forward with the divorce.

"Don't leave for me," she said. She was still in Seattle.

"I'm leaving no matter what. I want a chance to be happy."

I was already making plans for Kyshly and Kelssy to stay with me in Anaheim while they were out of school for the summer.

The following June, as defending World Series champions, the Angels flew into San Juan to play a three-game series against the Montreal Expos at Hiram Bithorn Stadium. Cheo and I bought about a hundred tickets. Mai and Pai invited everyone they knew to the house for a big party with onion steak, avocado and fried plantains, rice, and beans and chicken.

Nervous about playing in front of old classmates, cousins, aunts, and uncles, I struck out my first at-bat. Then I got four hits, including a home run in the eighth inning. I heard the crowd chanting my name as I rounded the bases. I pointed to the section filled with family and friends. Mai was bobbing up and down on her creaky legs, waving her hands over her head. Pai was on his feet, too, clapping and smiling. We locked eyes, and Pai pumped a triumphant fist at me.

A MESSAGE WAS waiting on my answering machine one night in July when I arrived at my Anaheim apartment after a game.

Jamie had been in a car accident. She had severe whiplash and hairline fractures in her neck, a dislocated kneecap, a broken wrist, fractured ribs, and a condition called temporomandibular joint disorder, which was causing so much pain in her jaw that she could barely eat. She couldn't work. I wanted to fly right up there. But I couldn't, so I sent flowers and more flowers. I called every day.

I didn't see her until we played in Seattle in September, two months after the accident. I went straight to Jamie's apartment from the airport. When she opened the door, I caught my breath. She was so thin I could see the ridges of her shoulder bones through her T-shirt. She had a cast on her wrist and a collar around her neck. Her face was pale and her eyes hollow, the result of bronchitis from the broken ribs.

I didn't realize I was crying until she wiped my face. It was a shock to see her so frail.

"I'm okay. It'll just take time."

"What can I do?" I kept asking. "How are you paying the rent? The doctor bills?"

"I have some savings and insurance. I'm getting by."

As we talked, I felt a deepening embarrassment that I still hadn't filed for divorce or looked for a place of my own in Yuma. If I were already divorced, or at least officially separated, maybe Jamie would have let me take care of her properly instead of from a distance, as if I were some well-regarded but casual acquaintance. She wanted no part of a married man's money.

I ENDED THE season with another Gold Glove and fourteen home runs, tying my highest total.

"You can hit twenty," Pai said when I was back in Puerto Rico for a visit in the off-season. "You stay healthy and you're capable of twenty."

Twenty? I smiled to myself. I wasn't a twenty-homer player. But I loved that he thought I was.

The following season, in June 2004, St. Louis called Yadier up to the big leagues. He was just twenty-three and had spent less than four full years in the minor leagues, about half the time Cheo and I did. I knew he'd get to the Majors quickly. We all knew. He'd been catching since he was five years old. His arm was like a grenade launcher. Like all of Benjamín Molina Santana's sons, Yadier didn't brag or show off. But unlike Cheo and me at his age, Yadier *knew* he belonged with the best in the world.

His arrival in the Majors prompted stories about the near impossibility of three brothers from one family becoming catchers in the Major Leagues.

"An explanation?" Yadier said, answering reporters' questions. "I don't have one. It's a thing of God, you know?"

Soon after Yadier was called up, Pai and Mai flew to the States to watch their sons play. They stayed a week with Yadier in St. Louis, then a week with Cheo and me in Anaheim. Pai was so soft with my girls. I watched him toss a Nerf ball to them in my living room, and when they threw it back, he pretended to fall backward from the force. Kelssy and Kyshly collapsed each time in giggles.

Pai doted on them in a way he never did with my brothers and me. He pushed plates of food at them—"*Mama*, you gotta eat." I remember one day when Kelssy was little we were at a hotel in Puerto Rico with one of Pai's Little League teams. They were there for a tournament. Pai was playing dominoes when Kelssy tugged at him and asked if he'd take her to the pool. Pai didn't interrupt his dominoes for anything, so I was about to pull her away and take her myself. But Pai was already summoning someone else to take his place at the table. He took his shirt off and jumped right into the pool with Kelssy.

My parents knew nothing yet of my disintegrating marriage. They didn't know I was sleeping on a couch downstairs when I was in Yuma and that I stashed the blanket and pillow in a closet before the girls woke up. During my parents' visit, I was the dutiful husband. I said the right things. I behaved as if all were well. I didn't even have to put much energy into playing the role. It was the default setting in my brain: I did what they expected me to do.

In July, a few days after my thirtieth birthday, we played a series in Seattle, and Jamie threw a small party in her apartment with some of her friends and family. She made onion steak, my favorite, and a chocolate Coca-Cola cake.

Her neck and back were still painful at times, but she was well enough to work. She told me she was moving back to California. She'd be doing freelance work again.

We'd been talking on the phone for five years by then. We'd been alone maybe four times. It was ridiculous when I thought about it. But it was perfect in a way, too. We knew each other so well from our hundreds of conversations. I bet we had talked more hours in those five years than most real couples talk in a lifetime.

Still, I didn't know for certain if she felt about me the way I did about her.

In his first season in the big leagues, Yadier's Cardinals reached the World Series, facing the Boston Red Sox, who hadn't won a championship in eighty-six years. Mai, Pai, José, I, and other family and friends descended on St. Louis to cheer on Yadier. The Sox swept the Cardinals. Still, Yadier had made it to the World Series. Some players spend their whole careers without ever getting there. Now all three of us had been.

IT WAS THE summer of 2005. The Angels were in New York to play the Yankees. Jamie was there for work. I walked into the hotel late one afternoon after visiting Mai's cousins in Brooklyn. It was an off day. When the elevator door opened, Jamie walked out.

"Hey," I said. "Where you headed?"

"Dinner."

We still had never been out for dinner, just the two of us. When she was on the road with the Angels, she usually ate with the guys from the crew or by herself. I usually got room service or went out with Cheo.

"Want some company?"

She smiled. "We can share a cab."

In the taxi, she said she hadn't been heading to any place in particular. And she wasn't really all that hungry. She just wanted to get out of her room. I suggested a movie. The cab dropped us at a theater, but every movie was sold out. So we strolled through Times Square, talking about the previous night's game, about music, about how two people from such small towns ended up with jobs that took them to Times Square. We talked about how weird fate could be. Our hands brushed. I slipped my fingers through hers. Neither of us acknowledged it.

Jamie looked spectacular even though she was just in jeans and a sleeveless top. Her hair was pulled back off her face in a ponytail that reached halfway down her back. I kept glancing sideways at her. We wandered into a park, where a guy in dreadlocks played a steel drum and young couples pushed baby strollers. There was a stone fountain, and people sat on the rim of the basin, relaxing in the warm evening air.

We stopped to watch the cascading water and listen to the steel drum. I turned toward Jamie and took her face in my hands. I leaned in and kissed her. I felt her arms wrap around me, and it felt as if we had done this a million times, as if it was the most normal thing in the world to be kissing in front of a hundred passersby at a fountain in a park.

"I love you," I said. "I think I've loved you since the first time I saw you in spring training."

Jamie laughed and said she never imagined being with me.

"But everything with you is so easy," she said. "We're such different people, but it's like we're soul mates."

She said she had realized she was falling in love a few years ago, and that was when she pulled away and didn't answer my calls for days and weeks at a time. "I knew I wanted to be with you and I couldn't. I knew it wasn't right to have feelings for a married man. I never wanted to be a factor in your decision to divorce."

I said my divorce was moving forward with or without her. She wanted to know about Kyshly and Kelssy. I'd get a house near them. It would be better for everyone, I said.

"You need to be sure."

I said I'd never been more certain about anything.

We stopped at Tower Records and I bought her a Mariah Carey CD. I wanted to give her love songs. We said good night before we reached the hotel and entered through separate doors. She didn't want to give anyone any ideas about "us"—she had her reputation to protect. But I was already thinking about what our kids might look like.

SOMETIMES, MY PRIDE could get the best of me. A catcher had to swallow his pride for the good of the team. Take the high road. Be the grown-up. I was still learning.

One game I noticed that whenever our pitcher gave up a hit, our shortstop shook his head. I didn't like the guy too much to begin with. He was all about himself. I'd sometimes see him texting and talking on the phone behind the dugout between innings. I had no respect for guys who didn't play the right way.

"Why were you shaking your head?" I asked him in the dugout.

"He should have thrown a fastball on a two-two count right there!" he said. I thought my head might explode. This guy was questioning my game-calling?

When he shook his head again the next inning, I called time-out and invited him to join the pitcher and me on the mound.

"Okay, you want to call the game, call it. Fastball touch your head. Curveball to the chest. Slider to the thigh. Shake your hand for the change-up."

I left the mound before he could answer and squatted behind the plate. The pitcher waited for my signal. I looked at the shortstop. He looked back at me. I waited. The pitcher looked at me, puzzled. I stared at the shortstop.

Bud Black, the pitching coach, called time and walked to the mound. I hustled over to join him and the pitcher.

"B-mo, what's going on?" he asked.

"We have a situation, Buddy. I think the shortstop is trying to tell us we don't know what we're doing. So I'm waiting for him to tell us what pitch we need to call in this situation."

"Come on, B-Mo, leave it till after the game."

I returned to the plate, squatted, and looked at the shortstop again. I waited a beat, then finally gave the sign.

Scioscia and Buddy called me into the office after the game.

"You could really hurt the team with that," Scioscia said. "You can't let those things bother you."

He was right. The guy was an idiot, and I let him get under my too-thin skin.

At the end of the season, we faced the Yankees again in the American League Division Series. My bat was so hot that Scioscia kept moving me up in the batting order. I hit sixth in Game 1, fifth in Game 2, and cleanup in Game 3. In the three games, I hit .455 with a home run in each game and five RBIs. When I was hit by a pitch and had to leave Game 3, Cheo took my place and hit a run-scoring single.

One day outside the clubhouse in Anaheim, I heard someone yell, "Hey, Big Money!" It was a janitor who was in the hallway every day. He had a nickname for everyone: Speeze for Spiezio, AK for Adam Kennedy, and so on. He had always called me B-Mo like everyone else did. One of the Angels broadcasters overheard him call me Big Money and used it on the air that night. Soon fans were waving "Big Money" signs in the stands. Other broadcasters picked up on it. The nickname stuck.

We beat the Yankees in five games to move on to the AL Championship Series. In the meantime, Yadier's Cardinals swept the Padres to reach the National League Championship Series. If we won and the Cardinals won, Cheo and I would play against Yadier in the World Series. It was crazy.

The *Wall Street Journal* dispatched a reporter to Espinosa to find out what was going on with the Molina family.

"Catchers are an idiosyncratic breed to show up three times in one family," the reporter wrote. He described Mai and Pai's house with "paint peeling on the ceilings and the windows held to their frames with masking tape." Mai and Pai were in the living room watching our games on TV. Mai apparently was yelling at the pitchers for making us dig balls out of the dirt and covering her eyes and praying when one of us came to bat.

José and I lost to the White Sox in the American League Championship Series. Yadier and the Cardinals lost to the Astros in the NLCS.

MY CONTRACT WITH the Angels was up, but I was confident they'd sign me to a new one. I had been with the organization for thirteen years. We had won a World Series together. In the off-season, I waited for my agent to call with their offer.

In the meantime, I found a smallish three-bedroom house with a little yard and a pool in a gated community in Yuma twenty minutes from the house my wife and I had bought. I still hadn't told Kyshly and Kelssy that I was moving out. They were twelve and nine, beautiful, dark-haired girls who danced and played soccer and knew how to field a grounder on a short hop. They attended Catholic school. Maybe because they had traveled so often to Mexico, Puerto Rico, and California, they seemed at ease no matter where they were or who they were with. They'd meet someone new and soon they were chatting as if they were old friends. I marveled at the ease with which they moved through the world. So different from me.

I told my wife about the new house and when I'd be moving in. Now I had to tell the girls. I practiced in my head what I'd say. When I sat with them in our living room, they were crying before I could get a word out. They already knew from their mother. They begged me to stay. I cried, too, and told them I wasn't leaving them, only the house. I was their father. I loved them and always would.

They crawled into the crooks of my arms, their faces buried in my chest, their shoulders heaving. My heart was breaking, but I wasn't changing my mind. This was the right thing. I wanted to give my daughters a happy, loving home. They'd never have that with their mother and me under one roof. I wanted Jamie in their lives. I wanted them to see her strength and independence as a woman, her kindness and compassion. I wanted them to see a healthy relationship where a man and a woman respected and admired each other and were deeply, completely in love. I wanted them to settle for nothing less in their own lives.

When I called to tell Mai and Pai, they already knew, too. My wife had beaten me to the punch.

"How could you do such a thing?" Mai yelled through the phone.

"This has been coming for a long time," I said, shaken that she was taking my wife's side in this. "You have to understand that if it didn't happen now, it would have happened a year from now."

"How can you do this? I don't understand!"

"There's no love anymore, Mai. We're fighting every day. We don't even speak. There's no relationship. I can't live like that anymore. I don't want the girls to live like that. Look, I'm not letting go of the girls. I'm going to be there for them. Whatever they need, I'm going to be there."

I wanted Pai to get on the phone. He'd help me figure out how to get Mai to understand. It hurt that she didn't trust me to make the right decision for my family. She yelled until she exhausted herself, and finally, thankfully, Pai got on.

"Pai—"

"Your girls are going to suffer!" he barked, livid. "You are the backbone of those girls. You are in charge. You don't just leave! How can you do this to them?"

I almost couldn't speak. Did he believe I didn't think this through? That I didn't struggle with the decision?

"Pai, you don't understand. This has been going on for so long. You think everything's so nice. But all we do is fight. The girls aren't happy. We can't go on this way."

"There is nothing more important than family. You need to go back to her. Go back to the girls. Do whatever it takes."

My whole life, Pai's words had been like notes from God. *If he said it, it must be true.* For the first time, I knew he was wrong.

"You need to trust me, Pai. I'm going to take care of them. It's the best thing for the girls and for me. They'll be happier. I'll be happier."

He was still steaming when he hung up the phone. I felt sick.

When I called the next day, Mai answered. She had calmed down but was still angry. After a few minutes, I asked to say hello to Pai.

"He won't come to the phone."

"What do you mean?"

"He doesn't want to talk to you."

I felt as if a truck had hit me. Pai not talk to me? When I needed him most? It was unthinkable. He had been there for me my whole life. He had believed in me. Made me push through the failures. Maybe I should have told him earlier about all this and explained what I had with Jamie, how the love and happiness I felt with her had made me feel whole. But I had been afraid to hear what he'd say. Good people don't divorce. Good men don't leave their families. Okay, but at least hear me out. At least consider my side. Was it some kind of cruel test?

"Let him cool off," Mai said. "He'll talk to you later."

But every time I called for the next few weeks, Mai made up some excuse why Pai couldn't come to the phone. He was eating. He was in the shower.

One day she said, "He's right here. Hang on."

Finally.

I heard Pai's voice in the background.

"Sorry, *mi hijo,*" Mai said, "he's going to the park."

"Oh, okay. Tell him '*Bendición.*'"

My whole life I had sought his blessing. I'd do anything for it. This time I couldn't. He thought I was tossing away his rules for my flawed ones. He couldn't see that I was, in fact, living by the values he taught me—family, love, responsibility. I was simply looking at them through my own lens instead of his.

In other words, I wasn't defying his values. I was, for the first time in my adult life, defying *him*.

I set up the girls' bedrooms first so they could start staying with me right away. They stayed at my house regularly, and we'd play Monopoly,

Pictionary, Scrabble. We played FIFA video games. Swam in the pool. I would drive them to school and pick them up as often as I could. When they weren't staying with me, I talked to them on the phone.

I talked to Jamie every day, too, during the off-season. She visited often from Los Angeles, helping me furnish and decorate. But it was too soon for her to meet my daughters.

"THE ANGELS ARE going with Jeff Mathis," my agent said, referring to the Angels' top minor-league catcher. It was the autumn of 2005.

I was out. Just like that. Another family broken. I was leaving the only franchise I'd known—all the clubbies, the cooks, the front office folks, the trainers, the coaches, Scioscia, my teammates. My own brother.

My agent said the Mets were offering $18 million over three years. "But I think we can get a few more million," he said.

"Yeah, you can try for a little more money, but make sure they know I want to make a deal," I said. "Tell them I'm excited to come to New York."

I had family back east—my mother's side in Brooklyn, my dad's not far away in Connecticut. It was a good fit. I told Jamie and Mai and my brothers that I was signing with the Mets. Now I could relax. I'd have good money for three years.

My agent didn't call for two days. It was weird. Why was it taking so long to get the deal done? I kept calling my agent and asking what was going on. No one at the agency called back. Four or five days passed. Then I got a message from a friend.

"Did you hear the Mets traded for Paul Lo Duca?"

My stomach dropped. Lo Duca was a catcher with the Florida

Marlins. They offer me three years then go and get Lo Duca? What was going on? I called the agency again and finally got a call back.

"What happened to the New York deal? I told you to accept it!"

"Oh, you didn't want to go there. New York is bad for you."

"I'm the one who decides where I want to go, not you!"

"I know, but I wanted to use the winter meetings to negotiate more money."

"I didn't tell you to wait for the winter meetings!"

I took a breath. I knew people would think I had rejected $18 million. They'd think I was greedy or an idiot. Probably both. I later learned rumors circulated that I was asking for $50 million. I wanted to punch a wall. Or my agent's face.

"So now what?" I snapped.

He told me not to worry. He was talking to other teams. But I heard a different tone in his voice. He wasn't as confident as he had been in October.

Suddenly I felt that familiar panic of running out of time—to get on a college team, to attract the attention of a pro scout, to climb out of the minors, to get to the big leagues. Spring training would be starting in two months, and I didn't have a team.

A month passed. Nothing. Most rosters were set. I just had the best season of my career, and I couldn't get a job? Scioscia called to see why I hadn't signed. I found out the Angels had offered a two-year contract—which my agent never passed on to me. He thought he'd be slick and get more years and more money. Jamie called to let me vent. My brothers called, confounded and worried. Mai called, furious.

"Estos cabrones! Son unos stupidos! Que no aprecian!" These assholes! They're stupid! They don't appreciate you!

Suddenly Pai was on the phone.

"You have to stay calm in a situation like this," he said, sounding like his old self. "The game will find you."

"But, Pai, I was the best catcher on the market."

"Listen, you can't control it. There is nothing you can do. So why do you worry?"

His voice calmed me as it always did. He was still there for me.

A week before spring training, Toronto offered one year at $5 million with an option year at $7.5 million. I knew the option was meaningless. It was a guarantee of nothing.

But of course I told my agent to accept the offer. Immediately. Then I fired him.

I flew to the Blue Jays' Florida training facility. I flew Jamie in, too. I could, for the first time, introduce her as my girlfriend. We were a couple from the start with my new team. There was no awkwardness or explanations, as there would have been with the Angels. After all those years, Jamie and I were together.

On Opening Day, I hit a grand slam to the fifth deck in left field. A few days later, I hit two more home runs. A week into the season, I was hitting over .400 with three homers. Maybe this would be the year I'd hit twenty homers, as Pai told me I could.

But when Toronto's starting catcher from the previous season came off the disabled list, the manager had us platooning—he started against right-handed pitchers, I started against lefties. It was insane. I was hitting the cover off the ball, and the manager was sitting me because we faced a right-handed pitcher? He had me batting cleanup against lefties, and I was completely out of the lineup against righties?

I was in the manager's office every other day. How could I keep any rhythm at the plate if I was playing only three days a week? How could I get to know our pitchers if I didn't catch them regularly?

One day when I called home I was particularly frustrated. Pai answered. We hadn't talked since the start of the season several weeks earlier and then only briefly. Mai always answered. I started to tell him what was going on. He stopped me and said he'd get Mai.

"Wait—what?"

But he was already gone.

Mai got on.

"Is Pai all right?" I asked.

"He's fine."

"He doesn't sound fine."

"He's fine."

But he didn't talk to me, not that day or for the rest of the season. I knew by this time that my ex was trashing Jamie and me every chance she got. Crazy, awful stories about us filtered back to me from Puerto Rico. As angry as I was about the lies circulating about Jamie and me, I was more hurt and shaken that Pai could think they were true.

THE SUN IN Yuma in July can bake your eyes right out of your head. But I couldn't wait to get there during the All-Star Break. The girls were spending three days with me. And so was Jamie. They would meet for the first time.

Jamie and I got the house ready with board games and Styrofoam noodles for the pool. The girls liked her right away. They were open and sweet. Jamie combed their hair after their showers. She and Kyshly played Kelssy and me in Pictionary. We swam and barbecued. We had a beautiful three days.

The girls couldn't visit me in Toronto because it was too far for them to travel by themselves. Mai and Pai never visited, either. Jamie, as always, got me through. She was still working in Los Angeles but not full-time. So she joined me as much as she could. When she was with me, even just watching TV or eating takeout, I was happy.

If Pai could have felt what I was feeling, he'd have known there was no other choice.

IT WAS WEIRD playing in Anaheim in a Blue Jays uniform. You never knew as a player whether the kinship you felt for the fans was truly reciprocal or if their affection ended when you changed teams. But when I walked into left field to stretch before the game, they stood and cheered.

"Bengie! We miss you!"

"Big Money! When you coming back?"

I stopped at the fence and signed autographs and thanked them for being so good to my brother and me.

It gave me goose bumps. I was still one of their own, even in a Toronto jersey. One of the regular ushers shouted down to me. Every time we had seen each other when I played with the Angels, we would salute each other. As I began to wave, he saluted. I saluted back. Another usher flashed me his usual greeting—the Hawaiian hang-loose sign. I flashed it back, as I had done for years. During batting practice, I hugged my old teammates, caught up with Scioscia, and made plans with Cheo to have dinner after the game. I couldn't help looking across the field at the Angels' bullpen, where I had caught warm-up sessions with the starting pitchers. Now coach Steve Soliz was working on footwork with Jeff Mathis, my replacement. I felt a tug of—what? longing? sadness?—the way I did every off-season when I returned to Dorado and was reminded yet again that it was no longer my home.

When I stepped to the plate for my first at-bat, the fans rose in a standing ovation. I was stunned. The cheers felt like a physical thing, a river flowing into me. I stepped out to raise my hand in thanks but also to gather myself. The cheers weren't for winning a game or hitting a home run. They were for me. *Me.* The long-shot kid from Kuilan. Who would have ever thought?

In the sixth inning, Cheo reached first base. The next batter up, he broke for second. My brother was stealing on me! I scooped the pitch out of the dirt and fired to second. Too late. Cheo had stolen just 6 bases in 278 Major League games. And he gets one against me.

The next inning, I singled. The third-base coach flashed me the steal sign. What? I had stolen exactly 2 bases in my 721 Major League games. I prayed the pitcher would be slow to the plate. He was. I took off. Cheo caught the ball and leaped to his feet. But no one was covering second! Why would they? Who would possibly expect me to steal? I slid in. No throw. Safe. The whole stadium of Angels fans hooted and hollered. I smiled at Cheo but couldn't tell beneath the mask if he was smiling back. I was guessing no.

After the game, Cheo and I gave each other crap. I said he got lucky. He said I'd have been out if anyone had been at the bag.

"Hey, man, we each got a stolen base, so who cares?" I said.

In the paper the next day, Sciosia said, "What are the chances of both Molinas stealing a base on the same night? What odds in Vegas would you get on that one?"

I started just 113 games that season, the fewest in my Major League career (when I wasn't injured). I was yanked before the end of a game twenty-nine times. Crazy. Still, I hit nineteen home runs.

While I headed back to Yuma for the off-season, Yadier and the Cardinals headed to the playoffs and reached the National League

Championship Series again. Their opponent? The New York Mets, the team I was supposed to sign with. I loved watching Yadier play. He was as quick as Cheo and threw even harder. The Cardinals timed his throw to second base at 1.7 seconds. The average is 1.9 seconds, which is what I usually threw. Over the course of the series, Yadier nailed nearly half of the Mets' would-be base stealers, a percentage on par with All-Star catchers like Pudge Rodriguez.

The NL Series went to a seventh game. The Cardinals were tied at one in the top of the ninth inning with a runner on base. Yadier stepped to the plate to face Mets reliever Aaron Heilman.

I yelled at the TV, "He's going to throw you another changeup! Sit on it, sit on it. That's what's coming."

Heilman threw a changeup. Yadier smashed it over the left-field wall for a two-run homer to put the Cardinals ahead, 3–1. He pointed to the camera, and I pointed back. "I told you!" Yadier had batted just .216 during the season but hit .358 in the Series. Another Big Money Molina.

Cardinals reliever Adam Wainwright loaded the bases in the bottom of the ninth. Yadier went to the mound twice to calm him. I could almost hear him: "Stay back, trust in yourself, keep your focus."

Wainwright struck out All-Star Carlos Beltran to clinch the pennant. Yadier was going to his second World Series in three years. Only two other catchers in history had played in two World Series before the age of twenty-five—Yogi Berra and Johnny Bench.

The Cards would play the Tigers, Pudge Rodriguez's team. Mai and Pai were there, which meant that among the 42,479 fans at Game 1 of the World Series in Detroit's Comerica Park was a quiet fifty-five-year-old factory worker who had coached both starting catchers.

I didn't go. I hadn't seen my girls since July and didn't want to leave them again. I watched every pitch on television with them and Jamie, and I called or texted Yadier every night. He couldn't fall asleep after games, so Mai, Pai, Cheo, Vitin, Tío Felo, and a few others stayed up with him until about 3 a.m., talking and laughing, playing dominoes, drinking beer, eating chicken wings, and analyzing the game.

Yadier was spectacular in the Series. He carved up the Tigers' pitching with seven hits in seventeen at-bats, including two doubles and an RBI.

The Cardinals won in five games. Jamie, the girls, and I danced around the living room and hollered every time we caught a glimpse of Yadier in the clubhouse drenching his teammates in champagne. I wished I could have seen Pai's face when Busch Stadium in St. Louis erupted after the final out.

Three sons.

Three catchers.

Now three World Series rings.

IN A SURPRISE to no one, the Blue Jays didn't pick up my option.

My new agent said he could get me three years with the San Francisco Giants. "Fifteen mil at least. Maybe eighteen, who knows?"

Sounded good to me. I asked about their current starter, Mike Matheny. He had been the starter for the Cardinals before Yadier was promoted to the position.

"He might be done," my agent said.

Every catcher in the league had been following the story of Mike Matheny, a veteran known as the Toughest Man Alive. He had taken a series of foul tips to his mask earlier that season. He stayed in the game for a few more pitches until his vision blurred and his head began to pound. He went to the Sports Concussion Program at the University of Pittsburgh Medical Center, where doctors put him through a battery of stress tests. He experienced the same symptoms every time: fatigue, memory problems, a tough time focusing, trouble seeing straight. He was diagnosed with "extensive concussion syndrome."

I went down the list of symptoms. Blurred vision. Headaches. Light-headedness. Check. Check. Check. After a foul tip to the head, I'd squint a few times to get my vision back. Take aspirin between innings. Once I took a foul tip so hard that I felt pain in the back of my head. But I didn't get it checked out. I didn't leave the game. I never left a game. I wondered sometimes why it was a much bigger deal when a batter got hit in the head but not a catcher. It was expected of a catcher. We were supposed to shake it off. But Matheny's situation got me wondering. How many blows could my head withstand without consequences? Would the next foul tip be the one that drove me into retirement? I put it out of my mind. You couldn't think that way.

"Please, tell the Giants yes," I told my agent.

"We can get more."

"Just tell them yes."

The final contract, if I earned all the bonuses, would be worth $18.5 million over three years.

I asked Jamie to move in with me. She said no. "Let's wait until we can do this right," she said. "When you can make a commitment."

The divorce was dragging on.

MAI WAS ALREADY outside when our rental car pulled up. It was a few weeks before Christmas in 2006. Kyshly and Kelssy tumbled out of the car and rushed into their *abuela*'s arms. I let out a long breath as if I'd been holding it in for months. I needed a dose of home. I needed to smell the *flamboyan* and eat some onion steak and lay eyes on my father. He hadn't taken my calls for months. He couldn't avoid me if I was right in front of him.

When he appeared in the doorway, the girls ran to him, and the three disappeared into the house. Mai hugged me tight. She squeezed my shoulders as she stepped back.

"What is it?" I asked.

"What do you mean?"

"I don't know. Everything all right?"

"Let's get your things inside."

She hauled out the bag of groceries I had bought on the way. I carried the girls' suitcases. Pai was in his usual chair in the living room. He was listening to the girls chatter about the flight and school. He didn't get up or look at me.

"Bendición, Pai."

"Dios te bendiga," he said without raising his eyes.

I hesitated, waiting for more. But he said nothing. I walked past him and into the kitchen to help Mai with the groceries.

The next day Pai was still distant. He didn't ask about the Giants contract. He didn't ask me to go to Junior Diaz's. I stayed in a hotel.

Yadier and Cheo lived about ten miles from Mai and Pai on the same block, seven houses apart, in a gated community. We went to Yadier's for dinner and talked about the World Series and cars and old friends and family. My new team, the Giants, was scheduled to play the Cardinals the first month of the season. Yadier and I had never played against each other.

"You try to get me out, because I'll be trying to get you out," I said.

"Don't worry!" he said, as if the thought of going easy on me had never crossed his mind. He was as competitive as anyone I knew. We were the closest of brothers, but not on the field. On the field, our teammates were our brothers.

That night at Yadier's, Pai played dominoes and pulled the girls onto his lap. He drank his Coors Light as always. But he was still not talking to me. My brothers told me Pai missed me. They said my living in Arizona instead of in Puerto Rico with the rest of the family probably didn't help, though they understood I had no choice: That's where my girls were. Maybe Pai felt that living in Arizona was some kind of rejection, and now the divorce was a second blow against the family. Cheo and Yadier didn't take sides. They loved Pai and they loved me, and they just wanted everything back to normal.

One day at Titi Graciella's, I ended up playing dominoes with Pai, my cousin Ramirito, and Pai's brother, Tío Tití. Pai couldn't help but look at me. He even made remarks in my direction. It wasn't a conversation, but I was having fun. He was there.

I stopped him one day as he arrived home from work.

"Pai, we're leaving in a couple of days. I'm sorry if I hurt you or Mai. I never wanted to hurt you. I know you're upset, but trust me, the girls are fine. You can see they're fine. They love Jamie."

"I'm not upset with you."

"You don't want to talk to me."

"I'm not mad."

Then he walked away.

When I called the following week from Arizona, he didn't come to the phone. I was disappointed, but I wasn't crushed. Progress. Maybe that was the test. Pai's rejection was forcing me to measure my need for Jamie against my need for him. Maybe, whether he realized it or not, he was giving me room to become my own man.

Jamie had been asking me for a month to join her in Cabo San Lucas, Mexico, in December for her family's annual trip. I said I couldn't. I had to go to San Francisco for a press conference. But I already had a plane ticket. I was going to surprise her.

When I arrived in Cabo, the front-desk clerk called Jamie's room to say there was a surprise for her in the lobby. She was on her way to the beach and said she'd get it later. No, the clerk said, you have to pick it up now.

Jamie emerged from the elevator and cried when she saw me. "I can't believe you're here."

I had gotten my own room but it wasn't ready, so we went to hers to stash my bag. "I can't wait for my parents to see you!" she said. "They're outside. I'm late already to meet up with them."

"Wait."

From my bag, I pulled out a new memory card for her camera. (She had told me hers was full.) I pulled out a bracelet with a dolphin charm. She loved dolphins. I pulled out a Brett Favre jersey, her favorite player.

"Thank you," she kept saying. "But let's do all this later. Everyone's waiting for me on the beach."

I couldn't wait.

I sank to one knee and opened a little white box. Jamie pressed a hand to her mouth. The ring was simple but beautiful: a cluster of little diamonds in a circle and two lines of diamonds down the sides. I wanted her to know I was for real and to wait with me through what was turning into a difficult divorce.

"Will you marry me?"

"Yes, yes!"

We were hugging and crying when we saw Jamie's mother,

Jennifer, marching up the garden path toward the sliding glass door of Jamie's room. She did not look happy.

Jamie flung open the door.

"We've been waiting—" Jennifer started to say.

"Mom! Look who surprised us!"

Jennifer's face lit up and I gave her a big hug. We toasted our engagement at the pool with Jamie's father and sister and family friends. It was the first time I'd spent time with Jamie's family, other than brief dinners after games. Her father and mother had remarried each other after their divorce when Jamie was younger. Their reunited family was happier than ever. We had a great three days. When I left, Jennifer told me she had never seen Jamie so happy.

I called Mai when I returned to Yuma. I knew the news of my engagement would not go over well. It didn't. This was one time I was relieved Pai wouldn't be coming to the phone. When I told the girls, they were worried more than angry or sad. Their mother and I had been apart for long enough that it was becoming the norm. "What's going to happen to *us*?" they wanted to know.

"Jamie loves you. We're a family. We're always a family. We'll just be a slightly bigger family."

PITCHERS AND CATCHERS report to spring training earlier than the position players. The *New York Times*' headline in January 2007:

"Three Weeks to Pitchers and Molinas."

The first thing I thought when I saw it: I've got to tell Pai. See what the Molina name has come to mean?

Then I remembered.

I told Mai instead. I knew she'd tell Pai, not only about the headline but also what I said about the Molina name. We were still tied together, even if his back was turned.

The Giants' clubhouse sounded like any other in early spring—the catching-up conversations, the clatter of new bats pulled from shipping boxes, the dull hum of faucets and showers. The guys were friendly and made me feel welcome, even superstar Barry Bonds, whom I had met during the trip to Japan in 2000. He gave me a big smile and a hug and announced, "This guy right here is the man."

But it didn't take long to see the cracks and ruptures. This team was Bonds and twenty-four other guys. Bonds kept himself so separate and held himself so above everyone else. I had gotten a taste of his personality during the All-Star trip to Japan. One day on the team bus, Bonds was talking loudly about how many houses he had, how many cars, how much money he had. In the beginning everyone listened, but then it got to be too much. Nobody said anything. It was Barry Bonds, arguably the best player in baseball. Suddenly Gary Sheffield stood up.

"Hey, Barry, why don't you shut up? Nobody here cares how much you have."

Bonds barked back at Sheffield, then Sandy Alomar barked at Bonds. The two had known each other since their fathers, Sandy Alomar Sr. and Bobby Bonds, played together for the New York Yankees in 1975. "I kicked your ass then, and I'll kick it now," Alomar told Bonds.

In the Giants' clubhouse, Bonds had the run of the place. I'd never seen anything like it. There wasn't much the Giants' new manager, Bruce Bochy, could do. All the rah-rah speeches in the world weren't going to turn a Barry Bonds team into a unified whole.

I threw myself into helping the Giants' young pitching staff, in particular a baby-faced rookie named Tim Lincecum. Timmy, a first-round draft pick, looked like the batboy—five feet, eleven inches tall and maybe 160, 170 pounds—but he pitched like Sandy Koufax. He threw 95 mph and had a great changeup, slider, and curve. But what made him so good, at least in large part, was he believed no one could hit him. People were already calling him "the Franchise."

"This kid is going to be unbelievable," I told Jamie on the phone one night, "once he really knows what he's doing."

He became my little brother in the clubhouse. He listened to everything. He never shook me off in a game. He was introverted and humble, especially for someone with such extraordinary talent and someone who was becoming so popular in San Francisco that he could barely walk out of his apartment without drawing a crowd.

Every day I found myself in quiet conversation in the clubhouse or dugout with one player or another, not just Timmy, offering encouragement to a guy on a bad streak, suggesting a particular approach against an opposing pitcher. As the season unfolded, I found myself echoing Pai:

"You got to just think about today, man."

"Don't try to do it all yourself. You got a whole team here with you."

"Just keep working hard every day. All-out, all the time. It'll turn around. You're too good, man, for it not to."

But I couldn't figure out the pep talk I was supposed to give myself when we blew another game. Every loss—even when we were nineteen games out of first place—cut me like a fresh wound. You'd think after all these years I'd have listened to my own advice—let it go, tomorrow's another day. But I slumped in the chair at my locker, unshowered, angry, frustrated, miserable.

When Jamie was in town, she waited in the family room across the hall from the clubhouse. By the time I emerged, she was the only one left. We walked back to the apartment I had rented near the ballpark. Jamie still lived in Los Angeles, doing freelance work. But she visited as much as she could.

"Let it rest," she said when I went on too long about a loss and the mistakes I had made behind the plate. She cooked something, then coaxed me into marathon games of dominoes or Boggle. She killed me in Boggle—she'd get thirty points to my seven or ten. But every new game, I'd think I was going to win. Eventually, late into the night, my mind was settled enough to sleep.

I'd show up at the field the next day convinced anew that we were going to win. I had no patience or respect for the guys who weren't. Some had stopped caring about wins and losses. They just wanted to pad their own numbers. Losing was bad enough, but losing that way, with no regard for the team? I confronted several of the worst offenders. But nothing changed. When I strapped on my gear and mask, they felt more than ever like armor. I couldn't tell sometimes if I was battling the opposing team or my own.

THE DIVORCE HAD turned even uglier, with grinding, exhausting battles at every turn. But I was happy. I loved being with Jamie. I loved watching her fly around my apartment cleaning this and that and me play-fighting with her because she wouldn't sit down. I had no interest in going to bars or hanging out with the guys. There was no place I'd rather be than at home with her, talking, playing Boggle, watching TV, eating dinner.

So Jamie surprised me one day when she said, "You're shutting me out."

"What? No, I'm not. I'm tired."

"You're depressed. You miss your father. It's killing you, Bengie. You know it is. You can't keep letting this drag on."

"What am I going to do? He won't talk to me."

"Call him anyway and keep calling. If you don't know what to say, talk about baseball. Ask him about when he played."

Jamie got a sheet of paper. "Write questions."

"He's not going to answer."

"Just write."

I sat at the kitchen table.

What was it like watching Roberto Clemente and Orlando Cepeda play?

What did you do to get out of a slump?

How did you lead your team when you were such a quiet guy?

Why didn't you go the Major Leagues?

I wrote pages of questions.

The next day, I dialed. Mai answered. I caught up on the news, then asked if Pai could come to the phone.

"He says to tell you hi."

"Tell him I want to ask him some questions."

"*Mi hijo,* let it alone. He'll come around."

One night in Colorado, during the first week of September, I snapped, breaking one of Pai's golden rules. After another bad loss, our fourth in a row, I blasted my Giants teammates in the press. Not by name. I was careful about that. But otherwise, I let rip a tirade unlike any in my life.

"It's an embarrassment what we're going through right now, losing so much, being in last place," I told reporters. "We came here to win. We didn't come here to be part of a country club just to pass the time, just to get paid. At least I didn't come here for that. I didn't come here to lose.

"People have got to understand, if you think only of yourself and your numbers and not the team, you're probably going to have a so-so year. But if you play for the team, to win, you're going to have way better numbers. If we have people here who are worrying about getting paid or just happy to be here and not worrying about winning, they're on the wrong team—or I am.

"We have a saying in Puerto Rico: 'I put my little piece in the puzzle.' What I do on the field is my piece. But I can't carry the team. Barry Bonds can't carry the team. Ray Durham, nobody. This has to be done together.

"Every guy has got to go out there between those lines and respect the game. Go all out for three and a half hours and respect your teammates. That's the biggest thing here, respect your teammates and work your butt off for nine innings. If you get beat, you can keep your head up. But if you beat yourself or you don't come out with the right energy or desire, if you're coming out just to get paid, it's hard on everybody."

Afterward, on my way home, I knew my teammates might be pissed when they saw the morning paper. Maybe even Boch would be pissed. I didn't fall asleep until the sun was rising. In the afternoon, when I arrived in the clubhouse, only one player felt offended. Bonds.

We snapped our losing streak that night. After the game Mike Murphy, our clubhouse manager, handed me a ball.

"What's this?"

"Your one hundredth home run."

"Really?" I had no idea.

Bonds had hit his 762nd home run that night, too, so none of the reporters asked about my little milestone. But this ball meant as much to me as any of Bonds's records. One hundred homers in the Majors when I couldn't even hit a ball to the hill at Maysonet Park.

I had to call Pai, though I knew he might not come to the phone.

By luck, he answered.

"Pai, I hit my hundredth homer today."

"Wow, that's pretty amazing. Congratulations."

"Now I'm only six hundred and sixty-two behind Bonds. I think I can catch up."

Pai gave me a little laugh.

The ice was breaking.

With a few games left in the season, Bochy called me into his office.

"Congratulations, Big Kahuna, you won the Willie Mac Award."

Named after the Giants' beloved Hall of Famer Willie McCovey, it went to the team's most inspirational player as voted on by the players, coaches, and training staff.

My Gold Glove in 2003 had been voted on by the media. This was different. This was from the people closest to you, who knew you best. I couldn't have been more honored.

In the off-season, Yadier landed a big multiyear contract with the Cardinals. The next day, he took Pai to a Toyota dealer.

"Why are you bringing me here? I don't need a car. I already got a car."

"This is so you can be more comfortable driving to work."

"I don't need it."

"I'm buying it."

Pai parked the FJ Cruiser 4x4 SUV in the driveway. He left it there for a month, with the plastic still on the seats and visors.

Mai called me to tell me they were throwing a surprise party for

Yadier to celebrate his new contract. Would I come? I knew Kelssy and Kyshly couldn't miss school, and I didn't want to go without them. I'd be leaving them again soon enough for spring training. I told Mai I couldn't get down there but I'd be thinking of them.

A few days after the party, I was talking to a friend from Puerto Rico who had been there. "You should have heard what your father said."

Pai had made a toast.

"I'm proud of my sons. I'm very happy with what they've become. We're only missing one thing here. My oldest son, Bengie. We're missing him here. I don't know why he didn't come. He should have been here. We're here having fun. *Pa'l carajo con el!*"

That destroyed me. *Pa'l carajo con el* means *To hell with him.* I would have been there had I known how important it was to Pai. I would have done whatever it took. Dropped everything.

I immediately called Mai and my brothers to apologize.

"I didn't know," I said.

Yadier said he didn't remember what Pai said. Cheo said Pai had too many beers. Mai said don't worry, it was fine.

I knew it wasn't fine. I knew Pai was thinking I was disloyal, that I didn't put family first. For Pai, that was the worst sin. It was confusing. I *was* putting family first. I was choosing my daughters over a party. I didn't know what was right or wrong with him. I didn't know how to make him happy. It seemed I couldn't win.

JAMIE'S APARTMENT BUILDING in Los Angeles was converting to condos. She had to buy one or move. I told her it was the fates telling her it was time to be with me. In February 2008, right before spring training, Jamie moved her stuff into my house in Yuma. In San Francisco during the baseball season, we rented a house in the Marina District with views of the bay and the Golden Gate Bridge. In July, with the girls out of school for the summer, Jamie flew from San Francisco to Yuma, met the girls at the airport, then flew back with them to San Francisco. Kyshly was thirteen and Kelssy nine, still too young in my mind to fly by themselves.

The four of us had a great time together. We went ice-skating at Yerba Buena, flew kites on the Marina Green, rented little "Go-Cars" at the Wharf and drove them—Jamie and Kyshly in one car, Kelssy and me in the other—down to the base of the Golden Gate Bridge (where we saw a dolphin in the bay), through the Presidio to Baker Beach and Sea Cliff. We ate clam chowder from bread bowls at Fisherman's Wharf. We went to Ripley's Believe It or Not, bought souvenirs. Kelssy chose an "Alcatraz Psych Ward Outpatient" jacket. We laughed so much our faces hurt. We took our ten-month-old Samoyed, Chico, for walks on Crissy Field and played soccer. At night when I got home from the ballpark, we played Scrabble, Boggle, or Rummy. I watched the girls with Jamie and thought if Pai could see them for just one weekend, all that worry in his heart would go away. I'd get my father back. But he wouldn't come visit, no matter how many times I asked Mai.

With Barry Bonds gone in 2008, there was already a more relaxed feel in the clubhouse. But his departure left a huge hole in the lineup. Now someone else was going to have to bat cleanup. Bochy made an unlikely choice.

Me.

Boch, a former catcher himself, made sure I knew my number-one job was handling an incredibly young, incredibly talented pitching staff. Tim Lincecum. Matt Cain. Jonathan Sanchez. Brian Wilson. Almost overnight, we changed from a hitting team to a pitching team.

In late May, seven weeks into the season, I went on a hitting tear. I'd had good streaks, but none like that. In one doubleheader in Miami, I went 6-for-7 with four doubles and five RBIs. (And I caught sixteen innings that day.) I hit .652 for the week. I was named National League Player of the Week, which came with a commemorative watch. Mai congratulated me after she read about it in the newspaper.

"Pai knows, right?"

"I'm sure he does. He reads the paper. But he's not here right now."

I called later, and he answered.

"Bendición."

"Dios te bendiga."

"Pai, did you see?"

"What a series you had in Miami."

"Yeah, every swing I had was a good one."

"Did you notice something? You got most of those hits to right center."

I laughed. "What you always told me. See? I listened."

"Congratulations on your watch. Okay, here's Mai."

The conversation was over.

When school started in August, the girls visited San Francisco on weekends if the Giants played at home, flying with Jamie or our friend Angie. Otherwise, they were in Yuma with their mother. One downside to baseball was being away from family. It was something you never got used to.

As September began, my hands looked like they always did toward the end of the season—like they belonged to two different men. The fingers on my glove hand were about one and a half times thicker than the ones on my throwing hand, and they were a different color—more purple than brown. The knuckles looked like misshapen knots on a tree. Two were fractured, but they'd have to wait until the end of the season to heal—not that there was really much to be done anyway. They just had to be left alone.

The toll of another season reminded me of how much time had passed. I had been with the Giants almost two years, and my father had yet to see me play.

The following week Mai called to say she was traveling to St. Louis to see Yadier, then wanted to visit with me during the Giants' end-of-the-season swing through San Diego and Arizona.

And one more thing. Pai was coming.

AN AIRLINE EMPLOYEE pushed Mai in a wheelchair into the baggage claim area of San Diego International Airport. She had bad knees, bad feet, and a bad heel, so she wore some sort of metal contraption on her foot. Vitin had taken to calling her the Hardware Store. Pai followed a few steps behind her. I hadn't seen him in almost two years. *Two years.* At fifty-eight, he was still barrel-chested and regal.

Jamie knew I was nervous. She squeezed my hand. "Your father is a good man and he loves you," she said. "Those two truths will win out."

I waved, but Pai didn't see. Mai did, and her face lit up: the slightly lopsided smile, the crinkled eyes, the pink cheeks. When she waved, Pai looked our way. He smiled and raised his chin in a nod.

"Bengie!" Mai said when they reached us. She pushed herself up from the wheelchair and held out her chubby arms.

"Bendición," I said, hugging her. My throat was dry and my eyes were wet. I had missed them so much.

"*Bendición,* Pai. Thank you for coming."

"Dios te bendiga."

He gave me a tight hug. I squeezed my eyes to stop more tears from falling. I stepped back and put my arm around Jamie's shoulders. *This is the person who has changed my life. This is the person who loves and dotes on your granddaughters. This is the person who completes my family.* That was what I wanted to say.

What I said instead: "This is Jamie, my fiancée."

Mai smiled and offered her hand, then Pai. No hugs.

"Un placer," Jamie said, smiling her thousand-watt smile. *Pleasure to meet you.* Jamie had taken a Spanish class in preparation for meeting my family.

We stopped at Denny's on the way to the hotel. Pai made a big show of stealing french fries from Mai's plate and teasing her about eating too much. Mai smacked his hand and told him she'd spear him with a fork next time. Jamie laughed and shot me an amused glance; this was the Mai-and-Pai routine she'd been hearing about all these years. Except Pai wasn't just relaxed and funny, he was almost giddy. I had never seen him so animated. He couldn't stop smiling. I imagine Jamie wasn't the ogre he had been hearing about the past two years. And I imagine he was as happy and relieved to see me as I was to see him.

We had arranged for Kyshly and Kelssy to drive in from Yuma with our friends José and Angie with their daughter, Christina. They didn't know *guelo* and *guela* would be waiting for them. Mai hid behind a big chair in the hotel room. Pai hid in the closet. When the girls arrived, they hugged me and Jamie. Then Mai and Pai popped out. Kyshly and Kelssy shrieked and fell into their grandparents' arms. They had seen one another just five weeks earlier on a visit to Puerto Rico with their mother. Their love affair was a strong one, unaffected by the freeze-out between Pai and me.

Soon Kyshly was sandwiched on the couch between Mai and

Jamie, and Kelssy was sprawled across my father in an armchair. My eyes welled up again. Finally, the people I loved most, all in one place.

At the game that night, Kelssy spent several innings on Jamie's lap. Though she was only nine, she was almost as big as Jamie. "You're going to kill her, Kelssy!" Pai had said. He saw how the girls hung all over Jamie and how she brushed their hair and protected them from foul balls and made sure they ate something other than hot dogs and churros. How she joked with them that they wouldn't go anywhere without Jamie holding their hands.

We spent three days together in San Diego. The girls snapped photos of Pai in a fluffy white robe with Kelssy's big toy eyeglasses perched on his nose. He sang along to his favorite salsa music into a room-service ketchup bottle and danced around the room, the girls dancing and laughing with him. He got on all fours, and the girls rode him like a horse. He was so gentle and playful, a side I rarely saw growing up. It was as if we had finally become what we wanted in the other: I had become the kind of leader and warrior on the field he had always expected of me; and he had become softer and more loving, qualities I had always looked for in him as a child.

Jamie earned points with Pai by fetching him six-packs of Coors Light.

"Only one more," Mai said. "You're drinking too much."

"Who are you to tell me? I'll take as many as I want."

Mai rolled her eyes. We stayed up talking, making up for lost time. Pai told a story about having to appear in court a few weeks earlier. "It doesn't matter why," he said before we could ask. Vitin was driving him, and on the way, Pai said there was a problem. He knew he was expected to show the judge his driver's license.

"I told Vitin I didn't have a license. I'd never had one. Vitin couldn't believe it. He said, 'You've been driving all these years without a license?'"

Pai laughed. "It was true. So I asked Vitin, 'What am I going to do?' He called someone he knew at the DMV. We went there, I passed the test and got my picture taken. When they handed me the license, I held it up and kissed it."

Pai mimicked kissing his license. "I said, 'I haven't seen you in fifty-eight years!'"

Mai shook her head and scoffed. "Oh, you had a license."

"Who's telling the story?"

Over dinner one night, Pai slipped a major announcement into the conversation.

"I'm retiring at the end of the year. You might be seeing me a lot."

"Finally!" I said "You and Mai could stay here for a month. Why not?" We could make up for lost time. We could get back to normal. I could ask all my questions.

"We'll see," Pai said. "I still have the Pampers League," referring to his team of nine- and ten-year-olds.

"Let somebody else carry the load. You've put in your time, Pai. You should relax."

"What, and hang around the house?" Mai said.

Before we left San Diego, my friend José pulled me aside.

"Your dad just told me something."

"What?"

"He said, 'Now I'm okay. Now I'm fine. I can go back home in peace.'"

"Really?"

"He said, 'I see how the girls are with Jamie. I know they're fine.'"

I let out a long breath. He saw.

We had an off day between our series in San Diego and our series against the Diamondbacks in Arizona. So I drove to Yuma with Jamie, Mai and Pai, and the girls. I had never heard Pai talk so much as on that drive. We stopped at my house so Mai and Pai could see it, but they spent the night with the girls at my ex's. The next day, Jamie and I picked up Mai and Pai, said good-bye to the girls, and drove to Phoenix.

I struck out three times against Cy Young winner Brandon Webb.

"I don't know how you don't hit that guy! I could hit him with my bare hand!" Pai said at the hotel afterward. "Why do you want to pull the ball? That's why you strike out. You never trust your hands. Go to right field! That's your strength!"

Jamie walked in with a six-pack of Coors Light. The beer kept him talking. I happily listened.

Later that night, Jamie told me about Pai and the son of one of my teammates. Mai, Pai, and Jamie were waiting in the guest relations lobby to pick up their game tickets. Also waiting were Jack Taschner's wife and their three-year-old son, Gradin, who had a glove and a plastic Wiffle ball. Pai didn't speak English, and Gradin didn't speak Spanish. Pai squatted down like a catcher and held up his hands. Little Gradin launched into a windup, complete with a leg kick, and fired the ball. Pai shook his hand as if the ball burned. He stood and gently showed the little boy how to grip the ball. Gradin arranged his chubby fingers the way Pai showed him and reared back and threw one pitch after another. No words passed between them. Just throw and catch.

"I never saw such a true smile on a man," Jamie said. "He was completely happy playing catch with that little boy. There was no language. Just baseball."

Mai and Pai left the next day. We'd had ten days together. Jamie and I gave Mai a bracelet, a watch, and some pretty blouses, and we filled a suitcase with new clothes and shoes for Pai. At the airport, Jamie hugged them and they hugged her back.

I told Pai I loved him and thanked him for coming. I said to take care of himself and Mai.

He hugged me. *"Dios te bendiga,"* he said.

His version of "I love you, too."

He and I had found our way back to each other. We were different from who we had been two years earlier. Now we connected as men. I no longer needed to ride on his shoulders. And he no longer needed to carry me.

That night, our last game of the Diamondbacks series, I came up to bat in the eighth inning. We were down 2–1. Juan Cruz, one of the Diamondbacks' best relievers, was on the mound. Pai's words were still fresh in my mind: Right field, right field. I got the pitch I wanted.

Home run over the right-field fence.

It tied the game, though we ended up losing in the ninth.

I called Pai the next day. He was at Junior Diaz's, but Mai made sure he called back as soon as he walked in the door.

"What you got for me, *mi hijo*?"

"I want you to know I got a base hit to right field, a line drive to second, and a home run to right."

"I never had a doubt about you. Right field is your power."

"I was really struggling for a while."

"When you're in a slump, just think about today as the first game of a new season."

He could have been talking about him and me. It was a new season. All the awfulness was behind us. I finally had my father back.

PART

5

I PUSHED MY phone deeper into my pocket to muffle the buzz. Nothing was going to disrupt my day at Legoland with Jamie and the girls. With the season over, I was all theirs. No baseball. No agents. No distractions. When the phone buzzed a second and third time, I yanked it out to see who was calling.

Ramirito, my cousin.

"Ramirito, I'm with—"

"Your father fell and hit his head!"

"What?"

Before he could answer, another buzz.

Yadier.

I hung up on Ramirito.

"Yadier, what's going on? Is Pai all right?"

I heard choked cries and yells and then a loud clap like a fist through a wall and suddenly Vitin was on the phone.

"What's happened?" I said, stepping out of line, my heart pounding. Fathers in baseball caps and cargo shorts pushed strollers crammed with sunburned babies and souvenir bags and half-finished bottles of water. *"Where's Pai?"*

"Bengie, your dad's hurting pretty bad." I could hear the effort of each word, as if he were speaking a foreign language. "You better make arrangements to come to Puerto Rico."

Pai had fallen at the park, he said. His Pampers League. Maybe a heart attack. Maybe his head. He was with the doctors in the emergency room.

Jamie had already pulled the girls out of line, and when I took off toward the exit, they broke into a run to keep up, calling after me to wait. Popcorn carts. A toppled ice-cream cone. Saw-toothed edges of Lego-block characters—a chef, a pirate. EXIT. Parking lot. Where was the car?

"Bengie!" Jamie grabbed my arm. Kyshly and Kelssy, sweating and out of breath, stared at me as if I had lost my mind.

Another buzz. Cheo.

"Do you know anything?" I asked. I knew he was still in New York, fresh from laser eye surgery after his season with the Yankees.

But instead of Cheo, it was my sister-in-law, Yalicia, crying.

"Your dad just passed away."

The sun kicked off the windshields and splintered into my eyes. My knees buckled. I felt the warm metal of a railing under my hand.

"What is it?" Jamie said. "What's happened?"

I bent over, feeling as if I were going to vomit. What came out instead was a scream.

"Dad!" The girls were crying. They had never seen me like this.

"Guelo," I said, choking out the word. *"Guelo* died."

The girls' faces twisted as if I had slapped them. I don't remember much else. The details—packing, checking out of the hotel, booking a flight—were swallowed up in the blur of that day and night. Jamie did everything. We arrived in San Juan late the next morning, still in our clothes from Legoland.

It was a Sunday morning, so La Número Dos was empty. But when we made the turn into Kuilan, a police officer stood at the end of our street diverting cars. I rolled down the passenger window of our hired van.

"Ah, Bengie," he said, recognizing me. "Too many people going in to see your mom."

Cars lined both sides of the street, tires tilted up onto walkways, bumpers poking into the road. People walked in the street, and we inched alongside, stopping to accept condolences through my open window. I knew almost all of them: cousins, neighbors, old teammates, Pai's coworkers, guys from Junior Diaz's, parents of Pai's players, former classmates of mine or my brothers.

"Is this all for *guelo*?" Kelssy asked.

"I think so, *mama*," I said. I am in Dorado, I told myself. In Espinosa. In Kuilan. Pai has died. He couldn't have died. We had just seen him. He had loved Jamie. We were a family again. We had plans.

On the street in front of Mai and Pai's house there were no cars. Instead, workers were erecting the skeleton of an enormous tent.

Mai was slumped like a rag doll in her chair in the living room, but her face was calm and open. Her brothers and sisters, and Pai's brothers and sisters, and a hundred other people, it seemed, filled every inch of the tiny house, the overflow spilling out to the carport and side patio and rolling into the street in both directions. It wasn't even 10 a.m.

Mai broke into a smile when she saw me.

"Mai, I'm so sorry," I said, bending to wrap my arms around her. I buried my head in her neck and sobbed.

"*Mi hijo,* he's resting right now. We have to be strong for each other. I'm okay," she said. "You need to be okay."

The words sounded like a recording, almost robotic but also clear and steady. Gladys Matta was tough. She wanted everyone to think she was fine. But I knew she was destroyed. The girls threw themselves into their *guela*'s arms. Mai pulled them onto her lap. When she saw Jamie lingering in the doorway, she waved her in. Jamie pressed her cheek against Mai's, enveloping my mother and my daughters in a hug.

One after another, my aunts and uncles held me close. They cried for my father but also for my return home. I had been away for two years.

When Yadier arrived, the sun was high enough to knife through the slats of the jalousie windows, turning Mai's crowded house into a sweltering bath. Yadier looked like hell. His face was blotched and puffy. We hugged hard. Cheo wouldn't be arriving until the following morning.

"No way, Yadier," I said. "No way! This can't be happening!"

Once he made the rounds, hugging everyone, he, Jamie, and I walked across to the ballpark with a friend who had been there when Pai collapsed. In the street, workers were positioning a huge rectangular air conditioner along the side of the white tent. Racks of folding chairs were being unloaded from a truck. Mai told me there had been talk of holding Pai's wake at the funeral parlor in Vega Alta by the elementary school. But she knew it had to be right here, on the spot Pai had crossed a million times with his bag of balls and bats. This was where he had lived, in the seam between baseball and family. And this was where, Mai said, he had taken his last steps.

He was crossing the street with new baseballs for the second game of a doubleheader with his team of nine- and ten-year-olds. Mai said she pushed open the front door and called after him.

"Did you take your pills?"

"Later!" he yelled back. Pai had high blood pressure.

One of the players' fathers was chalking the batter's box when Pai approached the backstop fence. "You fixed the whole field," the man said, protesting when Pai offered to take over. "Let me do this little part. Go get a beer."

Pai smiled and wedged the new baseballs into a bent opening in the fence where the umpire could easily retrieve them. He continued on to the cement bleachers by the first-base dugout, where parents and neighbors were settling in.

"He was standing right here," our friend said, leading us to the foot of the bleachers.

I pictured him there, chatting with the parents as his kids tossed the ball around on the field behind him, waiting for the game to start.

"Hilda," Pai had said to one of the mothers, "how do those baselines look to you?"

"Very pretty and well made," she said.

Pai turned toward the field, perhaps to watch his players, perhaps to check on the lines of the batter's box. I pictured the parents popping open cans of soda and beer and handing dollar bills to their children for the concession stand. On the street, cars would have been ambling by, people on their way home from the laundromat or

Saturday grocery shopping, slowing to holler at friends they spotted at the park.

Everyone said it had been a perfect day for baseball. Blue skies. Dry field. Slight breeze. Just like now. I looked out on Pai's field. The highest leaves of the *flamboyan* and tamarind trees fluttered in the outfield like flags.

Our friend described what happened.

Pai suddenly clutched the fence. Then he grabbed his chest and fell backward. The back of his head hit the bottom row of the bleachers. Then he crumpled to the ground.

People were shouting and stomping down the bleachers.

"Benjamín!"

Pai didn't respond. Foam bubbled up through his lips.

"Someone call 911!"

"Benjamín!"

Mai heard the shouting and hurried across the street. Her hands flew to her face when the crowd parted and she saw Pai. "*Benjamín!* Where's the ambulance?"

Someone had pulled a pickup truck to the bleachers. The decision apparently had been made to drive Pai to the hospital rather than wait for an ambulance. Former big leaguer Luis Figueroa climbed into the backseat and soon was cradling Pai's rigid body on his lap. Mai rode in the front, her hands still pressed to her face.

Luis could feel the thrum of Pai's racing heart.

"Benjamín," Luis kept saying, "hold on. You're going to be all right."

Then he heard a sound from Pai's chest he later described as "a little snap." Pai's body went limp and his heart fell silent.

Neither Yadier nor I said anything as we listened to our friend's account. Then Yadier told us about seeing Pai that morning. It was a fluke that he was even in Puerto Rico. He and his wife had been packing up their house in St. Louis for the off-season.

"We weren't scheduled to fly in until today," he said.

But his wife's father had fallen ill, and Yadier had been looking for an excuse to go home earlier. He couldn't wait to show Mai and Pai their newest grandchild, Yanuell, who was just five weeks old. So they left St. Louis on Friday with the idea of surprising Mai and Pai that evening. But when they arrived at the house with the baby, Pai was at Junior Diaz's. They waited with Mai until ten, then left to put the baby to bed. On the way home, Yadier drove by Junior Diaz's and honked.

Pai emerged with a big smile.

"What are you doing here?" he said, leaning into the window to get a look at his tiny grandson in the car seat.

"I'm surprising you!" Yadier said. "I have to get Yanuell home, but I'll see you tomorrow, okay?"

When Yadier returned to the house the following morning, he found Pai on the roof picking grapefruit for birthday cocktails that night with his friend Miguelito. He was between games of the doubleheader. He climbed off the roof and, as he hugged Yadier, he said, "I love you."

Yadier was moved and thrilled. Though Pai was more affectionate with Yadier than with José and me, he didn't toss around "I love you"s even to him.

"I love you, too, Pai."

Pai cradled and kissed Yanuell, then went into the house to fetch balls for the next game. Yadier and his family drove off to get groceries in Bayamón. He and his wife were in the supermarket when they got the call. They left the cart in the aisle and roared to the hospital in Vega Alta.

He said a crowd was already gathering in the parking lot and lobby when he arrived. Yadier burst into the ER, where Mai sat with Vitin, both of them stricken. Through the window of an exam room, Yadier could see a doctor shocking Pai with paddles. Again and again. Then the doctor stopped.

"You can't stop!" Yadier yelled, pushing open the door. "You have to keep trying!"

The doctor said he was sorry. There was nothing more he could do.

Yadier wheeled around and punched the wall. In the hall, he flipped over a gurney. He kicked a chair. He punched the wall again. Five or six quick, hard punches.

"Why did this happen?" Mai cried. "Why did you leave me?"

The doctor said Pai had suffered a massive heart attack.

Once Yadier exhausted himself, he sank into a chair next to Mai and took out his cell phone. He needed his brothers.

EVEN AFTER YADIER told me what had happened at the hospital, and even as I watched huge easels of flowers carried into the white tent outside, I kept thinking we'd find out all this was a mistake. Pai would emerge from the kitchen, popping open a Coors Light, teasing Mai about not being able to live without him.

"Do you believe this fuss?" he'd say. "For a bump on the head!"

So later in the evening, when the opportunity arose to see Pai before he was transported to the tent, I took it. Tío Felo knew the undertaker and had pulled me aside to take me to the funeral home.

La funeraria was a storefront business in downtown Vega Alta. The undertaker met us at the door, where Tío Felo then parked himself, wanting no part in seeing Pai's body. The undertaker showed me down a short hallway to a small chapel-like room. The room was cold, or maybe I was. There were rows of chairs and, atop a metal wheeled table, an aqua-colored casket as shiny as a showroom car. The lid was up.

I could see from where I stood Pai's head in profile, propped on a small pillow: white hair, flat forehead, wide nose, blunt chin. He was wearing glasses. My legs turned rubbery. I gripped the back of a chair. The distance from me to him, no more than a few yards, seemed too far to walk.

But the next thing I knew I was at the edge of the casket, looking down at my father's soft, peaceful face. He looked as if he were deep into an afternoon nap, as if he'd grunt or knit his eyebrows in annoyance if I shook his shoulders. His leathery workingman's hands were folded on his chest, a rosary laced between his palms. There was dirt from the field under his nails. He wore a crisp, gray collared shirt buttoned to his neck. I recognized it as one Jamie and I had bought for him at Macy's two weeks earlier. I remembered thinking how sharp he'd look in it.

"I'm sorry for not being here when you wanted me to be," I said, surprised this was the first thing out of my mouth. I meant Yadier's party.

Then I broke down. I cried in big heaves, as if all the feelings I ever held for my father—love, guilt, regret, gratitude, pride, anger, longing—came flooding out. How could he be taken away when I finally had gotten him back? I cried until I had nothing left.

I reached out to hold one of Pai's hands, but they were frozen in place. So I slipped the fingers of my right hand between his palms and with my left stroked his white stubbly head. He had always liked raking his fingers through his hair.

"Thank you for making me who I am," I said softly as if he were sleeping. "You're the reason I'm standing where I am in my life. Thank you for sacrificing so much for us. For teaching us baseball and respect."

I went on to say everything I wanted him to know.

"You can rest," I finally said. "Don't worry about anything." I promised to take care of Mai, his *gorda,* and his brothers and sisters the way he did.

I kissed his forehead.

"I love you, Pai," I whispered.

BACK IN MAI'S steamy living room, I found Jamie poring over the dozens and dozens of pictures that covered nearly every inch of wall space in the living room and hallway. There was Roberto Clemente on one knee in the on-deck circle. Jesus with his right hand raised in blessing. Kyshly and Kelssy as babies. But mostly the walls belonged to Yadier, Cheo, and me. Me in my Los Pobres uniform, an awkward skinny kid who had yet to hit a ball through the infield. Chubby little Yadier squatting behind the plate. Cheo in high school, serious as a priest, striking a big-league batting stance. Photos from the 2002 World Series and the 2006 World Series and from various ALCS and

NLCS series. Framed magazine covers. Plaques and trophies. Bobble-heads. Publicity shots and baseball cards and signed balls in plastic cubes. Everything bearing the Molina name.

Could Pai, who never made it to the big leagues himself, ever have dreamed this?

Jamie and I had planned to stay at Yadier's while the girls stayed with Mai, but as day turned to night, we made no move to leave.

Outside, the white tent rose to full height. Small vans arrived with tall easels of flowers shaped into crosses and hearts and even a baseball. Police arranged sawhorses and orange cones at the end of the street.

In the kitchen, I joined Yadier, my cousin Mandy, and other cousins and friends for a toast. Pai's Igloo coolers were still stocked with six-packs of Coors Light for Miguelito's birthday party. We each opened a can and, into a pan from Mai's cupboard, we poured out a little beer, the way Pai always did as a nod to the dead.

Out in the carport, Yadier put on Pai's favorite music, and people told stories, and we even laughed.

At around midnight, the hearse arrived.

The casket was wheeled into the tent and placed at the front, surrounded by enormous sprays of white lilies, birds of paradise, orchids, begonias, hibiscus. Relatives who had left earlier in the evening now reappeared as news spread that the casket had arrived. Titi Graciella took one look at Pai, screamed, and fainted into someone's arms.

Mai, on the other hand, didn't react at all. She just stared. Inside the casket was a ball signed by Pai's Little League team. Someone placed a Maceteros uniform patch by his arm. There were hats from the Giants, the Cardinals and the Yankees, and three photos from Pai's induction into the Puerto Rican Amateur Baseball Hall of Fame.

Someone attached to the casket a Kevlar balloon in the shape of a baseball.

Mai returned to the house and stayed, receiving visitors there.

Jamie and I sat in the white folding chairs next to the casket. After so much time away from Pai, I wasn't going anywhere. People arrived at 2, 3, 4 a.m. Police officers worked in shifts outside, redirecting cars to side streets. When I went into Mai's house to use the bathroom, waves of people flowed in and out with *pastalillos, alcapurrias,* six-packs of cold beer. Mai was asleep in her chair.

As the sun rose Monday morning, the man who carpooled with Pai arrived at about the time he and Pai would have headed to work. He said Pai's department at the factory had closed for the day so everyone could attend the wake.

Cheo arrived before noon. Even with large dark glasses protecting his laser-repaired eyes, his face looked puffed and pale. After we hugged, he slumped in a chair near the casket with his head down. I had never seen him or Yadier so broken. They were both happy and outgoing by nature, always cracking jokes and having a good time. Now Cheo's face was like an old man's, washed out and slack.

Hundreds of people streamed through the tent all morning. I recognized many of their faces. Pai's former players. Coworkers. Neighbors. Politicians. Shopkeepers. Children from Pai's teams. But there were so many I didn't know. Men and women I had never seen broke down in tears, telling Yadier, Cheo, and me what a great man Pai was. Some couldn't bring themselves to enter the tent. They didn't want to see him that way.

Deliverymen kept arriving with more flowers. When there was no more space around the casket, we lined them along the tent's walls.

When I stepped outside to use the restroom early in the afternoon,

I couldn't believe the number of people. The street was packed in both directions as far as I could see. Kyshly, who had just woken up, emerged from Mai's house as I was heading back to the tent.

"Dad!"

"Yes, *mama*?"

"All these people know *guelo*?"

"And more, *mama*."

But I was stunned, too. I knew he was known, but I didn't know how much. I knew he was loved, but I had no idea how deeply.

I stayed by the casket all day. Jamie stayed with me. We hadn't slept since the plane Saturday night. We had barely eaten. I told Jamie to go to Yadier's to get some rest. She wouldn't.

At nightfall, the music began out on the street. I could hear the thumping beat and rattle of the *pleneras,* the *maracas,* the *guirros.* I heard men's voices rise in singsong *bomba* verses, the lead singer delivering a four-line rhyme about Pai—about baseball, family, his integrity, sense of humor, Coors Light. The crowd answered with the chorus—*Hey, guy, get your woman out and start dancing bomba with us!* One verse after another. Hour after hour. When one singer left, another joined, an unbroken stream of music rolling through the streets of Kuilan through the night.

Yadier joined the throngs outside. This was how he took care of people. He made them feel welcome, the way Mai and Pai always did. Cheo joined in, too, at times, but I couldn't. I felt as if I'd be abandoning Pai, yet again, if I left his side.

Through the afternoon and evening, baseball players showed up—José Rosado, Pedro Feliciano, Juan Gonzalez, Carmelo Martinez, José Valentin, José Hernandez, and many of Pai's former Puerto Rican teammates and Hall of Famers.

The eight-year-old boy from next door was one of Pai's players. "He was like my second father," he told me.

One after another, men and boys I'd never met told my brothers and me that Pai had been like a father to them, too. He kept them in school, off drugs, out of jail, off the troubled streets. One boy couldn't stop crying. "Now what will I do?" he asked.

I thought about the crops that once covered the field where Pai coached us and so many other boys. It occurred to me that instead of growing sugarcane and grapefruit trees on that land, Pai had been growing young men.

"He was born for that," Jacinto Camacho said to me during our second long night at Pai's casket. "He was born and died for that. He died teaching. He died with the kids."

At some point, Vitin arrived with our local newspaper, *El Nuevo Día*. Pai's death was the top story. Vitin and I took turns reading it to Pai.

A late-season hurricane was developing off the coast. As Tuesday morning broke, wind whipped the tent. Intermittent bursts of rain pelted the roof. We would be burying Pai in the afternoon. My time with him was running out. I pulled my chair close to the casket.

"I'm going to hit twenty home runs," I told him.

I don't know why I said it. Maybe I thought hitting twenty home runs would be proof that his belief in me was so deep, so utterly complete, that it could work miracles. Maybe I thought it would be proof of how much I loved him.

Around noon, after a priest from Yadier's church led us in prayer and hymns, Cheo and Yadier used the microphone from Pai's beloved karaoke machine—which had been positioned next to the casket—to thank everyone for coming. I didn't trust myself to speak.

"If my dad were here, he would be very happy," Yadier said. "He would want everybody to be happy. For my part, I want to say thank you to everybody. To Bengie, Cheo, Mai. To my dad, I want to say, '*Mi viejo,* I love you so much.'"

A light rain fell as we carried Pai's closed casket out of the tent and onto the baseball field. The baselines and batter's boxes had been carefully chalked. The infield dirt had been raked and smoothed. In front of home plate, in large chalk letters, were the words: *Nunca te olvidaremos.* (We will never forget you.) *Kuilan.*

Jamie told me she had watched the man chalk the letters four or five times until they were good enough for Pai.

A thousand people filled the stands and crowded into the dugouts and outfield. The longtime mayor of Dorado, Carlitos Lopez, who had played Double A with Pai, stood with a microphone behind home plate.

"One of the best people in Puerto Rico, Benjamín Molina Santana!" he said as Pai's pallbearers—me, my brothers, Lusito, Junior Diaz, Vitin, and several others—carried the casket to home plate. The crowd roared. The mayor called Pai "a hero of the people, a pillar of Kuilan in the barrio of Espinosa, the best community role model."

He handed the mic to Cheo. "My mother and brothers and I are very happy for all those who saw Pai as their father, too," he said. "We didn't know Pai had so many children!"

We carried the casket to first base, then second and third. The mayor delivered a play-by-play of the action, as if Pai were rounding the bases. I picked up first base, Cheo second, and Yadier third. The mayor's voice grew louder and more excited as we carried Pai toward home. His last trip around the diamond. A thousand people leapt to their feet.

Pai's standing ovation.

"The most important base," the mayor said, "the one that brings Benjamín back to home, goes to a lady so supportive of her family and her husband. The home plate goes to Gladys Matta!"

The crowd went wild.

As we stood at home plate, I scooped up a handful of infield dirt and rubbed it on the lid of the casket.

In the rain, with a police escort, we walked behind Pai's silver hearse through the streets of Kuilan. On every block, people emerged from their houses, clapping and crying as we passed. Some held signs: "We will never forget you!" and "Rest in Peace, Benjamín" and "Thank you, Benjamín!"

Both lanes of La Número Dos had been closed to traffic to make way for Pai's funeral procession to the cemetery. Commuters stood by their cars in the rain, waving or holding their hats over their hearts.

The sky had turned black when we reached Cementerio de Monterrey. Mourners under striped golf umbrellas stretched across the lawn. People watched from balconies and rooftops on a ridge above us. We carried the casket into a small tent at the entrance to a row of crypts. We prayed, and each of us placed a single rose on top of the casket. Junior Diaz tried to speak but cried, and someone else took over. Mai thanked everyone for coming.

"I hope you know how much Benjamín loved every one of you," she said.

We carried Pai along a wall of vaults, each one marked by a square plaque. Toward the back, three up from the bottom, was an open square. I felt Jamie's hand on the back of my neck. I didn't know how long it had been there, but I knew it was the only thing holding me up.

We lifted the casket and slid it in. Pai's sisters began to wail. I heard distant shouts: "We love you, Benjamín! You'll never be forgotten!" Cemetery workers bolted the cover of the crypt and affixed a square of marble engraved with Pai's name, dates of birth and death, and "Beloved Husband and Father."

His entire life reduced, like a box score, to a few words and numbers.

For five or ten minutes nobody spoke. Nobody moved. Then we left. I didn't look back. I couldn't let myself think of him alone in that dark, cramped space. I kept moving forward.

At eight o'clock for the next nine nights a priest arrived at Mai's house to pray the novena. More than a hundred people showed up every night to join in, filling the patio and carport and overflowing into the street to pray the rosary and speed Pai's soul into heaven. Everyone stayed for soup and snacks, coffee and soda. Later the beer came out and we made more toasts and told more stories.

The talk every night at Mai's always turned to Pai's skills on the baseball field.

"Can you imagine if he hadn't missed those two years?" Pai's cousin Licinio said.

"What two years?" I asked.

"In Massachusetts."

"Massachusetts?"

Pai was sixteen years old and in love with Mai. He wanted to marry her but didn't earn enough playing Double A baseball to build a nest egg. He applied at all the factories, but unemployment then was in double digits. Sixteen-year-olds weren't getting hired.

Licinio had left home several years earlier and was working in

Lowell, Massachusetts. He told Pai he could get a job with him at the Jo-Ann Fabric factory as a fabric cutter. So Pai moved to Lowell, saying good-bye to his girlfriend and his brokenhearted grandmother. The cousins shared a cheap, cramped room above a store on Main Street.

"He was there for two years?" I asked. "When he was sixteen?"

Everybody knew sixteen was the prime age to attract the attention of pro baseball scouts. American teams liked to sign the Latin players when they were young so they could shape the raw talent themselves through the minor-league system. Pai had to have known this. He went to Massachusetts anyway.

"Maybe he thought he'd get more attention from scouts in America?" I asked.

Licinio said he didn't play baseball at all when he was in Massachusetts. "Chino thought only about making money for Gladys."

When Pai returned to Puerto Rico at age eighteen, he was immediately recruited by the Double A team in Utuado. He reestablished himself as a top player, earning seventy-five dollars a game. And he found a job at the Westinghouse factory. He and Mai resumed their courtship. Pai won the batting championship that year. He was better than he had ever been. The best in the league. Scouts came around. Everyone was certain he would be signed by a Major League club.

"He could have made it. No question," one of Pai's old teammates said.

We were on the front patio by the carport. A streetlamp across the street spilled a mist of light onto Pai's field.

"Of course! Look at Felix Millan!"

Millan was from Yabucoa, an hour outside San Juan. He gripped the bat halfway up the shaft the way Pai did. And he not only played in the Major Leagues as a second baseman for the Mets in the 1960s and '70s, he was an All-Star.

"But Chino never went to the tryout."

"Wait, what tryout?" I asked. I couldn't believe Pai never talked about any of this.

It was in the winter of 1973, they said. The tryout—at least according to everyone's best recollection—was with the Milwaukee Brewers. Everybody seemed to have a bit of the story.

"The guy had been watching Chino and wanted to sign him. I'm sure the money wasn't much at that time. Chino was small."

The scout gave Pai a time and place for the tryout. Other players had been invited as well. It was a big deal, especially because by this time Pai was twenty-two. On the appointed day, all the hopeful young men ran the bases, showed off their arms, and clobbered pitches to the outfield as the scout scribbled in his notebook.

"So what happened?" I asked.

"Benjamín didn't show up," Vitin said. "He was at a bar with his friends from the factory."

"What? Are you serious?" I said.

"He didn't go. Everyone said he was better than any of them."

This was crazy. He loved baseball more than anything. He had worked his whole life for that moment, his one big chance. It made no sense.

"Was he hurt?" I asked. I couldn't imagine what could have kept him away. "Was he scared?"

"Your father? Scared?" Vitin said, incredulous. "No!"

"What, then?"

Vitin leaned toward me in his lawn chair, his elbows on his knees, his big hand wrapped around his plastic cup of grapefruit and vodka. His face was hard, as if I had said something wrong.

"Your mother had just found out she was pregnant," he said. "He wouldn't leave her."

My eyes darted from one man to the next. They showed no sign of surprise. Did everyone know this? How could I not know? I sat in silence, stunned, trying to make sense of it. My father had let his dream walk right by him. He saw it, stepped aside, and let it pass. He spent the rest of his life at a factory, not once complaining.

I felt sick to my stomach. It was easier to think Pai had failed than to think he threw away his dream for us.

"I can't imagine that level of sacrifice," I said. "I wish he hadn't done it."

"Chino was the happiest man I knew," Vitin said.

"But he never got to do what he really wanted."

Vitin slapped his thigh, jostling his drink. "That man did exactly what he wanted," he said. "Don't you feel sorry for him."

"But he could have had such a different life," I said. I thought about all the times I had wished Pai could have felt the thrill of forty thousand fans cheering for him, the way his three sons had felt it.

"You have it all wrong, Bengie," Vitin said, rising from his chair. He seemed agitated. I watched as he poured another drink at a small table in the carport. The other men shifted in their chairs, sipping their cocktails and beer, watching a car slow down at our driveway, then continue on. The tent had come down. We could see Pai's field in the glow of the streetlamp: the outlines of the fences and backstop, the walls of the dugout.

Vitin sank into the lawn chair and slapped a mosquito on his bare arm. I waited for him to pick up where he had left off. But he said nothing, and soon the conversation turned to other topics. What did Vitin mean I had it all wrong?

WHEN A REPORTER called in November to get my comments on Tim Lincecum winning the Cy Young Award, it took me a moment to register what he was he talking about. The baseball season seemed like a million years ago.

Timmy was the second Cy Young winner I had caught in four seasons (the Angels' Bartolo Colon was the other). I texted Tim to congratulate him, and he texted back that he couldn't have won it without me. Typical Timmy. Generous, humble, and gracious. He said he was looking forward to seeing me at spring training in a couple of months.

But I knew I couldn't play baseball. Baseball died when Pai did. Baseball and Pai were a single thing. How could one continue without the other? Baseball was *his* passion, *his* great joy, *his* life's work. The game had no meaning for me if he wasn't around to share in it.

And I couldn't move past my guilt. I should have spent more time with Pai. I found myself blaming baseball. If I didn't play baseball, I could have stayed in Puerto Rico and helped him coach his Little Leaguers and played dominoes at Junior Diaz's. That's what Pai had done. Stayed with his family instead of going off to play baseball. I was out of my mind with grief.

I seemed to worry all day. I worried about Mai and about Pai's brothers and sisters. I worried about Pai's players. I worried about the cousins who had seen Pai as a second father. I worried about Cheo and Yadier. I called and checked in constantly, asking what they needed, what I could do. It was like a fifty-pound weight in my heart.

More than once, Jamie had to talk me out of moving to Puerto Rico. If it weren't for her, I'd have quit baseball right then and camped in front of Pai's grave, punishing myself for all our years apart.

"Take your time," Jamie kept telling me about playing baseball. "Don't make any decisions."

A month later, in December, Jamie found out she was pregnant. I wrapped my arms around her and, in the midst of my grief, felt a wave of gratitude for her and my girls and this new baby.

Of course I would go back to baseball. It was my job as caretaker of my family. It's what a man does. As long as I had my family, I knew I would be okay. Watching the girls grow and guiding them the way Pai guided me—what better way to spend my days? What more was there?

Then it dawned on me.

I suddenly understood what Vitin had meant. I had it all wrong about Pai sacrificing his dream for us.

I almost laughed, the way you do when you see how a magic trick is done; the answer had been in plain sight all along, if only you knew where to look. I thought about how Pai was the one who always watched over his sisters and their kids. How he stayed with Mai when she was pregnant with me. How he spent every afternoon after work on the baseball field with his three sons. How he never bragged about his Major League sons. How he stayed at the factory instead of letting us support him. How he kept coaching long after his own sons had left home.

Playing in the Major Leagues was not Pai's dream.

His dream was to be a good father and husband and raise good sons.

I thought about my first memory, when Pai hit that home run.

I remembered how his face lit up when he saw me at home plate. Now I understood that his joy wasn't just about hitting the home run but about sharing the moment with me. That's what baseball had always been about for him. Family.

He never craved conventional success. He measured his worth in his own way, not by any outside standard. He didn't need to play in Yankee Stadium to feel he had accomplished something. To him, baseball was baseball. Baseball on the field across the street was as true and beautiful as baseball in Yankee Stadium. Baseball delivered to this quiet and introverted man a means of connecting to his sons and to other people's sons. It was his way of becoming a father to every kid in the barrio, creating for himself an extended family of sons that had nothing to do with blood.

Through baseball, he taught all of us how to be men.

That was his life's work.

I remembered back to an afternoon soon after Pai's funeral when I visited with my great-aunt Clara Virgen. She lived on the same property as Titi Graciella and my other aunts. In the course of talking about Pai, I asked why their family, the Molinas and Santanas, rarely attended church. Clara Virgen was in her eighties then and seemed halfway swallowed up by the couch in her tiny cement-floor living room. Several grandchildren and great-nieces and -nephews had followed me into the house and sat cross-legged at her feet.

My great-aunt waved her hand, brushing away the question.

"This right here is the real church—yourself with some people in your house."

I kept thinking about that. Among all the comments from all the people I talked to about Pai, that one sentence from Clara Virgen captured so much of what I was trying to understand.

Family was my father's religion. Baseball was its sacrament.

In retrospect it seems obvious and inevitable that all three of Benjamín Molina Santana's sons would become catchers. Catchers are the caretakers, the counselors, the workhorses.

The fathers.

Of all the jobs on a baseball field, we found the one that positioned us at a spot called home. Our job was to protect it.

EPILOGUE

JAMIE AND I got married on Valentine's Day, four months after Pai's funeral. It was a fairly spontaneous ceremony, with just Jamie's parents, her sister, and our friends Angie, José, and their daughter, Christina. Kyshly and Kelssy were in school in Yuma, my brothers couldn't leave training camp, and Mai wasn't ready to travel yet. We held it in the park in front of the house we had rented in Scottsdale for spring training.

I brought with me to training camp a poster-sized collage of Pai's photos. I propped it in my locker in Arizona and then in San Francisco. My teammates gave me funny looks when I carried it onto the plane for road trips. I didn't care. It was my way of keeping him close. I also had patches stitched to the inside of my jersey: One read "Pai" and the other "Mai." On the underside of the bill of my cap I wrote the four words Pai drilled into us: "All-out every day."

Two days before the 2009 All-Star Game—Yadier had been voted in as the starting catcher—Jamie went into labor. Jayda Marie was born on July 11, nine months—almost to the minute—after Pai died. I held her at Jamie's bedside.

"She has his soul," I said.

I had been struggling at the plate through the season, working hard but still carrying my grief like a sack of stones. I hit well enough to hold on to my cleanup spot in the lineup. But my power numbers weren't great. I was hitting, on average, one home run for every nine games. Going into the last week of the season, I had eighteen home runs. We were playing a Wednesday game at home in San Francisco. There were just five games left, not enough time to reach twenty, given my season average.

I hit a home run in my first at-bat.

Nineteen.

Then, late in the game, I hit a pitch off the end of my bat and thought it was a pop-up. But it kept carrying. Home run.

Twenty!

As I rounded the bags, I felt as if my heart might swell right out of my chest. I put my head down, blinking back tears. I looked to the sky when I stepped on home plate.

"I did it, Pai. I promised you and I did it. You always said I could."

I held myself together in a TV interview after the game, but broke down afterward in the clubhouse. In the car on the way home, I called Mai even though it was after 2 a.m. in Puerto Rico.

"Hey, what's the matter? You okay?"

"Mai, I did it."

"What?"

"I got to twenty."

"What? You got another one?" She had seen the first one on TV then went to bed.

"I promised Pai."

She started crying.

"He's very happy for you right now."

IN OCTOBER 2009, Cheo earned his second World Series ring as a backup to the Yankees' Jorge Posada.

In November, Lincecum won his second Cy Young. "Bengie's half the reason I'm here," he told reporters in the press conference.

I signed a one-year contract with the Giants to play through the 2010 season. I'd be mentoring rookie catcher Buster Posey, a great talent and a great person. I loved working with him.

But at the end of June, the Giants traded me to the Texas Rangers. The team plane had just landed in Denver when my teammates looked up from their cell phones and began coming over to say how much they'd miss me. I had no idea what they were talking about. Then I saw a text message from Jamie: "Looks like we're going to Dallas." She had been getting texts for two hours about the trade. The news must have broken soon after we took off from San Francisco. With no Internet or cell service, none of us knew until we landed.

I was angry that I hadn't been told. Giants manager Bruce Bochy apologized and said he couldn't say anything because the trade hadn't been finalized.

No matter what any player tells you about baseball being a business and you can't take anything personally, it was a blow to be traded. That team was so much like a family, and being traded felt like being kicked out the front door. On the bus from the airport to the hotel, where I would wait for travel information from the Rangers, I stood up in the aisle.

"I want to say thanks for being such great teammates and for taking care of me," I said. "I'm really going to miss you guys. You have what it takes to win this whole thing. If you stick together as a team, you will do it. And I'm going to be watching as much as I can. You all have my number. Even if I'm not your teammate anymore, I'll always be your friend."

I was about to sit down when everyone started to clap. Then they stood and clapped. I was blown away. The best standing O of my career.

With the Giants, my jersey number had been 1. But another Rangers player already had it. The team said number 11 was available.

"Perfect!" I said.

Eleven had always been my number with Los Pobres.

Two weeks after I joined the Rangers, I hit for the cycle—a single, double, triple and home run in one game—for the first and only time in my career. Actually it was a grand cycle: the home run was a grand slam. As supposedly the slowest baseball player on the planet, I would guess the probability of me hitting a triple was almost zero, especially in tiny Fenway Park. When I got to third and looked in the dugout, my new teammates were going nuts. There is no better feeling as a player than to see your teammates cheer for you like that. After the game there were fifty-five text messages, many from my buddies on the Giants.

The Rangers kept winning. And the Giants kept winning.

We won the American League Championship. The Giants won the National League Championship. The Rangers would be playing the Giants in the World Series.

I became just the second player in history to play in the World Series against the team he had played for earlier in the same season. Among other things, it meant I'd get a World Series ring no matter which team won. (Any player on the roster at any time during a championship season receives a ring.)

Before Game 1 in San Francisco, a text arrived from Buster Posey: "Hey, B-Mo, good luck!"

I typed back: "Thanks, Buster. Enjoy the moment!"

Reporters in the Bay Area asked how I felt playing against teammates I considered like brothers.

"I've played against my real brothers," I said. "I think I'll be okay."

When I stepped into the batter's box against Lincecum, the kid I'd mentored since he arrived in the big leagues and had been his catcher during both his Cy Young seasons, I touched the bill of my cap, and he touched his.

The Rangers lost the Series. I watched from the dugout as my friends and former teammates swarmed the field to celebrate the franchise's first World Series championship since moving to San Francisco in 1958.

I retired a few months later. It was one of the most difficult things I had ever done. I had been playing baseball since I could walk. I was thirty-six. Could I have played another year or two? Yes. But I didn't want to lose any more time with my family. I had accomplished more than I had ever imagined. And the last game of my career came at the World Series. I'll take that kind of exit any day.

Mai continued to live in the same house in the same neighborhood, refusing to move. The field across the street fell into disrepair.

"It is dead," Jacinto Camacho told me during a visit. "When Benjamín died, from that moment on, it was as if it had been hit with an atomic bomb. Boom—everything disappeared. I stayed away for a long time. When I went back last week, it was like something tearing out of my heart."

I walked over to the field myself. The infield dirt was choppy and tufted with weeds. Tamarind pods rotted on the ground in left field. But along the baselines and around home plate were traces of white chalk. I could see the pockmarks of rubber spikes. A game had been played.

Like Jacinto, I wanted to stop time so everything stayed exactly as it was when Pai was alive. But you lay down chalk lines knowing they're going to disappear. That was another part of the beauty of baseball. You're not meant to hold on to things: the day-to-day failures and embarrassments, even the large and small triumphs. Let the strikeouts and dropped balls and home runs disappear into the dirt and grass. Let the trophies wash away in the floodwaters. Baseball is about what you get and give up, what you earn and relinquish.

I watched Yadier's and Cheo's games on TV. Cheo was with the Toronto Blue Jays, and Yadier was on his way to winning another World Series championship with the Cardinals in 2011.

In 2012, Yadier spent close to a million dollars turning Pai's field into one of the best youth ballparks in Puerto Rico. Pai's many, many sons in Espinosa have a home again.

After Pai died, Mai's house was as busy as a bus depot, people stopping in all day and into the evening to check on her or sit on her sofa and catch up. They drove her to the pharmacy to get her meds. When Yadier bought a house in Jupiter, Florida, near the Cardinals' spring training complex, Mai began to split her time between there and Puerto Rico. With Cheo playing in Tampa, she saw him a lot, too. And I'd make trips with Jamie and the girls.

I saw her even more in 2013, when, two years after I retired, I joined the Cardinals as the assistant batting coach. Jamie knew I needed baseball and encouraged me to accept the job, even though it meant packing and moving and time apart when I was on the road. She always knew, even when I couldn't imagine baseball without Pai, that my love for the game was as true as his.

I loved seeing Yadier every day at the field. We won the National League pennant that year—marking the seventh time in nine years that a Molina appeared in the World Series. I've been to the World Series three times now—the first with José in Anaheim, the second on my own in Texas, and the third with Yadier in St. Louis. How could that have happened—sharing a World Series with each of my brothers? Who would be crazy enough to dream that?

I thought about this when I was talking to Vitin during a visit to Puerto Rico not long ago. He asked if I knew he had collected the belongings from my father's body at the hospital. I didn't. That's when he told me about the three things in Pai's pockets: a Little League rulebook, a measuring tape, and a lotto ticket.

The items seemed so ordinary, but they felt like a message, too. In those three things were nearly all of Pai's lessons to my brothers and me.

Through baseball, he gave us the rules and codes to live by. Integrity and humility. Respect. Play hard and unselfishly. Accept that failure is a normal part of life and move on. Pai weathered setbacks and losses with such grace because he understood that what is done is done. He couldn't change the fact the flood happened. So he let go of everything he had lost and started over in a different house.

He taught us that the measure of a man is in the attributes that can't be timed, weighed, scored, or tallied. A baseball field is precisely measured—exactly ninety feet between the bases, exactly sixty feet six inches between home and the pitcher's mound—but the players can never be. You can't measure what's inside them. I think Pai believed, as I do now, that the single greatest measure of a man is how fiercely he's willing to follow his heart, on and off the field.

By that standard, my father was the most successful man I've ever known. He married a great woman and raised three sons who measured themselves by him, a factory worker. And to his last breath Pai did exactly what he loved in the place and with the people he loved. The ultimate success is to live your life in your own way, by your own measure, inspired and guided by core values. Pai did that every day. To the public, my brothers and I were stars. But my father was always the real star. The true Hall of Famer.

Now I'm happy to be following in Pai's footsteps as a coach. I spent the 2013 season with the Texas Rangers as first-base coach and catching instructor. In the off-season I coach kids in my youth baseball program. I want the baseball field to be, as it was for me, the place where they learn how to be good men. And where, for all their failures and flaws, someone believes in them as much as Pai believed in me.

ACKNOWLEDGMENTS

THIS BOOK IS as much Jamie's as it is mine. She encouraged me to share the story of my dad, along with my own unlikely journey to the big leagues. She pushed me to fill in the gaps of my father's life and to capture the heroism in a life lived with humility and integrity. If she had not come into my life, this book would not have happened. She is my love, my life, my Black Pearl.

Although this book is about my father, my mother was as powerful an influence on me and my brothers as he was. While Pai was working, Mai was always there for us, teaching us respect, making us laugh, pushing us to work hard, and instilling in us the kind of strength and love she has shown all her life.

My daughters, Kyshly, Kelssy, and Jayda, inspire me to be as good a dad to them as Pai was to me. Thank you, Kyshly and Kelssy, for bringing so much happiness to your grandfather's life. You were such lights in his life. Jayda never got to meet her loving *abuelo*, so I hope this book will help her to know him.

My brothers, Cheo and Yadier, are great ballplayers and even better people. For all their success, they are still as humble as they were as kids hitting bottle caps with taped-up bats on the field across the street.

So many family and friends helped with background and details of my father's life. I am so grateful for the hours they spent being interviewed, telling priceless stories and digging up old photos. I want to thank on Mai's side of the family: Titi Norma, Titi Charo, Titi Ivonne, Tío Paquito, Tío Felo, Tío Papo, and Titi Rosalia. And on Pai's side: Titi Panchita, Titi Nenita, Titi Graciela, Titi Pura, Titi Pillita, Titi Guia, Tío Chiquito, Tío Tití, Tío Gordo, Tío Blanco, and Titi Virgen.

Other family and friends who helped either with interviews or logistics: Luisito Samot Molina, Junior Diaz, Jacinto Camacho, Mandy Matta, Vitin Morales, Morayma Arroyo, José Olivo Miguelito and Lourdes Rivera, Eliut Rivera, Pedro "Cucho" Morales, Jare Morales, Joel Morales, and Carlitos Lopez.

Thanks to Jamie's parents, Jennifer and Wayne Weimer, and her sister, Wendy Weimer, for offering feedback on an early version of the manuscript. Thanks also to my cousin Jennifer Cruz for her help in holding down the fort while Jamie and I worked on this project.

Finally, a huge thank-you to the coaches and teammates who have been my teachers and brothers throughout my career.

—Bengie Molina

I am grateful to Bengie, Jamie, and the entire Molina family for allowing me to step into their lives and help tell Benjamín's powerful story. So many people not only shared their memories during my visits to Puerto Rico but drove me around Dorado and fed me at their kitchen tables.

Several books helped with background on baseball and culture in Puerto Rico: *Clemente: The Passion and Grace of Baseball's Last Hero* by David Maraniss (Simon & Schuster, 2006); *Puerto Rico's Winter League: A History of Major League Baseball's Launching Pad* by Thomas E. Van Hyning (McFarland & Company, 1995); and *Puerto Rico in the American Century: A History Since 1898* by César J. Ayala and Rafael Bernabe (University of North Carolina Press, 2007).

I am indebted to translator Elsie Parra for her patience and professionalism.

Thanks also to my editor, Jofie Ferrari-Adler; my agent, Betsy Lerner; and to those who helped me brainstorm and read early drafts: Barry Tompkins, Erin Becker, Rob Becker, Lorna Stevens, Gary Pomerantz, and Ken Conner.

—Joan Ryan